THE CONSTITUTIONAL PROTECTION OF CAPITALISM

In 1945 a Labour government deployed Britain's national autonomy and parliamentary sovereignty to nationalise key industries and services such as coal, rail, gas and electricity, and to establish a publicly-owned National Health Service. This monograph argues that constitutional constraints stemming from economic and legal globalisation would now preclude such a programme. It contends that whilst no state has ever, or could ever, possess complete freedom of action, the rise of the transnational corporation nonetheless means that national autonomy is now significantly restricted. The book focuses in particular on the way in which these economic constraints have been nurtured, reinforced and legitimised by the creation on the part of world leaders of a globalised constitutional law of trade and competition. This has been brought into existence by the adoption of effective enforcement machinery, sometimes embedded within the nation states, sometimes formed at transnational level.

With Britain enmeshed in supranational economic and legal structures from which it is difficult to extricate itself, the British polity no longer enjoys the range and freedom of policymaking once open to it. Transnational legal obligations constitute not just law but in effect a de facto supreme law entrenching a predominantly neoliberal political settlement in which the freedom of the individual is identified with the freedom of the market.

The book analyses the key provisions of WTO, EU and ECHR law that provide constitutional protection for private enterprise. It focuses on the law of services liberalisation, public monopolies, state aid, public procurement and the fundamental right of property ownership, arguing that the new constitutional order compromises the traditional ideals of British democracy.

The Constitutional Protection of Capitalism

Danny Nicol

·HART·
PUBLISHING

OXFORD AND PORTLAND, OREGON
2010

Published in North America (US and Canada) by
Hart Publishing
c/o International Specialized Book Services
920 NE 58th Avenue, Suite 300
Portland, OR
97213-3786
USA
Tel: +1-503-287-3093 or toll-free: 1-800-944-6190
Fax: +1-503-280-8832
Email: orders@isbs.com
Website: http://www.isbs.com

Hart Publishing Ltd
16C Worcester Place
Oxford
OX1 2JW
Telephone: +44 (0)1865 517530
Fax: +44 (0)1865 510710
Email: mail@hartpub.co.uk
Website: http://www.hartpub.co.uk

British Library Cataloguing in Publication Data
Data Available

ISBN: 978-1-84113-859-6

Typeset by Hope Services, Abingdon
Printed and bound in Great Britain by
TJ International Ltd, Padstow, Cornwall

To my mother and father

PREFACE

This book sprung from my dissatisfaction with British public law scholarship—especially my own. Like many public lawyers at the turn of the century, I became preoccupied with the Human Rights Act (HRA) 1998 and the way in which it would change the constitution. The HRA raised many interesting and important questions about the way in which power would be shifted to the judiciary and whether the hybrid structure of the HRA, with its delicate balance of preserving parliamentary sovereignty whilst augmenting judicial authority, would allow for a culture of controversy over the meaning of rights.

As the years went by, however, I started to wonder if my work had focused on the most important thing in life. The HRA, sadly, failed to usher in a new era of liberty. Faced with the tidal wave of the 'war against terror', it was not strong enough to withstand the gradual emergence of the surveillance society. It proved unequal to the task of extending civil liberties. But at the same time I started to question the centrality of the very issues on which HRA litigation tended to focus. These issues were undoubtedly important, not just to the people bringing the cases but to our comfort that we are living in a civilised society. Yet they had little bearing on the happiness of the broad mass of the population. Aside from the HRA's undermining of the position of complainants in sexual assault trials, which affected a large number of people—overwhelmingly women—the bulk of the population were largely unaffected by the Act, save for a general perception that the country's civil liberties had, if anything, diminished and the sentiment, perhaps unfair, that the Act seemed largely to benefit the criminal fraternity. The HRA is important and worthy of study, not least because what it tells us about the expansion of judicial power, but in terms of impact on the broad mass of the British population, most 'classical' civil liberties issues appear to be dwarfed by issues of economic policy, in terms of the human contentment or human misery that they generate.

At the same time, the first faint signs of economic calamity were starting to materialise. The catastrophic blunder of banks and financial institutions investing in sub-prime mortgages was beginning to show its consequences in terms of unemployment, insecurity, home repossessions and widening inequality. The British Prime Minister of the day, Gordon Brown, emphasised at every turn that the economic problems were not the result of national economic policy but global problems requiring global solutions. Brown's argument was not altogether convincing: the 'New Labour' government elected in 1997 had pursued neoliberal globalisation with vim and vigour and had embraced the cause of 'light-touch' regulation. Britain's banks had been allowed to make a free choice over their purchase of the infamous 'poisonous' securities. Furthermore, the 'global solutions', when they finally materialised, were rather paltry. But be that as it may, the dire consequences of the credit crunch made me think that public law was not focusing on the most important issues. Whilst the study of the HRA remained important (irrespective of popular sentiment), analysis of the relationship between economic policy and public law seemed far more so. In my research, it became alarming to discover the extent to which free trade was acting as a cover for the security of private enterprise, as well as the extent to which contestable ideas had been constitutionalised at a transnational level. The study gave me cause to question, too, whether the study of public law should be so fixated on the state at the expense of transnational institutions and, indeed, even transnational corporations. Furthermore, whilst there had been considerable academic controversy about the merits and demerits of the shift in power from politicians to the judiciary, I came to see this shift as being part of a bigger picture, the evolution of a neoliberal constitution.

I would like to thank the following for the help they have given me in writing this book: Gavin Anderson, Kyungu Gordon-Walker, Carol Harlow, Adam Łazowski, Luke Martell, Mike Meehan, Harriet Samuels, Lisa Webley, Alison Young. I would like to thank Andrew Le Sueur and *Public Law* for allowing me to reproduce material on the negotiations of the European Convention on Human Rights that featured in my 2005 article 'Original Intent and the European Convention on Human Rights'. I am also thankful for participants in lectures and seminars at University College London, Glasgow and London Metropolitan University for their constructive remarks. Finally, this monograph also benefited from several anonymous reviewers, whom I would like to thank for their helpful criticisms and suggestions. In the nature of things, each of these reviewers proffered widely differing advice, so I hope they will forgive me if I have not be able to follow each piece of advice in the depth that I would wish.

Danny Nicol
London
July 2009

TABLE OF CONTENTS

Contents

TABLE OF CASES

United Kingdom

WTO

TABLE OF LEGISLATION

EU LEGISLATION

Decisions

Directives

Regulations

1

Transnational Regimes and the Constitution

S HOULD THE BRITISH constitution elevate a certain form of capitalism above politics? This book argues that this is essentially what has happened and is continuing to happen, owing to a process of constitutional globalisation. It contends that there has been a constitutional 'transnationalisation' that has introduced a far more severe ideological bias into the constitution than has hitherto existed, certainly since the ending of the veto power of the House of Lords in 1911; this in turn has seriously compromised British democracy. By placing the power of private enterprise on a more secure footing than was previously the case, this transnationalisation has significantly restricted policy choice, thereby narrowing the scope for legitimate, democratic politics. In particular, the free choice of economic policies—on such matters as state aid, public procurement, state regulation and, above all, the choice between markets and public sector monopoly—has increasingly been rendered constitutionally impermissible. Only the strength of neoliberal consensus amongst the present generation of politicians has served to conceal this democratic diminution.

At a time of economic depression when we are witnessing 'the self-immolation of the neoliberals on the funeral pyre of greed and excess',[1] ideas of state intervention are enjoying a revival, and so it may seem odd to claim that the constitution affords protection to a version of capitalism particularly wedded to the security and freedom of private enterprise. Yet the organising principle of the new constitutionalism is not free market dogma but rather class interest. The new constitutionalism is sufficiently nuanced to allow the state to come to the aid of private enterprise at times of recession whilst in no way undermining the principles that the private sector should dominate the economy and that regulation imposed upon the private sector should be subject to judicial review. As such, the new constitutionalism is intended to make substantive policy commitments designed to withstand the test of time by binding future governments.

This forms a stark contrast to traditional conceptions of the British constitution. For much of the twentieth century, the British constitution's main ideological commitment was to representative democracy. To this extent the constitution was perceived as being based on procedures rather than on substantive outcomes.[2] Thus although no constitution can ever be wholly neutral, the British constitution

---

[1] Larry Elliott, *The Guardian*, 20 April 2009.
[2] Alder (2007) 4.

1

at least enjoyed a certain measure of political neutrality in substantive terms. This position, however, has now changed to a considerable extent, owing to the evolution of international agreements and, more especially, international organisations that commit Britain to substantive aims. Until recently, international agreements have not generally been perceived as part of a country's constitution, but this book argues that the time has come to modify our perceptions and to do so. This book also contends that these international agreements and organisations conform predominantly (albeit not exclusively) to one particular creed: neoliberalism. Such a constitutional commitment to a *substantive* political ideology raises profound democratic concerns.

Although this book is concerned with 'international organisations', the text generally eschews this familiar verbiage in favour of the term 'transnational regimes'. There are two reasons for preferring this term. First, the use of the word 'regime' is intended to convey the idea that the organisations that form the subject matter of this book are not politically neutral. Rather, they are teleological: each embodies a substantive ideological content. Accordingly, they are not simply forums that change the structure and locus of political decision-making. If they were, they would raise fewer democratic concerns. Instead, the agreements on which they are based enshrine substantive policies, and these policies, considered together, entrench a distinct ideology. Secondly, the use of the word 'transnational' is intended to reflect the blurred line that now exists between the international and the supranational. The orthodox assumption has been to view the European Union (EU) as supranational and everything else as international. But in recent times a more complex and nuanced constitutional landscape has emerged. 'International law' has increasingly assumed a variety of different strengths which corresponds to the diverse processes of globalisation itself.[3] The three transnational regimes analysed in this book—the World Trade Organization (WTO), the European Union and the European Convention on Human Rights (ECHR)—all lie at the more 'federal' end of the international law spectrum. The substance is increasingly constitutional, even when the form remains international. As such, it will be argued, it is misguided to exclude such transnational regimes from considerations of the British constitution.

It is widely acknowledged that the European Union in particular enjoys a quasi-federal status vis-à-vis national law, by virtue of the role of the national courts in enforcing the doctrines of direct effect and supremacy of EU law. As Eric Stein famously observed, 'tucked away in the fairyland Duchy of Luxembourg and blessed, until recently with benign neglect by the powers-that-be and the mass media, the Court of Justice of the European Communities has fashioned a constitutional framework for a federal-type Europe.'[4] The ECJ has created this constitutional framework by, in effect, recruiting the national courts as its police in the Member States to prevent national governments and parliaments from violating

---

[3] Sand (2004) 52.
[4] Stein (1981) 1.

its rules. This strategy has given Community law unique authority within the national legal systems. In effect, every national court has become a EU court, every national judge has become a EU judge. Only EU law has gone so far as to assert the right to determine its own legal effects within the national legal systems. But this is not to say that other forms of transnational law are bereft of federal characteristics. The story of the evolution of the transnational regimes has been one in which a constant widening of substantive scope has gone hand in hand with increasingly effective enforcement machinery. The chapters on the World Trade Organisation and the European Convention on Human Rights will chronicle how initially weak mechanisms of compliance were progressively replaced by stronger systems of enforcement. This was in large measure due to the willingness of national politicians in the participating states to approve rule changes that would guarantee greater respect for regime policies but also partly due to the constitutional jurisprudence of the juridical bodies of the regimes themselves.

Two Conceptions of Neoliberalism

The major thesis of this book is that these regimes, armed with their more effective supranational enforcement structures, form a 'supra-constitution' that goes above and beyond the domestic British constitution and evinces an ideological commitment to a certain form of capitalism—neoliberalism, the ideology associated with the variety of capitalism ushered in by Margaret Thatcher and Ronald Reagan. But what precisely do we mean by neoliberalism? David Harvey has argued that in fact there are *two* competing interpretations of neoliberalism.[5] The first conception relates to a utopian theoretical design based on 'a model of societal relations in which government regulation and social welfare guarantees are reduced in order to foster the play of market forces driven by private enterprises pursuing profit maximization'.[6] It involves 'an almost doctrinal fixation on free trade, privatization and small government, and unfettered markets to foster economic growth and wealth generation, as opposed to government action and collective bargaining to promote social and economic equality'.[7] The ideological founding father of this grand design of neoliberalism was Friedrich A Hayek, whose books *The Road to Serfdom* and *The Constitution of Liberty* ran against the grain of socialist and social democratic thinking in the 1940s and 1950s.

The second interpretation of neoliberalism put forward by Harvey is very different from the first. It perceives neoliberalism as a political project designed to restore the power of economic elites. In other words, neoliberalism is essentially

---

[5] Harvey (2005) 19.
[6] Shaffer (2003) 4.
[7] Shaffer (2003) 5.

about the promotion of class interests, not about adherence to free market *principles*. Harvey argues that in practice it is this second conception of neoliberalism that is dominant. Indeed, he insists that the theoretical utopianism of neoliberal argument works primarily as a system of justification and legitimation for whatever needs to be done to achieve the goal of restoring the power of an economic elite, even if such actions conflict diametrically with neoliberal orthodoxy. On this reading the economic status quo is not some natural, organic order of things. Rather, it is an order that has been created and maintained as a matter of public policy and government power. As Antinori has observed, 'laissez-faire is a myth, and the question is never between government regulation of the economy and no government regulation: the question is always what type of government regulation.'[8] Accordingly, neoliberal theory is essentially window-dressing: it provides the indispensable normative basis for neoliberalism, the arguments of principle based on liberty and democracy that seek to justify the system of private enterprise. But when neoliberal principles clash with the need to sustain elite power, then such principles are either abandoned or twisted out of all recognition.

It may be, however, that some neoliberals stand firm in their adherence to neoliberal nostrums—believing that if corporations commit major policy blunders, they should be allowed to fail—whilst other neoliberals adopt a more pragmatic approach. Thus on the basis of Harvey's distinction it is possible to identify two types of neoliberal: the minority are 'free market principle neoliberals' who keep to neoliberal dogma, whilst the majority are 'class interest neoliberals' who are ready to abandon that dogma in defence of the interests of the economic elite. We can perceive the two types of neoliberal in opposition to each other during the banking crisis of 2008, since the question of state aid to private corporations is one on which the difference between the two conceptions of neoliberalism has been most keenly felt. According to neoliberal principle, the state's role should be to maintain a system of competition; to rescue firms by eliminating the sanction for imprudent business decisions would jeopardise that system of competition. But sometimes class interests require corporations to be kept in existence with public funding but under private sector control. An example of this division of opinion is afforded by the split in the Republican Party in the US House of Representatives in September 2008, when 133 Republicans voted against the bank bailout, whilst others joined with the Democrats in favour. Another example is provided by the disagreement between the Governor of the Bank of England, Mervyn King, and the British government over bank bailouts. King supported a fundamentalist, free-market orthodoxy and was adamant that foolish commercial banks should pay for their own mistakes, whilst the government favoured a bailout that gave itself ownership whilst denying itself control.[9] The division between the two types of neoliberal is significant since it helps explain why some aspects of transnational constitutionalism, such as the restrictions on state aid, are more flexible than

---

[8] Antinori (1994–95) 1838, 1846.
[9] Brummer (2008) 68–69.

others, such as the free movement of capital and services. The latter unites the two types of neoliberal, whilst the former divides them.

It deserves to be emphasised that the series of neoliberal governments since 1979 were not introducing a new doctrine when they brought in neoliberalism. Neoliberalism, as defined above, has in fact usually been the dominant governmental doctrine in Britain since the birth of capitalism itself. Thus the Thatcher government and its successors essentially brought about neoliberalism's powerful *re*introduction. And just as the neoliberals of the eighteenth and nineteenth centuries could rely on elements of constitutional design in order to guarantee respect for corporate property rights—such as the structure of the British Empire, an international legal order that protected foreign capital[10] and the veto power of the House of Lords[11]—so too have the recent succession of neoliberal governments understood full well the importance of constitutional design as a means of ensuring that the economic status quo is not only fundamentally retained but actually made more favourable for corporate interests.

The Idea of a Constitution

It will be readily apparent that this book intends to challenge the conventional limits inherent in the definition of a constitution. It is argued that globalisation obliges us to depart from established tradition. As Thomas Poole has observed, British public lawyers 'have come late to the globalisation debate, and there is a sense in which the issue remains peripheral to the study of constitutional law'.[12] Our very idea of 'the constitutional' remains heavily dependant on the assumption that the state is the basic constitutional unit, reflecting this reluctance to engage with globalisation. Thus British constitutional scholarship for the most part tends to focus on Britain's internal institutions. Yet a preponderant focus on the internal is, it will be argued, increasingly unsustainable. Under conditions of globalisation the established academic boundary lines no longer correspond to patterns of contemporary governance. The state no longer possesses the primacy it once enjoyed, and it becomes necessary to draw the transnational regimes themselves—not only the European Union but also others, such as the World Trade Organization and the European Convention on Human Rights—within the scope of our definition of the constitution.

This transformation has been facilitated by the strengthening of the system of transnational law in two ways. First, the scope of transnational regulation has expanded. It now intrudes deeply into fields of activity that were previously considered the exclusive domain of the state. In particular, more and more aspects of

---

[10] Lipson (1985).
[11] See, eg, Blackstone's idea of a 'balanced constitution' in Craig (1991) 234–37.
[12] Poole (2007) 606.

economic policy are set at a transnational level. This gradual erosion of the barriers between policy areas regarded as national and those regarded as international has meant that national authority has slowly been eroded, and the power of the state to make choices between distinct economic policies has gradually been challenged.[13] To emphasise this trend towards constitutional globalisation is not to hark back to some mythical golden age of absolute national autonomy but rather to assert that, although states may never have enjoyed complete freedom of action to pursue their own choice of internal policies, there has nonetheless been a discernable whittling-away of the policymaking discretion of national governments and parliaments, in part by due process of constitutional law. Nor has this development been ideologically neutral: behind globalisation lies marketisation.[14] Indeed, politicians tend to deploy the rhetoric of free trade to obscure other priorities.[15] Chief amongst these has been the consolidation of private enterprise as the dominant economic form: the marketplace has increasingly been legally institutionalised at global and regional level,[16] and international legal regimes have lent an almost constitutional character to the principle of free competition.[17] These changes require British public lawyers to orientate themselves towards the substantive law of the transnational regimes and to consider the way in which it impacts on economic policy—for there is nothing peripheral about the policies that have been entrenched. They do not represent a mere erosion of sovereignty 'at the edges'. On the contrary, they represent very fundamental policy choices.

The second element of strengthening is that certain international law regimes have become more effective. In making this claim it is important not to exaggerate the impotence of international rules in the past. *Pacta sunt survenda* has long been a principle of international law, meaning that 'in exercising their sovereign rights, including the right to determine their laws and regulations, states should conform with their obligations under international law. A state may not invoke the provisions of its municipal law as justification for failure to fulfil its obligations under international law.'[18] In addition there is a natural propensity for states broadly to comply with their international obligations. As one author put it, most states obey most international law most of the time.[19] Nonetheless, since the Second World War there has been a discernable trend towards the establishment of more effective enforcement of international rules. This trend became stronger in the 1980s and 1990s, as states increasingly sought to guarantee compliance with international rules. As a result, 'national sovereignty' can no longer be 'a magic wand that one waves in order to ward off any entanglement in the international system'.[20] At least

---

[13] Luard (1977).

[14] Rodrik (1997) 85.

[15] Bello (2005) 105.

[16] Sand (2004) 42.

[17] *Ibid*, 54.

[18] Lukashuk (1989) 518. This principle applies provided that there is reciprocity on the part of the contracting parties.

[19] Henkin (1979).

[20] Jackson (1998) 77.

in the case of some transnational regimes, the relative ease with which obligations can be breached is largely, albeit not wholly, a thing of the past.[21]

Constitutional globalisation has also been characterised by a shift towards American legal style.[22] This includes a broad empowerment of private actors to assert rights.[23] Trade liberalisation—opening international markets for capital, goods and services—has allowed new actors to enter previously closed markets and to participate in areas of economic activity in which markets were previously nonexistent. This development has required re-regulation on more formal, legalistic and transparent lines, to match the lack of close ties between industry and government. These changes correspond to those which took place in the United States at an earlier stage because liberalisation commenced earlier there.

Moreover it is arguable that globalisation has followed not only American law but American constitutional design, with an emphasis on quasi-federalism, judicialisation and insulation of policy against political forces that may come to power in the future. The World Bank has promoted a stronger role for the judiciary in promoting and underpinning the business climate on the American model. It has also pressed for the adoption of a US-style separation of powers, both horizontally (executive, legislature and judiciary) and vertically (devolution, federalism) as well as for a looser party system. The Bank has argued that 'the broader the separation of powers, the greater will be the number of veto points to be navigated to change any rule-based commitments. Thus the separation of powers increases confidence in the stability of rules.'[24] Most significantly, the Bank accepts that these US-style constitutional attributes, if not present in the domestic constitution, can be provided by international institutions such as the European Union and World Trade Organization.[25]

It might be argued that it is inappropriate to view transnational regimes as part of the constitution since in the final analysis a nation state can always withdraw from an organisation. There are, however, two compelling objections to this argument. The first is that merely because a constitutional arrangement is capable of being altered is no reason to deny its constitutional status. Ultimately *all* constitutional arrangements can be changed. Such arrangements acquire their constitutional status not because of pretensions to permanence but because they comprise, as long as they are in force, the ground rules for governance.

The second argument is that there is in any event a strong de facto entrenchment of our membership of the transnational regimes. On this reading there is no need for formal legal requirements, such as special parliamentary majorities or referenda, in order to entrench a country's membership. Rather, the very nature of the organisation, combined with the commercial context in which it operates, constitutes a means of entrenchment. According to some globalisation scholars, a

---

[21] Jackson (2006a) 107.
[22] Kelemann and Sibbert (2004) 103.
[23] *Ibid*, 106.
[24] World Bank (1997) 100.
[25] *Ibid*, 7–8.

process of 'denationalisation' has taken place whereby the authority of the state has been replaced by markets and by regional and global forms of governance. This has led in turn to a relationship of interdependence that is costly to break.[26] Furthermore, membership of these regimes forms a package deal in which individual elements cannot be 'unpicked' from the whole, and this constitutes an entrenching device. Whilst states retain their theoretical ability to change course, the World Bank has pointed out that they need to calculate the costs and benefits of withdrawal, including the threat of international censure.[27] The source of such censure is not only states but transnational corporations. If we free ourselves from our conventional preconceptions about constitutional thinking, there is no compelling reason why such de facto entrenchment ought not to be regarded as a means of *constitutional* entrenchment.

Thus the strengthening of the transnational regimes obliges us to rethink the boundaries of our discipline in the face of this 'denationalisation of constitutional law'.[28] Hitherto it has often been said that the most important feature of British constitutional law is the legislative supremacy of Parliament, that is, the acceptance by our judiciary of Parliament's right to make and unmake the supreme law of the land in the form of Acts of Parliament.[29] But perhaps we have reached the point at which, in ever wider fields, the most important element of Britain's constitution (and indeed, the constitutions of other countries) is no longer Parliamentary sovereignty but rather transnational regulation. Such regulation involves the imposition of limitations on national governmental activity and a bypassing of national governmental processes. If this shift in our conception of the constitutional is accepted, then vast swathes of substantive transnational law, much of it concerning economic policy, would need to be seen as falling within the ambit of our own public law.

Significantly, the traditional, state-based conception of the constitution is not shared by many international economic lawyers. Whilst the question of whether the WTO Agreements form a constitution remains controversial,[30] the idea that the Agreements provide important legal *elements* for the national constitutions is beyond dispute for international economic lawyers. For example, John Jackson, a leading scholar in WTO law, argues that the trends in international law since the Second World War compel attention ever more towards the 'constitutional law' nature of international regimes. He argues that the GATT/WTO and EEC/EU systems have established an astonishingly 'rule-oriented' landscape in which state

---

[26] Bartle (2005) 13.

[27] World Bank (1997) 101.

[28] De Búrca and Gerstenberg (2006).

[29] The existence (as opposed to the content) of Parliamentary sovereignty is relatively uncontroversial in English law and the law of Northern Ireland, but is this the case in Scots law? The dictum of Lord President Cooper in *MacCormick v Lord Advocate*, 1953 SC 366 that parliamentary sovereignty is a distinctly English doctrine with no counterpart in Scots constitutional law is well known. It may be argued, however, that judicial inaction speaks louder than words. In the three-hundred-year history of the Union, no Scottish court has invalidated an Act of Parliament.

[30] Cass (2005).

sovereignty no longer immunises states from international measures that affect internal or domestic governmental activities.[31] In the same vein Henry Schermers highlights how the idea of sovereignty as unlimited state power over matters within a state's domestic jurisdiction has been seriously weakened during the latter half of the twentieth century.[32] Similarly Ernst-Ulrich Petersmann emphasises how market economies have been protected by means of a supranational 'economic constitution'. This constitution, he argues, is based on a coherent set of constituent principles such as monetary stability, open markets, private ownership, freedom of contract, liability and policy coherence.[33] The finding that international economic lawyers view constitutions in such broad terms should give national public lawyers cause to question our own, more limited conception of the constitutional. The arguments for including the transnational regimes within our definition of the constitution are therefore rather compelling, even though to do so would mean a departure from conventional thinking.

An even more radical proposal is that pursued by Gavin Anderson in his book *Constitutional Rights after Globalisation*.[34] Anderson argues that transnational corporations also merit inclusion in our definition of the constitution. He contends that our notion of 'the constitution' should fully encompass how society is organised and how it functions. In other words, our conception of the constitution should embrace the entire regime whereby power is exercised.[35] This argument is timely. There is a growing recognition of the variety of techniques of governing being extended from law and politics to encompass the economic; markets are increasingly seen as having governmental functions on a par with politico-legal systems, and corporate actors are seen as governmental actors in addition to the political and sovereign actors to which we are accustomed.[36] We shall see that corporations, not just states, have acted as protagonists in the constitutional evolution of the EC Treaty and WTO Agreements.[37] It may be that public law's preoccupation with 'public actors' and its pervasive defensiveness towards private actors need to be reconsidered.[38]

If we expand our conception of constitutional actors to include transnational corporations, then this would mean that their commercial actions, actual or

---

[31] Jackson (2006a) 205–6.

[32] Schermers (2002) 192.

[33] Petersmann (2001) 88

[34] Anderson (2005). Anderson argues that the state does not have a monopoly on law, so we need to rethink the nature and location of political authority and to conceive corporations as major political actors. He argues for the rejection of state-centred accounts of constitutional law-making in favour of ones that acknowledge multiple sites of governance. In a review of the book, Hans Lindahl, whilst supporting Anderson's expanded conception of constitutionalism, criticises Anderson's understanding of constitutional norms as coming from two sources, public and private. Instead, Lindahl argues that private law *is* public law, and accordingly, acts of norm-creation by 'private parties' such as corporations should be conceived as acts of *state* officials (Lindahl (2007) 149).

[35] Teubner (2004).

[36] Sand (2004) 44–45.

[37] Emberland (2006) 10.

[38] Freeman (2000); Muchlinski (2001).

threatened, come to be regarded as a means of constitutional entrenchment. This would fly in the face of an orthodox conception of 'the constitutional', which would view the constraints presented by corporations not as constitutional constraints, but rather as being of a 'factual' nature, a 'political' restriction, as part of 'reality' or as the deeds of 'autonomous actors'. Yet there is nothing that dictates conclusively what we should regard as 'constitutional' and what we should not consider 'constitutional'. Accordingly, there is a strong case for reclassifying the external economic factors that circumscribe the freedom of action of government as being, in fact, constitutional. The transnationalisation of the corporation is a major reason why it may now be more than ever appropriate to consider corporations as part of the constitution.

In the 1970s Stuart Holland argued that the rise of multinational companies constituted a fundamental change in the structure of capitalism, which meant that power was now concentrated in the hands of a miniscule class of enormously powerful top managers.[39] This multinationalisation, he contended, had rendered ineffective the traditional Keynesian means of governmental control of the economy such as monetary and fiscal policy, as well as tariff barriers, common market and customs union policies. In short, the new domination of monopoly-multinational capital had deprived the nation state of its power to control its own economic destiny.[40] Such analyses of economic globalisation—pointing to the significant augmentation of power of multinational corporations vis-à-vis states[41]—should prompt us to rethink the locus of political authority and therefore recognise the close connection between the constitutional and economic realms.[42] Moreover the argument that corporations form part of our constitution is particularly difficult to refute now that under transnational law, their rights have been more formally constitutionalised. Put bluntly, corporations are the beneficiaries of fundamental rights.

If we adopt Anderson's wider conception of the constitution, we might regard the WTO and EU judiciaries as providing effective constitutional sanctions for breaching the WTO Agreements and EU Treaties, whilst the risk of retaliation from transnational corporations, from the transnational regimes themselves and from their participating states, provide effective constitutional sanctions to deter secession from the WTO and EU. All these constraints can be regarded as constitutional constraints since after all there is no compelling reason to regard legal enmeshment as the only form of constitutional enmeshment. Perhaps, indeed, we should conceive enmeshment itself as making a rule or regime constitutional, the source of that enmeshment (legal, economic, cultural or political) being of secondary importance.[43] Such a broad approach would in fact chime well with the

---

[39] Holland (1975a)

[40] *Ibid.*

[41] Anderson (2005) 26.

[42] *Ibid*, 33.

[43] Consider, for instance, British adhesion to the European Convention on Human Rights. It would perhaps be easier for Britain to denounce the ECHR than to extricate itself from the WTO and EU. (We can therefore discern a sliding scale of enmeshment.) Yet the reasons Britain is unlikely to do so relate

extra-legal traditions of the British constitution, whereby many of the most important rules are not laid down by the law.[44]

This monograph does not have as its focus the constitutional role of corporations, a subject that would require another whole book. Instead, this book focuses on the transnational regimes—WTO, EU, ECHR—arguing that they are essentially part of our constitution and that they bind us to a certain form of capitalism. We will therefore not pursue any further the argument that transnational corporations form part of the constitution. Nonetheless, the inclusion of corporations within the definition of the constitution enables us to appreciate the full degree of entrenchment enjoyed by the transnational regimes within the constitution. Rejecting the characterisation of corporate actions as 'factual' constraints as opposed to constitutional constraints means that the acts of corporations cannot be treated as a 'given' to be borne by constitutional scholars without comment. Under the expanded conception of the constitution, a constitutional scholar can treat corporate power as contingent and contestable, just like any other feature of the constitution. Corporations are not thereby distanced from governance by being perceived as 'independent actors'; rather, they are treated for what they are: governing institutions.

If we accept this expanded definition of the constitution, then a wholly different picture of the British constitution emerges. Many of our beliefs about our key constitutional characteristics and doctrines will need to be reconsidered.[45] For instance, if we accept the idea of a globalised public law, it may no longer be appropriate to perceive Britain as having an unwritten constitution. Instruments such as the EU Treaties, WTO Agreements and the ECHR can be seen as providing, in essence, a fragmented multiplicity of written constitutions, each enjoying a high degree of entrenchment, de facto and de jure. Similarly, the separation of powers doctrine would need to be radically reconsidered if the institutions of the transnational regimes come to be seen as part of a system of checks and balances. As for the rule of law, if, as Lord Bingham proposes, it embraces an obligation to comply with international law, it could be seen as reinforcing constitutional globalisation.[46] Most importantly, however, we would need to rethink the constitution's relationship with democracy.[47] The greater the degree of policy entrenchment, the less is open to democratic contestation. There is the danger therefore that elections are increasingly providing democratic window-dressing for an entrenched reality. This state of affairs provides material for a vigorous normative debate: can the property, contract and trading rights of the EU and WTO legal systems be treated as containing an a priori goodness, or should such matters be determined by democratic politics?[48]

partly to the desire not to set a bad example to ECHR states with poor human rights records such as Russia (political) and partly to the normative and rhetorical 'pull' of human rights (political/cultural).

[44] After all, it would be difficult to abolish conventions of the constitution such as the rule that the Queen acts on ministerial advice, but not because of any risk of judicial intervention.

[45] De Búrca (1999) 61.

[46] Bingham (2006).

[47] Rosenfeld (2008) 415.

[48] Trachtman (2006) 482.

A Revolution from Above

What brought about this constitutional transformation? The established view is that the modern international institution was born with the creation of the League of Nations in the wake of the First World War.[49] The League has been described as 'caught between the promise of a new politics and the debacle of an old regime'; it is seen as having been positioned between deference to sovereign autonomy and the international authority of its own organs.[50] In response to the failure of the League there was an intensification of institutionalisation after 1945. In the economic sphere, the General Agreement on Tariffs and Trade (GATT) came into existence and the European Economic Community (EEC) was established. At their inception these organisations were characterised by the toleration of a variety of capitalisms and had relatively weak enforcement processes. However, from the 1980s onwards, the election of neoliberals in key countries such as the United States and Britain gradually led to the establishment of a neoliberal consensus among world leaders, which in turn came to be reflected in a sharpening of the neoliberal ideology of transnational constitutionalism. This was to have important ramifications in terms of both substantive policy and enforcement machinery.

It will be readily apparent that globalisation is the lynchpin concept, the prism through which the contemporary constitution needs to be analysed. Neoliberal leaders have constantly deployed the rhetoric of globalisation in order to advance key neoliberal demands such as the free movement of capital and services. Yet globalisation did not happen merely by dint of business decisions or technological advances: globalisation above all has *political* foundations. Had national politicians opted to maintain trade barriers in the wake of the Second World War, globalisation would have been less extensive. It was the forces of globalisation unleashed by the GATT and EEC, along with the relaxation of capital and regulatory controls by national governments, that fostered greater multinationalism of corporations, and this in turn gave corporations greater leverage over governments.

What, then, do we mean by globalisation? In simple terms, globalisation can be defined as 'the widening, deepening and speeding up of worldwide interconnectedness in all aspects of contemporary social life'.[51] It constitutes 'a social process in which the constraints of geography on economic, political, social and cultural arrangements recede, in which people become increasingly aware that they are receding and in which people act accordingly'.[52] Beyond such straightforward definitions, however, there is fierce debate about the true nature of globalisation. David Held, Anthony McGrew, David Goldblatt and Jonathan Perraton identify three competing theories, which they dub 'hyperglobalist', 'sceptical' and 'transformationist'.[53]

---

[49] Kennedy (1986–87) 842.
[50] *Ibid*, 980.
[51] Held, McGrew, Goldblatt and Perraton (1999) 2.
[52] Waters (2001) 5.
[53] Held, McGrew, Goldblatt and Perraton (1999) 3–9.

The hyperglobalist thesis views the traditional state as becoming an unnatural, even impossible business unit. Hyperglobalists perceive a 'denationalisation' of economies, as a result of which a single global market has emerged. Within this market governments are relegated to little more than transmission belts for global capital. Hyperglobalists emphasise that the needs of global capital impose a neo-liberal economic discipline on all governments, thereby reducing the scope of politics to sound economic management. The hyperglobalist prognosis is that globalisation will ultimately lead to the demise of the nation state and its replacement with a truly global civilisation (or 'market civilisation'), defined by universal standards of economic and political organisation.

In stark contrast, the sceptical thesis is that globalisation is a myth. Observing that the present degree of economic integration remains far less significant than the level prevailing in the late nineteenth century, sceptics argue that contemporary levels of economic interdependence are by no means unprecedented. Moreover, they contend that the enduring power of national governments to regulate international economic activity must not be underestimated. The forces of internationalisation themselves depend on the regulatory power of national governments to ensure continuing economic liberalisation. Accordingly, governments are not the passive victims of internationalisation but rather its primary architects.

Finally, the transformationalist thesis argues that globalisation is a central driving force, bringing about rapid social, political and economic changes that are reshaping societies and the world order. However, the direction of this 'shake-out' remains uncertain, since globalisation is an essentially contingent historical process replete with contradictions. Thus transformationalists make no claims about the future trajectory of globalisation. They believe that globalisation is reconstituting the power, functions and authority of national governments by strengthening the institutions of international governance and the constraints of international law. They argue that a 'new sovereignty regime' is thereby displacing traditional conceptions of statehood as absolute, territorially-exclusive public power. In short, the world order is no longer state-centric. Powerful new non-territorial entities, such as multinational corporations, transnational social movements and international regulatory agencies, are coming to the fore. Governments are obliged to become more outward-looking and to create international regimes to manage the growing array of cross-border issues. Thus the powers of the state are not necessarily diminished by globalisation; rather, states are being reconstituted and restructured in response to a more interconnected world.

Analysis of the legal regimes covered in this book tends to vindicate the transformationalist argument more than those advanced by hyperglobalists and sceptics. The transformationist thesis is particularly attractive because of its rejection of historical determinism. It can indeed be convincingly argued that there has been nothing inevitable about the extent of globalisation or the ideological form that it has taken. Yet some supporters of neoliberal globalisation insist that the process has been inevitable. For instance, Jackson has argued that developments in communications, transport and weapons have played the predominant role in the growth of globalisation.[54] Claims of historical determinism are nothing new but thankfully neither are its critics. Ironically, foremost amongst those critics is the ideological leading light of neoliberalism, Friedrich A Hayek. Hayek wrote his classic book *The Road to Serfdom* in 1944, during an era when, according to Hayek himself, socialism was seen as an inevitable result of technological change.[55] He argued that in reality, the forward march of socialism should be attributed to its political popularity: 'it is because nearly everybody wants it that we are moving in this direction. There are no objective facts which make it inevitable.'[56] The same pertains to neoliberal globalisation: it has happened because nearly everybody among the political and business elite has wanted it to happen. By the same token the future of globalisation cannot be predetermined either. In this respect, it is appropriate to recall Isaiah Berlin's denunciation of the idea of historical inevitability as 'one of the great alibis, pleaded by those who cannot or do not wish to face the fact of human responsibility'.[57]

Another attractive feature of the transformationalist thesis is that whilst it does not envisage the total demise of the state, neither does it see things as remaining much the same as they were in the past. It thereby charts a course between the hyperglobalist Scylla and the sceptic Chaybdis. The transformationist narrative of a reconstituted state corresponds most acutely to the way in which national policy-making autonomy has been eroded by the legal instruments discussed in this book. It also corresponds with the normative ideal of a teleological state advanced by the European Court of Justice in cases such as *von Colson* and *Brasserie du Pêcheur and Factortame*, in which it posited national judiciaries and legislatures as duty-bound to help secure the achievement of EU objectives.[58] The transformationist thesis does not necessarily involve a wholesale weakening of national institutions: thus for instance, the judicial branch is actually made more powerful[59] not in order to give courts policymaking freedom but rather for the teleological purpose of ensuring that government and parliament abide by their duty to facilitate EU aims.

It is certainly valuable, as globalisation sceptics suggest, to look back in history at previous waves of globalisation. But such comparisons may serve to highlight the unique elements of the present era. To be sure, during the nineteenth century the process of globalisation, in terms of international trade, accelerated on an unprecedented scale, benefiting from relative world peace. Empire and force of arms could be deployed to enforce free trade. As a result there was a rapid increase in the number and size of multinational corporations and a global upsurge in

---

[54] Jackson (2006b) 427.
[55] Hayek (1986) ch. IV.
[56] *Ibid*, 3.
[57] Berlin (2007) 164.
[58] Case 14/83 *Von Colson* [1984] ECR 1891, [1986] CMLR 430; Joined cases C-46/93 and C-48/93 *Brasserie du Pêcheur and Factortame* [1996] ECR I-1029.
[59] Craig (1997b).

foreign investment.[60] This went hand in hand with the spread of international property law, which guaranteed property rights on a virtually global basis. These rights were secured by the growth of *bilateral* commercial treaties, which protected alien property. The core principle of these treaties was that the property of foreigners could only be taken if there was prompt and full compensation. This system of bilateral treaties proved effective: until 1914 there were no major expropriations of foreign property.[61] After a reversal of globalisation during World War I and the inter-war years, the aftermath of World War II saw the beginning of the construction of the new global economy. By this point there were many barriers to the free movement of economic factors. In contrast to the earlier era of globalisation, the legal solution was the creation of international organisations. The reduction of world trade barriers through the GATT in 1947 and the creation of the large 'common market' of the EEC in 1957, in combination with the 'political herding' of national leaders towards neoliberalism from the 1980s onwards, led to an intensification of the pace of globalisation. Crucially it facilitated a further growth of transnational corporations, such that by 2000 two-fifths of world trade was actually intrafirm.[62]

Thus in terms of legal strategy, the difference between the globalisation of the late nineteenth century and the globalisation of the second half of the twentieth century was profound. Whilst the globalisation of the Victorian era had relied on bilateral treaties, the globalisation of the post-War era was characterised by the rise of transnational regimes.[63] The creation of these regimes had profound consequences for constitutional governance, as John Ruggie explained:

> [I]t created principal–agent problems that had not existed before. Any form of organizational mediation is capable of affecting outcomes, of introducing elements into the substance or process of decision making that previously were not present. A multi-purpose, universal membership organisation complicates that situation by involving itself even in areas in which no normative consensus exists . . . Second, multilateral forums increasingly have come to share in the agenda-setting and convening power of states. For example, such forums increasingly drive the international conference diplomacy game. Third, and perhaps most important, multilateral diplomacy has come to embody a procedural norm in its own right—though often a hotly contested one—in some instances carrying with it an international legitimacy not enjoyed by other means.[64]

Thus transnational regimes took on a life of their own. Part of this autonomous existence involved the vast growth of the international judiciary.[65] For some, indeed, the global expansion of judicial power constituted the most important development of the post-Cold War age.[66] The creation and evolution of regimes

---

[60] Jones (2005) ch.2.
[61] *Ibid*, 24–25. See generally Lipson (1985).
[62] Jones (2005) 41.
[63] Alvarez (2005) 555.
[64] Ruggie (1983) 23.
[65] Alvarez (2005) 646.
[66] Romano (1998–99) 709.

with their own juridical systems radically altered the way in which governmental power is exercised at national level.[67] As states came to vest the transnational regimes with real authority to fashion international standards, the transfer of power to interpret and enforce those standards naturally followed.[68] This new situation has turned on its head the traditional argument that claims that the judiciary is the 'least dangerous branch' of government since it has no particular political axe to grind.[69] The teleology of the transnational regimes has endowed the transnational judiciary with just such definitive political objectives. The European Court of Justice developed a particularly strong system of remedies, but the trend towards broad scope and strengthened enforcement soon spread to other regimes. As Karen Alter observed in 2001,

> As late as the 1970s and early 1980s, the European [Community] experience appeared to be quite exceptional. But in the late 1980s and the 1990s, there have been signs of a broader trend towards international law influencing state behaviour. The European Court of Human Rights is increasingly active in European human rights issues. The new World Trade Organization dispute resolution system has been hearing a number of cases with broad implications for national policy.[70]

The increase in judicial power is only one aspect of transnational constitutionalism, albeit an important one. In many instances the bare words of transnational provisions are clear enough to rule out political options without the need for recourse to judicial elucidation. In any event, irrespective of whether rules derive from the clear meaning of treaties or the interpretation of courts, the policy discretion of governments and parliaments is ever more tightly structured by a continuous expansion of legal constraints, a process known as judicialisation.[71]

Furthermore, in the 1980s and 1990s the ideological focus of the transnational regimes sharpened. This was a result of political victories of neoliberals at national level, which gradually created a neoliberal consensus. In turn, this consensus was ultimately reflected in a greater neoliberalisation at transnational level. By the late 1980s and early 1990s, leaders throughout the world seemed to have come to a consensus that business—economic organisation in the form of the market or the firm—should become the dominant form in the world's economies.[72] Liberalisation and privatisation have since become hegemonic political practice, taking the place of public ownership and direct ministerial scrutiny, not just in Britain but throughout the world. David Levy-Faur argues that this hegemony can partly be attributed to a herding phenomenon, whereby in many political situations one's choice is determined not only by one's own preferences but by the signals of others.[73] Privatisation in Britain inspired liberalisation at EU level, which led in turn to a constitutionalisation of liberalisation by means of Community law. The same phenomenon was

[67] Alvarez (2005) 647.
[68] Romano (1998–99) 729.
[69] Bickel (1986); Steyn (2007). Cf Griffith (1997).
[70] Alter (2001) 230.
[71] Stone Sweet (2000) 1.
[72] Trachtman (2006) 15.
[73] Levy-Faur (2002).

reproduced at global level but with the United States as well as Britain forming the privatising vanguard. Thus a large group of states took their cues from early national programmes of privatisation, notably Britain's; in this way, a contagious process of imitation took place in which pressure from a global corporate elite was transformed into a set of ideas and rhetoric to win over those social groups unlikely to benefit.[74] In this way the convergence of national preferences towards international liberalisation and privatisation in the 1990s and early 2000s became a distinctive feature of globalisation.[75] Moreover this convergence determined globalisation's constitutional design. By the time of the WTO negotiations most national politicians perceived that privatisation was desirable, and this was reflected in the WTO provisions.[76] Similarly, the EU provisions on free movement came to be embellished, by EU legislation and ECJ interpretation alike, in a manner that reflected a preference for the expansion of the private sector. The same consensus encouraged the European Court of Human Rights (ECtHR) to go far beyond the original intentions of the ECHR framers to strengthen the right of private property ownership.

For British politicians, neoliberalism had an allure because of the economic and industrial problems of the 1960s and more particularly the 1970s. Both the Edward Heath and James Callaghan administrations culminated in major industrial unrest. Under Margaret Thatcher's leadership and under the influence of Sir Keith Joseph, the Conservative Party swung in favour of a more neoliberal stance. The long period of Conservative rule in the 1980s gave the Party the opportunity to implement neoliberalism into British policy and law. Most importantly, however, the British left was also gradually won over to neoliberal ideas, with the Labour Party progressively discarding its socialist and social democratic credentials, a process that culminated in its decision in 1996 to abandon its constitutional aim of an economy based on public ownership. Ultimately, New Labour's commitment to neoliberalism assumed an almost evangelistic zeal,[77] so that far from putting Thatcherism into reverse, on taking office they supercharged it.[78] Nor did a change of leader herald a change in ideology: Tony Blair was replaced by Gordon Brown, a politician whose commitment to privatisation is said to border on the messianic.[79] Thus both main parties became actively committed to the cause of neoliberal globalisation.[80] The transnational constitution therefore arose largely as a result of the rough and tumble of the democratic process, namely the election of successive neoliberal governments in Britain and the United States, combined with a conversion to (or toleration of) neoliberalism on the part of governments and transnational regimes elsewhere. It was truly 'a constitution established by the victorious class after a successful battle'.[81] However, the mere fact that the

[74] Bartle (2005) 35–36.
[75] *Ibid*, 26.
[76] Blank and Marceau (1997) 49.
[77] Evans (2005) 71.
[78] Jenkins (2007) 206.
[79] *Ibid*, 258.
[80] Martell (2008).
[81] Letter from Friedrich Engels to Joseph Bloch, 22 September 1890.

neoliberal constitution has been the product of the democratic process does not serve to make that constitution itself democratic.

Although British Conservatives and American Republicans sought neo-liberalism, they were emotionally committed to national sovereignty and had to reconcile this attachment with the adoption of transnational constraints. The way they did so is revealed in IM Destler's account of the US debate on WTO membership:

> The WTO raised concerns that the new trade institutions and procedures would override US laws . . . Supporters brought in conservative jurist Robert Bork to quash the sovereignty question, and Bork declared that the WTO took away no authority from US institutions and could not force any changes in US law. The Heritage Foundation weighed in with the same analysis. Together with the strengthened dispute settlement procedures, however, the WTO could produce legitimate decisions that US laws violated US trade commitments. And while it could not force changes in these laws, it could sanction retaliation by other nations if the laws were not changed.[82]

The same confusion is evident in the views of Thatcher. Thatcher's much-trumpeted support for parliamentary supremacy and national sovereignty may well have been sincerely felt, yet her government approved the Single European Act, a revision of the EC Treaty that drastically reduced national autonomy. Such an erosion of sovereignty was made psychologically acceptable only by adhering to the formal analysis urged by Bork, which posits a sharp divide between national constitutional law and international rules.[83]

The narrative of neoliberal constitutionalism offered in this chapter is not par-ticularly fanciful. No belief in any grand conspiracy is required (although we can-not discount the possibility that such a conspiracy existed). All that is being argued is that the neoliberal consensus among the world's political leaders was, and remains, extremely strong. Accordingly, when neoliberal leaders were called upon to make constitutional choices, they naturally enough opted for constitutional arrangements that benefited the attainment and retention of their own favoured policies. In so doing they could not resist the temptation of privileging those poli-cies over considerations of democracy, by means of entrenchment. They consid-ered the perpetuation of their policies to be more constitutionally valuable than the retention of policymaking choice.

Ran Hirschl in his book *Towards Juristocracy* has advanced the theory that transnational constitutionalism is the product of interplay between three groups.[84] First, ruling political elites felt threatened by democracy and wanted their business-friendly policy preferences to be less effectively contested under new constitutional arrangements. Secondly, economic elites—namely transnational corporations—sought the constitutionalisation of rights, especially property and mobility rights, to promote privatisation and ward off socialistic encroachments by states. They

---

[82] Destler (2005) 221.
[83] Thatcher (1986) ch.18.
[84] Hirschl (2004) 1–16, 38–49.

sought to place economic liberties beyond the reach of majoritarian control. Thirdly, judicial elites saw the new constitutionalism as a way to advance their political influence and international status.

Hirschl's narrative seems broadly to correspond to the findings in this book, though a couple of refinements might usefully be added. First, whilst all three elites have at different times taken lead roles in the creation of the transnational constitution, it can convincingly be argued that the political elite has played the dominant role. Secondly, whilst the judiciary wanted to improve its institutional position—pure and simple judicial empowerment was undoubtedly a factor in encouraging transnational judicial bodies and national courts to transform their constitutional position[85]—neither should we ignore the fact that judges, like all of us, hold political beliefs. The teleology demanded by the transnational regimes was rather similar to the ideological commitments that had guided the common law and is therefore one that the judiciary found attractive: an ideology based primarily on 'strong' business rights and 'weak' individualised civil rights.[86] Whilst the nature of the transnational regimes required judges to be more explicit about ideological aims, they could claim merely to be deciphering the genetic codes transmitted by those who framed the transnational agreements. At the same time the new constitutionalism had the advantage, from the judicial perspective, of prevailing over statute either in actual or in normative terms.

Transnational Constitutionalism as Insurance

The constraints of the new constitutionalism have thus been obscured and camouflaged by the seamless succession of neoliberal governments. British governments of both parties have embraced neoliberalism with vim and vigour, and this consensus has served to achieve two things. First, it has helped to bring about a degree of constitutionalisation of neoliberal policy. Matters of contemporary consensus are precisely those that are most likely to become constitutionally entrenched. Secondly, however, consensus has also served to mask the very constitutionalisation that has occurred. Inevitably, with governments and oppositions broadly united on ideology, the constitutionalisation of this ideology largely fell under the radar, due to the lack of serious resistance. It is against this backdrop that the transnational constitution can be perceived as a kind of insurance policy guaranteeing the preservation of a particular variety of capitalism. Its object is to lock in place a system of privatisation and commercial liberty, so that things will not change very much when new governments are elected. Thus the new constitutional law serves to guard against the possibility that future governments might abandon the creed of private enterprise. The particular type of market economy

---

[85] Weiler (1999a) 197.
[86] Griffith (1997); Ewing and Than (2008).

thereby protected is one that guarantees an expanded role for private enterprise in the 'public utilities', as well as safeguards the private sector's more traditional preserves of finance and the wider economy. It is also one which guarantees that governmental regulation can be subjected to independent review on proportionality grounds to ensure a generous measure of commercial liberty. The transnational constitution was fashioned by those who sought homogenous political parties committed to these policies. There has undoubtedly been a smoothing-out of Britain's traditional political cleavage,[87] but this has been placed on a more secure foundation by the elevation of a body of transnational law above politics.

The objection might be raised that if such an 'insurance policy' were genuinely 'in force', then this would surely be evidenced by numerous instances of neoliberalism being enforced by judicial fiat, whereas in fact it is rare for courts to upbraid states for failing to apply the basic WTO or EU rules to their leading markets. But it is in the nature of insurance policies that they only need to be called upon in exceptional circumstances. Over the last thirty years, the attitudes of politicians have in fact been wholeheartedly in tune with the policies enshrined in the governing instruments of the transnational regimes and the courts charged with interpreting them, such has been the strength of the neoliberal consensus. Thus the elected leaders of the last three decades have broadly wanted to run their countries in conformity with these norms. In other words, most neoliberal governments obey most neoliberal laws most of the time *because they wish to do so*; and this explains the lack of litigation on basic issues. By the same token, it is unconvincing to argue that the 'threat' of adverse judgments has acted as a shadow, deterring politicians from policies that veer from neoliberal orthodoxy. No such deterrent has been necessary, since politicians from the mid-1980s onwards have craved neoliberalism. The real purpose of transnational constitutionalism is to ensure the stability of policy in the event of today's neoliberals being succeeded by politicians of a different ilk.

Was the insurance policy really necessary? It is in the nature of insurance policies to guard against eventualities that are unlikely but nonetheless possible. Perhaps the strength of neoliberal ideological hegemony is such that neoliberalism does not really require constitutional protection. But one never knows. Neoliberal politicians did not wish to take that risk. Nor did corporations, since for them business stability has a value that easily overrides the value attributed to democracy, and policy stability is a precondition of business stability. It was necessary, therefore, to strengthen neoliberalism as the dominant ideological hegemony by increasing the political price of deviation. It was thus in the interests of both national neoliberal leaders and transnational corporations to promote the entrenchment of neoliberal policies at the expense of democracy.[88]

It is important to recognise that the constitutional 'insurance policy' has protected neoliberalism not only because it provides a set of legal remedies to nullify

---

[87] See generally Oborne (2007).
[88] de Sousa Santos (2002) 165.

'deviant' policies. As David Schneiderman has observed, the very existence of constitutional limitations has served to frame political possibilities. Whilst the rules and structures of constitutional law are not entirely determinative of political life, constitutional rules nonetheless help to reproduce particular understandings of state–society relations.[89] Constitutionalism can indeed provide a powerful cultural imperative that can prevent rival policies from even materialising. All in all, therefore, political actors can be profoundly influenced by the limitations imposed by constitutional democracy.

The Criterion of Democracy

This book does not concern itself with whether the constraints of constitutional globalisation are 'just' or 'unjust'. Judgments on the general fairness or unfairness of the new constitutional arrangements depend on one's political position. The justice or injustice of the new arrangements cannot therefore be subject to objective scrutiny, since as Jeremy Waldron has observed, 'there are many of us, and we disagree about justice.'[90] For those with a tenderness towards private enterprise, the de facto entrenchment of EU and WTO membership may be seen as fair and just. A government that is unable to provide a legal framework offering security to foreign investors will contribute to the existence of a high-risk environment in which only risky or speculative investments will probably be attracted.[91] Membership in a wider free trade area may also make a host country a more enticing location.[92] If a government imperils these attributes by threatening withdrawal from the transnational regimes, corporate retaliation in the form of a threat to withdraw investment may be seen as 'just'.

Conversely, from a more egalitarian perspective, the entrenchment of a pro-private enterprise economic policy may be considered unfair and unjust, in that corporations can be seen as benefiting from constitutional rights without the burden of constitutional responsibilities and accountability. Moreover entrenched commitments to private enterprise compromise the long-term ability of countries to provide a welfare state for their citizens based on considerations of the public interest.[93] These disagreements have been, and will continue to be, the subject of extensive scholarship and polemical writings. For this reason, this book adopts a narrower focus: the implications for *democracy* of the transnational constitution. Democracy, after all, allows the political community some say in what it regards as 'just' or 'unjust' in any given point in time. Thus the book will question whether the constitutional constraints ushered in by legal globalisation make Britain more

---

[89] Schneiderman (2008) 11.
[90] Waldron (1999) 1.
[91] Jones (2005) 9.
[92] *Ibid*, 9.
[93] Leys (2003) ch.7.

or less democratic. This will require an engagement with some of the normative arguments regarding sovereignty in the present era of globalisation, with ideas of cooperative rather than exclusive sovereignty, with conceptions of democracy that encompass the post-national era and with the neoliberal conception of democracy.

In summary, the remainder of this chapter puts the case for a normative ideal of democracy based on three democratic attributes: contestability, ideological neutrality and accountability. Assessed on this basis, it can be argued that Britain's pre-globalisation constitution offered a superior degree of democracy than is available under today's more globalised arrangements. The chapter will finally go on to consider some of the normative arguments used to justify the new constitutional status quo.

The first democratic attribute is contestability. Contestability means that since people disagree about everything, there can be no universal or self-evident truths that can be enshrined as supreme law.[94] Accordingly, everything that government does needs to be democratically contestable.[95] This should be the case irrespective of the issue involved. Thus, policies and decisions should be contestable regardless of whether they involve basic liberal political rights, the fundamentals of economic policy or social rights. There is no principled basis on which these different aspects of policy can be disentangled from each other. Rather, they blur into one another. Thus free movement rights are regarded as the 'fundamental freedoms' of the individual and the corporation, and the human right to peaceful enjoyment of one's possessions fuses with the corporate ownership rights of private property. The bottom line is that there can be no entrenchment of favoured policies, since entrenchment would cocoon such policies from the full rigour of contestability. Entrenchment would also serve to hive off decision-making from the political community at large to a judicial elite.[96] There should therefore be no division between 'ordinary' politics and 'constitutional' politics.[97] Moreover, the constitution should guarantee the *permanence* of contestability. Melissa Schwarzberg has argued that the ability of a representative assembly to modify the law, to revisit decisions and to innovate has rightly been a defining characteristic of democracy since the days of the Athenians, who generally rejected entrenchment as a means of self-binding so that a temporary passion (such as our present passion for neoliberalism) would not overwhelm them. All in all, therefore, the democratic constitution should not privilege substantive outcomes but should represent the structure for reaching collective decisions in a democratic way.[98]

The second democratic attribute is ideological neutrality. The idea of ideological neutrality is closely related to the contestability of individual policies, but on a grander scale: it represents contestability writ large. It rests on the assumption that most political actors do not attach themselves to a motley ragbag of policies on an

---

[94] Waldron (1999).
[95] Pettit (1997) 277.
[96] Waldron (1993) 18.
[97] Bellamy (2007) 24–25.
[98] *Ibid*, 4.

eclectic, pick-and-mix basis; their choice of individual policies instead has some coherence, in the sense that they flow from ideology, a worldview of how society should be organised and how life should be lived. In providing the framework or structure by which these ideological differences are resolved, the constitution ought to maintain as neutral a stance as possible, favouring neither one substantive ideology nor another. Rather, the constitution's enduring ideological commitment must be to democracy itself, thereby permitting the country to be drawn in whichever ideological direction reflects the will of the political community. Such a constitution should be preferred over one with an inbuilt bias in favour of one substantive political creed at the expense of others, since this would detract unacceptably from the power of the people to determine their own future.

The third democratic attribute is accountability, which enables citizens to hold decision-makers to account and allows decision-makers to advance policies and laws with the legitimacy of electoral consent. When electors come to vote in a general election, they never start with a blank canvass: every election is a re-election. Elections afford an opportunity to judge the performance of the government, set against the backdrop of the other potential governments on offer. A system of accountability cannot guarantee that governing institutions will necessarily track the interests of those to whom they are accountable.[99] Rather, it provides an opportunity. Ultimately governments are as accountable as the electorate wishes to make them. If voters give considerable latitude to their politicians, that is the electorate's choice. Accordingly it is not necessarily the case that voters get their way on each and every issue, sometimes not even in the long run: governments do not, in other words, replicate the views of the electorate in the way envisaged by AV Dicey, who saw the constitution as 'self-correcting'.[100] On the other hand, the very fear or anticipation of electoral rejection itself conditions political conduct to some extent. The need for power-holders to compete for re-election is what makes them responsive to the public.[101] Thus the idea of democratic accountability—that it is possible to replace political office-holders through elections—is one that has great resonance.[102] It is fundamentally important to us that those who rule in our name are in the end answerable to us.[103] For this reason, as Carol Harlow has observed, accountability has become the framework for government and the precondition for all democratic rule.[104] Whilst the language of accountability has expanded in recent years to embrace weaker forms of public dialogue not involving the possibility of sanction,[105] there surely need to be compelling reasons of principle (such as, for example, the need to guarantee the independence of the judiciary) to justify a weakening of accountability in the case of those who wield very substantial governmental power. In the normal run of things, if accountability is to ensure that

[99] Tomkins (2005) ch 2.
[100] Dicey (1962) ch 1. Cf Craig (1990) ch 2.
[101] Lord (1998) 80.
[102] Harlow (2002) 8.
[103] Dunn (1999) 342–43.
[104] Harlow (2002) 8.
[105] Le Sueur (2004) 73–74.

rulers are responsive to those they rule, it needs both to be regular and to permit the sanction of dismissal.

In the pages that follow we shall adopt a somewhat artificial imagining of the constitution that separates its internal from its transnational aspects. The argument that will be advanced is that the three criteria of democracy—contestability, ideological neutrality and accountability—are values to which our internal constitution gives expression, however imperfectly,[106] but that by contrast, the transnationalisation of the constitution has fatally compromised our constitution's adherence to these three attributes.

The British Model and Contestability

The British model of constitutionalism can be said to facilitate a high degree of contestability. The propensity to disagree is deeply engrained within the British psyche, and this has been aided by 'the colonisation of large areas of the constitution by party politics'.[107] However, contestability means not only being able to argue for legal change; it also means actually being able to change the law. In Britain, parliamentary sovereignty means that there are no legal limits to the legislative change that citizens, parties and politicians can seek and that Parliament can enact through its normal legislative procedure. Dicey famously defined parliamentary sovereignty as meaning that Parliament enjoys 'the right to make or unmake any law whatever; and, further, that no person or body is recognised by the law of England as having a right to override or set aside the legislation of Parliament'.[108] Unlike many countries with codified constitutions, therefore, we do not have legal arrangements that enable policies or values to be insulated from contestability by forms of entrenchment. Since nothing can be entrenched, nothing is set above the ordinary, everyday process of political contestation. This longstanding constitutional doctrine seeped into and affected political culture. At least three hundred years of parliamentary sovereignty served to give Britain the underlying ethos of a contestatory democracy in which it was difficult to remove anything from the sphere of contestable politics. This situation is nicely encapsulated in the words of Richard Crossman, a Labour minister in the Wilson government, who apparently shocked American audiences by informing them that 'British politicians have no profound belief in natural law, largely because we have no written constitution or Supreme Court. If we don't like a law, we just change it.'[109]

---

[106] These imperfections are substantial, but considerations of space preclude an analysis of them. They include the excessive concentration of executive power in the hands of the Prime Minister at the expense of the Cabinet and the homogeneity between the political parties.

[107] Daintith (1997).

[108] Dicey (1962) 39–40.

[109] Mount (1993) 206.

This political culture has added a certain vibrancy to the British political scene.[110] The endless controversies regarding the Human Rights Act 1998 provide a good example.[111] Far from being venerated as some kind of supra-party 'bill of rights' that should rightly limit the legislature, the Act has from its inception been seen as intensely contestable. Among journalists, politicians and academics alike, the Act has its doughty defenders and vehement detractors.[112] For good measure it has divided parliamentarians on party lines. It evidently lacks, therefore, the unifying normative 'pull' of, say, the German Basic Law or the United States Constitution.[113]

Economic policy provides another prize example of 'contestability in action'. In democratic theory, legislative majorities, as the repositories of sovereignty, are endowed with sole authority to implement policy choices regarding matters such as the economy.[114] This is reflected in the British constitution. Since the Second World War, approaches to economic policy have been subject to radical change over the years. Provided the political will was there, there have been scant constitutional obstacles to such change. In the 1940s neither Labour nor the Conservatives favoured economic liberalism. Both accepted that the days of laissez-faire were over and that Britain should, to some significant extent at least, plan its economic life in the light of social needs through government intervention.[115] By the 1970s, the economy was stagnating, and the Labour Party was showing interest in the further extension of state control. Socialist economists highlighted the new phenomenon of multinational corporations. They argued that these Leviathans were highly efficient in terms of pursuing their own self-interests but highly inefficient in terms of pursuing the public good.[116] Public ownership could be utilised to achieve real control of leading manufacturing firms, enabling the government to harness the power of large companies to achieve job creation, investment, technological development and so on.[117] According to one key Party document,

> Public ownership, to everyone except the extreme political bigot, has now proved itself. We therefore propose, on grounds of the national interest, economic efficiency and democratic advance, to define a substantial further extension of the public sector.[118]

This solution—whilst popular with Labour's grass roots—did not find favour with the Party's parliamentary leadership, who disregarded the decision of the party conference to substantially extend public ownership. Yet public ownership nonetheless

---

[110] Nicol (2004); O'Cinneade (2004).

[111] See, eg, David Cameron's speech of 26 June 2006 to the Centre for Policy Studies, London, 'Balancing Freedom and Security: A Modern British Bill of Rights'.

[112] See, eg, Ewing (2004); Lester (2005); Ewing and Than (2008).

[113] For an argument that democratic contestability must extend to constitutional arrangements, see Waldron (1999) ch 13. Cf Laws (1995).

[114] Antinori (1994–95) 1838.

[115] Gardner (1956) 31.

[116] Holland (1975a).

[117] Holland (1975b) 43–61.

[118] Labour Party (1972) 28.

remained an important element of the social democratic economy. By 1979 state-owned industries had been established in almost every economic sector, touching the lives of almost every British person. The public sector accounted for 14 per cent of total economic investment, 10 per cent of gross domestic product and 8 per cent of employment.

However, the election of Thatcher's government in 1979 heralded a fundamental change in economic policy, as a result of which Britain in the 1980s and 1990s undertook the earliest and largest privatisation programme in the world. The programme was motivated by neoliberal beliefs: government was too large, the market was better at allocating resources; private ownership would mean greater competition, choice and efficiency, and greater political freedom. Privatisation would thus reverse the corrosive and corrupting effect of socialism.[119] The Conservatives' 1983 manifesto argued:

> Few people can now believe that state ownership means better service to the customer. The old illusions have melted away. Nationalisation does not improve job satisfaction, job security or labour relations . . . A company which has to satisfy its customers and compete to survive is more likely to be efficient, alert to innovation and genuinely accountable to the public.[120]

By the late 1980s the country entered a period of vanishing political cleavage,[121] with the Labour Party being increasingly won over to the merits of private enterprise.

There is now the possibility of political opinion gradually turning full circle, with the credit crunch casting doubt on the private sector's efficiency, and the social effects of a privatised economy remaining contentious.[122] In any event, it is clear that economic policy and the debate over the merits and demerits of public and private ownership have been central to British politics since the Second World War. Against this backdrop, there is democratic merit in the fact that the British model of constitutionalism presents no obstacle, in terms of constitutional law, to either nationalisation or privatisation. Economic policy surely should remain contestable: even Jackson, a leading authority on WTO law, has conceded that 'national societies may have vastly different views about the efficacy and fairness of the way in which markets work' and that these views differ from subject to subject as well as from society to society.[123] But in addition, and crucially, national views also legitimately vary over *time*.

This temporal element is indispensable to the maintenance of contestability. The British model does not insist that the political community place its faith in the

---

[119] Miller (1997).

[120] Conservative Party (1983).

[121] de Sousa Santos (2002) 314.

[122] Research in 2007 confirmed that Britain is moving back towards levels of inequality in wealth and poverty last seen more than 40 years ago. The general pattern is of increases in social equality during the 1970s, followed by rising inequality in the 1980s and 1990s (Dorling et al (2007)).

[123] Jackson (2006a) 235.

wisdom of some particular 'constitutional moment', since the wisdom of such a moment is always contestable. Instead the doctrine of parliamentary sovereignty embodies the rule that Parliament cannot be bound by its predecessors.[124] As Ian Loveland has put it, 'Parliament's unconfined legislative power is created anew every time it meets, irrespective of what previous Parliaments have enacted.'[125] This rule against self-binding serves to prevent previous generations from ruling from the grave over future generations. It makes contestability a permanent feature of the political landscape by facilitating a *continual* struggle between competing visions of the common good.[126] In this way, as Conor Gearty has observed, parliamentary sovereignty functions 'as a kind of empty vessel into which the temporary victors in the endless political fray could pour their ever-contingent versions of right and wrong'.[127] Through parliamentary sovereignty, the British model seeks to secure the perpetuity of political contests, treating rights and law as part of politics rather than as instruments for the closure of politics and thereby avoiding the displacement and depoliticisation of political questions.[128]

This traditional view of parliamentary sovereignty whereby Parliament cannot be bound in any way whatsoever is to be contrasted with the so-called 'new view' of 'self-embracing sovereignty' whereby, although Parliament cannot bind itself as to the substance of future legislation, it can bind itself as to the manner and form by which future legislation is to be enacted.[129] 'Self-embracing sovereignty' would allow Parliament to entrench provisions by procedural means. Parliament could, for example, require a two-thirds majority in either or both Houses, or a referendum, before legislation could be amended or repealed. This approach marks a departure from the orthodox view whereby the courts would disregard any attempt to bind Parliament's successors as to the form of future legislation, out of concern to preserve Parliament's status as a perpetually sovereign institution.[130] However, in the era of transnational regimes, many political actors, including judges, no longer see self-bindingness as a constitutional affront. With our political community bound by an ever-expanding body of transnational rules, the case for retaining Parliament's own 'continuing sovereignty' now seems less compelling. Thus Baroness Hale expressed support for the 'self-embracing' view in *Jackson v Attorney General* when she opined: 'if Parliament can do anything, there is no reason why Parliament should not decide to re-design itself, either in general

---

[124] See, eg, *Ellen Street Estates Ltd v Minister of Health* [1934] 1 KB 590.

[125] Loveland (2006) 37.

[126] Ackerman (1991) 206.

[127] Gearty (2004) 23.

[128] Honig (1993) ch 1.

[129] For an attack on 'self-embracing' sovereignty, see Young (2008).

[130] *Ellen Street Estates Ltd v Minister of Health* [1934] 1 KB 590. Maugham LJ held that 'the Legislature cannot, according to our constitution, bind itself as to the form of subsequent legislation, and it is impossible for Parliament to enact that in a subsequent statute dealing with the same subject-matter there can be no implied repeal. If in a subsequent Act Parliament chooses to make it plain that the earlier statute is being to some extent repealed, effect must be given to that intention just because it is the will of the Legislature'.

or for a particular purpose.[131] Nonetheless, it is submitted that the 'self-embracing' version of sovereignty ought to be rejected on normative grounds, since in practice 'self-embracing' parliamentary sovereignty is likely to mean no parliamentary sovereignty at all. For instance, if the government of the day enacted through Parliament a procedurally-entrenched Bill of Rights and if such a Bill of Rights contained a provision permitting the judicial invalidation of 'ordinary' statute, it would essentially become the supreme law of the land: parliamentary sovereignty would in substance have been replaced by constitutional sovereignty. In such circumstances it would remain contestable whether the enactment and entrenchment of the Bill of Rights represented a moment of constitutional wisdom or of constitutional folly, but those who took the latter view would be severely disadvantaged in their efforts to secure change.

Parliamentary sovereignty went hand-in-hand with a certain albeit limited measure of national sovereignty or national autonomy. Before the Second World War, international law was very weak by comparison to domestic legal systems. States were wilful actors who only grudgingly and rarely irreversibly gave up their sovereignty.[132] Such international regulation as existed tended to focus on the frontiers of states rather than what happened within those frontiers. The modern trend has seriously compromised this autonomy. In particular, states no longer have the same ability to change their laws and policies over time. As Miles Kahler has observed in the context of the 'legalisation' of international agreements,

> Government commitments are more credible under precise agreements of high obligation; delegated authority to interpret these commitments may also strengthen compliance. *Legalization may be particularly important in providing an institutional solution to commitments fulfilled over an extended period of time.* NAFTA's precision, for example, was part of the Mexican government's strategy to bind successor governments to its policies of economic openness. As the large literature on central bank independence suggests, *delegation to a relatively autonomous agency may also serve to reduce time-inconsistency problems.* Judicial or quasi-judicial agencies in legalized regimes may serve similar purposes by restricting future freedom of action by politicians.[133]

Thus those who seek to bind governments to particular domestic policies, including those governments themselves, undoubtedly choose judicalised international institutions in order to do so.[134] They thereby strengthen the confidence of international investors who value policy stability—but at the expense of democracy, which requires the freedom to effect periodic political change. Thus, for instance, the World Trade Organization cannot create obligations that states do not agree upon in principle at a particular point in time, but having made those commitments, it is less easy for states to evade them.[135] To be sure, rule-based

---

[131] *Jackson v Attorney-General* [2005] UKHL 56, [2005] 3 WLR 733 [160] (emphasis added).
[132] Hudec (1993) 358.
[133] Kahler (2001) 279 (emphases added).
[134] *Ibid*, 285.
[135] Grieco and Ikenberry (2003) 302.

policy coordination, such as in the WTO and EU, means that governments do not need to make continuous choices about economic relations.[136] Yet by the same token, the supposed economic gains from free trade are offset by a loss of governmental autonomy and control over its national economy—in fact, a loss of democracy.[137] States sacrifice the *ongoing* right of the political community to choose between different economic arrangements.

Thus the contestability that characterises the British model contrasts dramatically with the transnational constitution that has superseded it in crucial spheres. Constitutional globalisation has involved a relative decentring of the state as an actor in the world system[138] and a strengthening of the principle of the market over the principle of the state.[139] The chapters that follow will aim to show that transnational provisions do much to determine the most important elements of the structure of our society. For example, it will be argued that the WTO and EU free trade provisions effectively determine that private enterprise rather than the public sector will be the dominant means of providing goods and services, including so-called public services. Provisions on public procurement and state aid also presuppose an economy in which private enterprise is dominant. In addition, property ownership is itself classified as a fundamental right, a 'human' right that benefits corporations.

The rising importance of the transnational regimes dovetails with the rise from the late 1980s onwards of 'common law constitutionalism' as a normative theory amongst British academic lawyers. This is the view that the courts should discard their traditional allegiance to parliamentary sovereignty in favour of the protection of fundamental rights somehow inherent in the common law.[140] Common law constitutionalists therefore want the courts to restrict democratic contestability, albeit within limited spheres. Intriguingly, however, it seems unlikely that the common law constitutionalists themselves were fully aware of the way in which transnational provisions were changing the constitution in a far more sweeping way than they themselves were proposing. For instance, the common law constitutionalists often distinguish between matters of 'principle', which should be guaranteed by the courts even if this means overriding statute, and matters of 'policy', which Parliament should have the power to decide.[141] A similar distinction is made between 'negative rights', which must be safeguarded by the courts, and 'positive rights' (health, education, environment etc), over which Parliament is necessarily and rightly supreme.[142] But the transnational constitution simply does not respect any such distinction. In areas such as health and education, once the free market has been opened up, it simply is not open to Parliament to change

---

[136] *Ibid*, 293.
[137] *Ibid*, 290.
[138] de Sousa Santos (2002) 198.
[139] *Ibid*, 196.
[140] Allan (2001); Laws (1995); Laws (1996).
[141] Dworkin (1977) ch 4; Dworkin (1986) 221–24.
[142] Laws (1996).

tack. Individual rights are not placed normatively higher than nor independent of matters of policy.[143] Indeed the transnational provisions expose the incoherence of the very distinction between 'principle' and 'policy', since whilst from one perspective the public or private provision of health care involves the allocation of scarce resources and is essentially a matter of 'policy', from another perspective private sector involvement within the National Health Service involves the fundamental freedom of transnational service provision and should accordingly be considered a matter of 'principle'. Nonetheless it is arguable that, wittingly or unwittingly, the common law constitutionalists have through their long-term campaign for judicial review of Acts of Parliament endowed the transnational constitution with an academic veneer of respectability that it might otherwise not possess.

Thus, on a very wide array of issues—economic policy, social policy, fundamental rights (all these flow into each other in any case)—contestability is increasingly being replaced by incontestability. Under the transnational constitution, moreover, the sheer weight of unchallengeable law, the cumulative effect of so much that is incontestable, is having a depoliticising effect.

Some may welcome the demotion of the state. Ferdinand Mount, for example, argues that we should relish the limitations ushered in by transnational trade law:

> A really dedicated free-marketeer surely ought to welcome the installation of a supranational legal framework which would take the principles of free trade out of reach of the political lobbyists. He would look for a constitutional settlement which would include assertions of principle on the scale of those contained in the US constitution.[144]

Thus for Mount, the idea that states should retain democratic choice in such matters is perverse, since it amounts to a 'campaign for the right to pursue economic policies one regards as abhorrent'.[145] The privatised free market is the 'correct' policy to pursue for all time, so any other economic policy should be made constitutionally impermissible. The inconvenient possibility that others may disagree with Mount as to the abhorrence of this or that economic policy is disregarded. Yet as Chantal Mouffe put it, 'to negate the ineradicable character of antagonism and aim at a universal rational consensus—this is the real threat to democracy.'[146] The inescapability and permanence of political disagreement ought to be the keystone of our democratic constitution.[147]

---

[143] Ball (1996) 345.
[144] Mount (1993) 242
[145] *Ibid*, 245.
[146] Mouffe (1996).
[147] Gee (2008).

The British Model and Relative Ideological Neutrality

Fairness demands that the constitution should be as impartial as possible between those of differing democratic political philosophies. It should strive neither to favour nor to discriminate against substantive ideological tendencies, be they of Right, Left or Centre. Accordingly, the constitution should maintain a reasonably level playing field between those who seek to preserve the status quo and those who pursue varying degrees of social change. The desire for substantive ideological neutrality in the constitution is frequently articulated: there is a widespread feeling, as Jack Straw put it, that 'the constitution doesn't belong to any one party and should not be used as a partisan tool.'[148] Ideological neutrality is intimately related to the two other democratic attributes of the British model, contestability and accountability. It is the logical consequence of the idea that everything is contestable. Relative ideological neutrality also fosters accountability, since it means that ideological entrenchment cannot serve as a constitutional 'alibi' for government failures. As Keith Ewing has observed,

> One of the great virtues of the British constitution—and parliamentary sovereignty as one of the two foundation principles—has been its relative neutrality. There is of course no such thing as a truly neutral constitution: all constitutions reflect certain economic structures, and are designed to ensure the political influence of dominant economic interests. But for those wishing to promote social change, the British constitution provided one of the best opportunities for this to be done, particularly after the introduction of universal suffrage and the reform of the House of Lords in 1911 and 1949 . . . There were no institutional restraints on a legally sovereign legislature and a politically sovereign electorate.[149]

This relative neutrality means that rather than enshrining a particular conception of social justice or representing one particular political dogma as the one true path for the British people, politics is viewed as a way of handling conflicting choices between a *multiplicity* of moral maps, continuously struggling with the eternal question of how life should be lived.[150] It was not always so. In the Middle Ages and later, most writers maintained that a right to property formed part of the fundamental law of England. This fundamental law bound Parliament and the Crown, although the courts had only a limited power to enforce it against either body. But with the assertion of parliamentary sovereignty after the constitutional struggles of the seventeenth century, the strength and practical relevance of fundamental law waned considerably.[151] Statute came to prevail over common law.

---

[148] Jack Straw, Leader of the House, 19 June 2007 to the House of Commons Constitutional Affairs Committee.

[149] Ewing (2001) 104.

[150] Loughlin (2003) 156.

[151] Allen (2005) 15.

On the other hand, the relative neutrality of the modern era should not be exaggerated. As Ewing pointed out, there has probably never been such a thing as an entirely neutral constitution. In any system of government, no administration can escape the ideological 'pull' of a country's history, traditions and form of economic organisation. Thus the democratic potential of parliamentary sovereignty has always been counterbalanced by the inbuilt establishmentarian bias of the House of Lords, civil service and judiciary.[152] Nonetheless, constitutional neutrality is a matter of degree: assuming that the 'self-embracing' view of parliamentary sovereignty is rejected, British constitutional rules at least preclude Parliament from being bound by its predecessors on matters of legislation; and this serves, at least to some limited extent, to prevent the party that was previously in office from imposing its ideals on the party currently in office. The British model of constitutionalism, whilst it rightly shows an ideological commitment to representative democracy, does not explicitly pre-commit the political community to *substantive* political or economic goals. In this way parliamentary sovereignty has operated as 'a value-free response posed by the absence of consensus about core values'.[153]

True enough, during periods of greater national autonomy, Britain's parliamentary sovereignty has allowed dominant political tendencies of different eras to fine-tune the constitution to their needs, whilst at the same time crucially preserving the ability to change the constitution in some other direction in the future: the radicalism of the 1906 Liberal government, the welfare socialism of the 1945 Labour government, the Wild West capitalism of Thatcher and Blair, and so on. Thus Ewing has identified over the last century and a half a Victorian Tory constitution, a Liberal constitution, a Social constitution and now a constitution based on the metaphor of the market.[154] Vernon Bogdanor argues that the constitutional changes inaugurated by the Blair government were created for the benefit of liberalism, whilst he associates the pre-1990s constitution with the social democratic tradition.[155] In this manner our internal constitution, by virtue of its flexibility, has provided a fair procedure to work through our disagreements about justice and, when necessary, come to collective decisions for the time being.[156] In this respect at least, the internal constitution operates in a way that shows a reasonable, if imperfect, degree of ideological neutrality.[157] By contrast, the transnational constitution—with its rigid ethos of 'capitalism first, democracy second'—limits us to one particular ideology, so that even if it were to become discredited, we would be stuck with it.

The British model thereby avoids the danger that the values espoused by constitution-framers or constitution-interpreters will gain more purchase than they merit. By contrast, the founding fathers of the US Constitution had a definite

---

[152] See, eg, Benn (1982).
[153] Feldman (2005).
[154] Ewing (2000). Cf Allan (2000).
[155] Bogdanor (2004) 260–61.
[156] Bellamy (2007) 20.
[157] See further Sah and Daintith (1993).

substantive ideological agenda. In *The Federalist Papers* James Madison argued that the Constitution must guard against groups seeking the equal division of property, which he described as an improper and wicked project.[158] This can help explain the way in which some of the express entrenchment of values in the Constitution, such as the takings clause,[159] as well as the Constitution's overall institutional design, is designed to favour the retention of the status quo to the detriment of greater social equality. The US Constitution, with its federalism and system of checks and balances, was consciously fashioned in an effort to minimise the perceived problem of 'faction', whereby a group of citizens (be they a minority or majority), united by a common impulse or passion adverse to the rights of other citizens or detrimental to the public good, seeks to bring about political change. The British model lacks such institutional restraints and thereby provides the best means for social reform, if reform (of whatever variety) is what the political community opt for.[160] In addition, parliamentary sovereignty acts as the democratic corrective to any ideological bias of the common law. According to John Griffith's famous monograph *The Politics of the Judiciary*, judges preserve the existing order, with a strong emphasis on protecting individual property rights.[161] If so, the primacy of statute over common law leaves Parliament with the ultimate ideological choice—to accept the case law of the courts or to override it by changing the law.

It is conventional to conceive international agreements as 'bargains' from which Britain receives a 'benefit' and 'burden'. Viewed in this way, it would be wrong for a state to reap the benefits but shirk the burdens. The 'packages' that constitute an international agreement cannot be unpicked or their provisions cherry-picked, since they form part of a broader web of mutual concessions that can hardly remain unaffected by cutting out a part of it. The problem with this depiction is that it depoliticises international agreements, distracting attention from their primarily ideological nature. In particular, it obscures and downplays the way in which the transnational agreements tend to privilege one particular type of market economy over others. Such a depoliticised depiction serves to enmesh the commentator within the worldview of the agreement being analysed, thereby blunting criticism. But in fact international agreements are primarily ideological rather than contractual, and they ought to be critiqued on that basis. In addition, the bargain metaphor portrays states as having stable interests divorced from ideology, when in fact the identification of national interests depends on prevailing political ideology, which can change over time in line with national politics.[162] The personification of 'the state' as actor and contractor masks the fact that it is the

---

[158] Madison, Hamilton and Jay (1987) 122–28.

[159] Article V of the Bill of Rights provides that 'nor shall private property be taken for public use, without just compensation'.

[160] Ewing (2001) 104.

[161] Griffith (1997) ch 9.

[162] For example, there was nothing inherently 'in the British interest' about promoting, for example, the free movement of services. The identification of this policy objective as a British interest was the result of the election of neoliberal governments.

politicians of the day and civil servants who identify and pursue what they see as the state's interests.

The transnational constitution resembles the American more than the British model, insofar as it is widely perceived as being tied to a particular substantive ideology based on its own particular vision of the good life, namely market liberalism.[163] Commentators point to the ascendancy in the 1980s and 1990s of the so-called 'Washington consensus'. This was a tacit but powerful agreement among political, academic and business elites in favour of such reforms as the minimal state, the deregulated market, fiscal constraint, free trade, reduced welfare spending and lower taxation.[164] The transnational constitution can be regarded as having elevated a once obscure strand of economic thinking into the constitutional imperative.[165] Under the sway of the Washington consensus the GATT and EEC abandoned such ideological ambivalence as they once possessed, the state has been reconfigured to meet the interests of market forces, and transnational corporations have been elevated as global political and legal actors.[166]

Global constitutional law aims to buttress this one-ideology world with the routines of democracy acting as window-dressing for the pursuit of a single ideology. The state, rather than becoming impotent through globalisation, has itself become teleological; it intervenes copiously but is constrained to deploy its power principally to advance the demands of transnational market forces.[167] Against this vista it is hard to disagree with Michael Mandel's idea that the propertied classes have changed everything (in constitutional terms) so that everything (in terms of the oligarchy of wealth) can remain the same.[168] Yet, in a society where we disagree about justice, there is no compelling normative justification for giving the Washington consensus a privileged position or unfair advantage. Neoliberalism, rather than relying on constitutional cocooning, should stand on its own two feet in party and electoral politics.

The British Model and Accountability

Political democracy has been described as a system 'in which rulers are held accountable for their policies and actions in the public realm by citizens, and where competing elites offer alternative programmes and vie for popular support'.[169] Under the British model there is an appreciation that in order to have genuine accountability, governments need first to have the opportunity to govern.

---

[163] Alder (2007) 219.
[164] Anderson (2005) 19.
[165] Cerney, Menz and Soederberg (2005).
[166] Monbiot (2000).
[167] Leys (2001) 11.
[168] Mandel (1998) 253.
[169] Andersen and Burns (1996) 227.

Constitutional provisions should not therefore prevent an administration from pursuing the programme on which it was elected, since this would break the chain of accountability. To be sure, the government is constitutionally responsible to Parliament, and this in itself is a valuable tool of accountability.[170] Indeed, since the 1970s, the evidence suggests that backbenchers have become ever more assertive in taking the government to task.[171] Yet it may be argued that under the British model, accountability to Parliament and accountability to the electorate are complimentary: a party's backbenchers serve to remind the government of the political principles for which their party is in business,[172] and at the end of the day the electorate forms a judgment on the performance of that party in office.

It is tempting to assume that more institutions and more elections mean more accountability, but this is not the case. A surfeit of institutional checks and balances can be inimical to accountability. In a piece entitled 'A Plethora of Parliaments?' Harlow has drawn attention to the way in which a superfluity of accountability mechanisms tends to reduce the centrality of any one of those mechanisms, with the consequence that a democratic deficit is brought about by a 'democratic surplus' or fragmentation of power.[173] It is in fact the subjection of a concentration, rather than a division, of power to the regular judgment of the electorate that makes for the strongest form of political accountability. Vivien Schmidt has characterised the British political system as a 'simple polity' where governing activity is traditionally channelled through a single authority, suggesting that transnational regimes like the EU have submerged Britain's 'traditionally polarized, partisan politics'.[174] Yet it is precisely this form of politics that enables the most meaningful accountability to take place.

This political accountability goes hand in hand with the absence of judicially enforced constitutional restrictions on legislation. Under the British model of constitutionalism the legislation of the accountable officers of the state was hierarchically preeminent over that of the state's non-accountable officers. Thus the role of the courts was not to challenge or invalidate statute but rather to obey and enforce the latest expression of Parliament's will.[175] Furthermore, the courts had to discern the will of Parliament without taking too many liberties by way of over-imaginative statutory interpretation, since to do so would be to usurp the role of the legislature.[176] Thus, as Adam Tomkins has observed, the British model emphasises the political control of accountability in preference to a focus on legal controls.[177]

By contrast, the transnational regimes frequently (though not exclusively) shift the locus of legal change away from those who are accountable to those who are not.[178]

---

[170] Tomkins (2005).
[171] Norton (1975); Norton (1985); Cowley (2002); Cowley (2005).
[172] Butt (1967) 437.
[173] Harlow (2002) 84; Scott (2000) 52.
[174] Schmidt ((2006) 3.
[175] *British Railways Board v Pickin* [1974] AC 765.
[176] *Magor and St Mellons RDC v Newport Corporation* [1951] 2 All ER 839, 841 (per Lord Simonds).
[177] Tomkins (2005) 1–6.
[178] See generally Schwartzberg (2007).

Frank Vibert, in his book *The Rise of the Unelected*, has reflected on the present-day state of affairs whereby

> Unelected bodies now perform many of the practical day-to-day tasks that enable demo-cracies to function. Their rise poses an enormous challenge both to the theory and to the practice of modern democracy. At a practical level the traditional democratic institutions seem to be relegated to a role of merely symbolic actors. Even worse, parliaments, prime ministers and presidents appear to maintain a smokescreen of democratic organization while concealing the apparently undemocratic means through which societies actually work.[179]

Vibert talks of 'unelected bodies', and in this regard it is worth noting that whilst globalised governance has lead to a strengthening of the role of judicial power,[180] it has led more generally to the rise of unaccountable bodies. Indeed, one cannot maintain a sharp distinction between judicial bodies and non-judicial unaccount-able bodies; neither can convincingly be regarded as 'impartial', since they pursue a strong ideological attachment to the objectives and values underlying the transnational regime of which they form part.[181] They are teleological rather than accountable. Griffith observed that judges cannot be politically neutral because they are placed in positions where they are required to make political choices as to where the public interest lies. They are part of established authority so their con-ception of the public interest is conservative: they have a tenderness towards pri-vate property and are generally concerned to preserve and protect the existing order.[182] If this were the case before constitutional globalisation, in the context of the vague and unwritten common law, it is yet more valid in the globalised era in the case of transnational agreements, which charge courts and other unaccount-able power-wielders with *explicit* political goals. Any pretence at neutrality wears thin.

On this reading, there is less difference than might be supposed between, say, the European Court of Human Rights, the panels of the WTO, the European Commission and the European Central Bank. All are unaccountable bodies to which governmental power has been transferred. These unelected bodies, Vibert has argued, demarcate the boundaries between state and market.[183] Essentially, therefore, they determine the very boundaries of politics. This in turn erodes both national and sub-national democratic decision-making. In particular, in all three transnational regimes states have transferred to non-accountable juridical bodies their responsibility to strike a balance between the interests of the private sector and competing public interests. This is evident from cases (which ought to be

---

[179] Vibert (2007) 166.
[180] Martinico and Pollicinio (2008) 97.
[181] See, eg, Nicol (2005) 167–70.
[182] Griffith (1997) 336.
[183] Vibert (2007) 167. John Jackson has noted that most experts (economists and others specialists) tend to accept the value of free markets as a societal mechanism to best achieve economic development, which in turn increases the probability of individuals satisfactorily pursuing their own chosen goals. See Jackson (2006a) 86.

regarded as amongst the landmark cases of British constitutional law) such as *Shrimp–Turtle* in the WTO, *Cassis de Dijon* in the EU and *Sporrong* in the ECHR.[184] Yet this balancing function, which is not a technical but a value-laden exercise,[185] is the essence of governance.

Under the transnational constitution, responsible government is replaced by a bewildering array of international organisations, leading to a depoliticised world managed by courts, commissions and panels of experts, with no parties with projects to rule and no aspiration of self-government.[186] Moreover, in the transnational regimes the power of the judicial branch appears to be particularly strong, since, as Martin Shapiro has shown, judicial power is at its strongest when necessitated not merely by a rights instrument but above all by a division-of-powers arrangement.[187] This 'governance by experts' conforms to neoliberal theory in being profoundly suspicious of democracy, since democracy may threaten property rights and entrepreneurial liberties. Accordingly, key institutions must at all costs be liberated from democratic pressures.[188] The object of the exercise is to instil an understanding of the 'proper limits' of politics, under which 'there can be no question of blaming everything on the government'.[189] Unaccountable bodies are thereby deployed to erect a boundary between the constitution and politics, presenting constitutional argument as a learned discourse as opposed to a political discourse.[190] The central role accorded to unaccountable bodies within international regimes may permanently change the nature of domestic politics, prompting national politicians to change their expectations, modify their behaviour and promote yet further transfers of power to the unaccountable.[191]

On the other hand, it is arguable that transnational law has not reduced accountability as such: it has simply changed the identity of those to whom our leaders are accountable. Not only are politicians who implement 'imprudent' policies likely to be punished economically by transnational corporations, but now the transnational constitution has reinforced these 'economic' sanctions by the sanctions of global public law.[192] Thus the state is being made tightly accountable to corporations through the medium of the transnational regimes, whilst its structure is being changed to reduce governmental exposure to the pressure of the electorate.

---

[184] *United States Import Prohibition of Certain Shrimp and Shrimp Products* WT/DS58/AB/R, adopted 6 November 1998; Case 120/78 *Rewe-Zentrale AG v Bundesmonopoluerwaltung für Branntwein ('Cassis de Dijon')* [1979] ECR 649; *Sporrong and Lönnroth v Sweden* (A52) (1982) 5 EHRR 85.

[185] See, eg, Weiler (1999b) 368.

[186] Koskenniemi (2007) 28–29.

[187] Shapiro (2002).

[188] Harvey (2005) 66.

[189] Mount (1993) 266.

[190] Anderson (2005) 110.

[191] Goldstein, Kahler, Keohane and Slaughter (2001) 15. See further Koh (1998) 623–82. Michael Mandel has argued that the underlying rationale for the modern fashion for legislatures to be hemmed in by constitutional limitations, enforced by judicial and quasi-judicial bodies of every size and shape, national and international, is to operate as an antidote to democracy, in order to safeguard the existing balance of wealth and property. See Mandel (1998) 251–52.

[192] Wriston (2002) 9.

Limited Democracy: The Triumph of Hayek

Aspects of today's constitution are strikingly similar to that advocated by the intellectual godfather of neoliberalism, Hayek, who initially delineated his ideal constitution in the 1940s and 1950s, at a time when his views were marginalised. He argued explicitly that it was undesirable to extend democracy to its maximum possible scope. Rather, he maintained, a *limited* democracy was preferable, since this would help preserve the conditions that made democracy workable.[193]

It was in this context that Hayek famously advanced his own conception of the rule of law.[194] He argued that the rule of law could be achieved only if there were the greatest possible reduction in executive discretion.[195] This would have the consequence that any governmental policies aimed at bringing about greater substantive distributive justice would 'find themselves obstructed at every move' by the rule of law.[196] The rule of law, he insisted, had to govern the entire economic policy of government. It meant that the legal system had to recognise the principle of private property and provide a precise definition of this right as applied to different things.[197] The rule of law also precluded government from claiming for itself the exclusive right to provide any service other than those that would not otherwise be supplied at all. Public sector enterprise was only acceptable if it were conducted on the same terms as private enterprise. Furthermore, regulation of private enterprise had to be restricted to measures that could be verified by an impartial court as being necessary to achieve the general effect aimed at by the law. Any control of quantity and price was impermissible as being too discretionary and arbitrary. It had to be possible for the market to function adequately.[198] Hayek is sometimes assumed to have been a supporter of *laissez-faire* capitalism, but in fact he repeatedly insisted that the state had the positive role of intelligently designing and continuously adjusting an effective system of competition. He welcomed the planning required to create such a competitive system: he was critical only of planning that was intended to be a substitute for competition.[199]

Hayek was also keenly aware of the way in which the institutional design of a political community could help to rule out certain 'undesirable' policy options.

---

[193] Hayek (1978) ch 7.

[194] As Paul Craig has observed, 'the phrase the "rule of law" has a power or force of its own. To criticise governmental action as contrary to the rule of law immediately casts it in a bad light. Such criticism . . . demands clarity as to the particular theory of justice which informs the critique' (Craig (1997a) 487). John Griffith was even more scathing: '[W]hat becomes sacred and untouchable is something called the Rule of Law. The Rule of Law is an invaluable concept for those who wish not to change the present set-up . . . Statutes may be contrary to the Rule of Law . . . but the common law, it seems, can never be' (Griffith (1979) 15). It might be argued that Hayek's use of the term proves Griffith wrong: the rhetoric of the Rule of Law can be used to 'change the present set-up' in a more capitalist direction.

[195] Hayek (1986) 54.

[196] Hayek (1978) 232; Hayek (1986) 59.

[197] Hayek (1986) 28.

[198] Hayek (1976) ch 15.

[199] Hayek (1986) 31.

Thus he was disarmingly frank as to why he favoured federalism as part of his ideal 'constitution of liberty'. Federalism, he insisted, is the most efficacious check on democracy, curbing not only the will of the majority but the power of the whole people. Hayek maintained that this was particularly the case when it came to economic policy:

> [C]ertain kinds of coercion require the joint and co-ordinated use of different powers or the employment of several means, and, if these means are in separate hands, nobody can exercise those kinds of coercion. The most familiar illustration is provided by many kinds of economic control which can be effective only if the authority exercising them can also control the movement of men and goods across the frontiers of its territory. If it lacks that power, though it has the power to control internal events, it cannot pursue policies which require the joint use of both. Federal government is thus in a very definite sense limited government.[200]

Hayek therefore canvassed a supranational form of government that would prevent states from regaining unfettered sovereignty in the economic sphere by being able to veto their economic policy measures. The need for such a supranational authority was all the more pressing, according to Hayek, in view of the post-war tendency of governments to become units of economic administration, actors in rather than merely supervisors of the economic scene. This sort of supranational federalism would foster the 'democracy with definitely limited powers' craved by Hayek. At the same time, however, Hayek insisted that 'there can be no international law without a power to enforce it.'[201] Hayek therefore seems to have been envisaging a kind of 'municipal state', with nation states becoming more like local authorities relative to the institutions of global governance. As we shall see in the ensuing chapters, the transnational constitutional comes close to Hayek's broad design in a number of respects.

Transnational Democracy: Hayek's Heirs?

Some present-day supporters of transnational governance make more extravagant claims than Hayek. Hayek, after all, admitted that his scheme of things would actually mean less democracy, but he thought that this was desirable since limited democracy would paradoxically allow democracy to be preserved. By contrast, some contemporary commentators argue that transnational governance can actually mean more democracy. In an article entitled 'Democracy-Enhancing Multilateralism', Robert Keohane, Stephen Macedo and Andrew Moravcsik advance the argument that 'under some plausible conditions', supranationalism can in fact enhance the quality of democracy at home.[202]

---

[200] Hayek (1978) 184–85.
[201] Hayek (1986) 172–73.
[202] Keohane, Macedo and Moravcsik (2007).

The authors concede that majority opinion is against them: most analysts, regardless of disciplinary background or political allegiance, believe that transnational institutions threaten democracy. Most incline to the view expressed by Jed Rubenfeld that international organisations are 'bureaucratic, diplomatic, technocratic—everything but democratic'[203] or to the opinion of Ralf Dahrendorf that internationalisation 'almost invariably means a loss of democracy'.[204] Keohane, Macedo and Moravcsik observe that there are, however, three 'conventional' defences of transnational governance, and they believe that these can now be supplemented by new arguments.

Let us first consider these conventional defences. The first is that transnational institutions are in fact directly accountable to their member states and thus indirectly accountable to the publics in the democracies themselves. In reality it is questionable whether there is much accountability of national decisions to endorse transnational legislation. But in any event, this argument pays scant regard to the ongoing ability or inability of a political community to *change* such legislation once it is in force. This applies in particular to the difficulty of changing primary legislation, such as treaty provisions. The second conventional argument is that power is delegated democratically and could always be rescinded in the same way. Yet the fact that membership in transnational institutions is subject to national consent does not serve in itself to make those institutions democratic. Moreover, this argument ignores the element of de facto enmeshment, which occurs when a state joins a transnational regime such as the EU or WTO. The third conventional response is that even if democracy is degraded by passing power to transnational regimes, the ends justify the undemocratic means, since a pooling of sovereignty allows states to achieve policy goals that none could realise alone. Whilst there are certainly objectives that states cannot achieve on their own, the argument presupposes that the policy goals being pursued are incontestably desirable. This is often a questionable assumption, as the substantive chapters of this book aim to show.

Let us move on to the new arguments put forward by Keohane, Macedo and Moravcsik. Their broad contention is that multilateralism may actually improve the functioning of domestic democracy. They proceed by spelling out their preferred version of democracy. They argue that whilst popular elections are essential to democracy, democratic systems above all require constitutional rules and institutions to constrain the power of governments and temporary majorities. These constraints are necessary for the people to be able effectively to make political decisions and to be assured of continuing to make them. Competing public institutions and a system of checks and balances, including politically independent courts and agencies with specialised expertise, can help ensure that policy choices are defended against robust criticism and that errors are identified and corrected. The authors argue that such well-designed constitutional constraints enhance

---

[203] Rubenfeld (2004) 2003.
[204] Dahrendorf (1999) 16.

40

democracy, understood as the ability of the public on due reflection to govern itself over the long run. They insist that transnational decision-making helps to achieve this sort of democracy in three ways: by combating special interests, by protecting rights and by fostering robust public deliberation.

It will be readily apparent that the version of democracy favoured by the three authors is far removed from the British model of constitutionalism. The authors give short shrift to contestability, constitutional neutrality and accountability as democratic attributes. Instead, they embrace a Madisonian conception of 'deliberative democracy' based on the American model of constitutionalism, which they extol for ensuring that 'much of politics is deliberately insulated from direct majoritarian control'. Unlike the British model, Madisonian democracy renders certain values practically incontestable by means of constitutional entrenchment; it compromises neutrality by privileging the economic and social status quo (as noted by both Hayek and the World Bank), and it undermines accountability by establishing its system of checks and balances. If one fails to endorse the view of the three authors as to the superiority of Madisonian constitutionalism, then their arguments largely collapse. Nonetheless, they advance three arguments, and an attempt will be made to tackle these in turn.

First, Keohane, Macedo and Moravcsik insist that transnational institutions help combat special interests or 'dominant factions'. They give the example of trade policy, arguing that institutions such as the WTO and EU provide mechanisms by which democratic publics can limit the influence of minority (protectionist) factions by *committing in advance* to a set of multilateral rules and practices that require trade policies to be defended on the basis of public reasons. This has proven effective partly because it is reinforced by the principle of reciprocity; partly because multilateral trade liberalisation shifts control over the domestic trade agenda into the hands of the executive branch which represents a broader national constituency than the individual members of the legislature; and partly because of the establishment of impartial international adjudication such as the WTO panels, WTO Appellate Body and the ECJ. The democratic credentials of this argument are, however, questionable. For a political community to 'commit in advance' to any set of rules or practices is in itself democratically suspect, since to do so compromises its ability to change law and policy over time. The authors are right to observe that transnational decision-making tends to shift power from national legislatures to national executives, but it seems strange to trumpet this as a democratic gain. Similarly it seems curious to parade as an increase in democracy the shift in power from national politicians, who are accountable, to transnational adjudication agencies, which are not.

Secondly, Keohane, Macedo and Moravcsik argue that transnational institutions help protect individual and minority rights. Protection of such rights in sovereign democracies, they contend, is imperfect and uneven, and transnational institutions may improve such protection. Even on their own terms, the authors suffer from the fault of sweeping generalisation; indeed, they ultimately concede (in the context of post-9/11 anti-terrorist measures) that multilateral institutions can and do actually deprive individuals of their traditional civil liberties. The greater flaw in their argument, however, is their pervasive assumption of the *incontestability* of rights.[205] The WTO system, for example, safeguards transnational private enterprise and therefore constitutionalises the transnational capitalist system. This system has resulted in a distribution of wealth in which the world's 225 richest people have a combined wealth of over US$1 trillion, equal to the annual income of the poorest 47 per cent of the world's people.[206] Are these 225 individuals the 'minority' whose 'individual rights' are being protected? Conversely, the cost of achieving and maintaining universal access to basic education, health care, food, safe water and sanitation would be less than 4 per cent of the combined wealth of the same 225 richest. Against this backdrop it is arguable that the shift to marketisation constitutionalised by the WTO has led to a *diminution* of the social and economic rights of billions of individuals. Some may disagree with this analysis, but if they do so, this merely serves to illustrate the inherent contestability of rights.

Thirdly, Keohane, Macedo and Moravcsik contend that transnational institutions foster collective deliberation. They argue that individual democracies can utilise information, expertise and debate even more effectively when they participate in multilateral institutions and networks. The wider scope, greater diversity, expert staff and political insulation of multilateral forums mean that information and critical insights are generated and utilised effectively, and this improves democracy.

It may conceivably be argued that certain international forums, such as the Intergovernmental Panel on Climate Change, specialise in the dissemination of invaluable information and scientific insights. To generalise this to all transnational institutions, however, conveys a depiction of a world of apolitical technocrats with no ideological axes to grind: competent experts in insulated forums will promote 'best practices' unsullied by partisan politics, leading to wiser decision-making by national leaders. Alas, this is not what has been constructed. First, it is scandalously misleading to depict transnational regimes as mere purveyors of information on the basis of which national democracies can dwell and deliberate; many such institutions do not merely provide information to accountable national leaders; rather, they actually *take decisions.* It would be ludicrous to characterise the institutions discussed in this book—the WTO panels and Appellate Body, the European Commission and European Court of Justice, and the European Court of Human Rights—as advisory bodies. Rather, there has been a transfer of power to these bodies.

Secondly, the portrayal of impartiality and objectivity is equally disingenuous. Many institutions are established with firm ideological objectives. This applies not only to the WTO, which exists to promote global economic interpenetration,[207] but to the EU, which is charged with establishing a common market on the basis

---

[205] On the contestability of rights generally, see Waldron (1999); Campbell (1999); Nicol (2006).
[206] UN Development Programme (1998).
[207] Article III, Marrakesh Agreement Establishing the WTO (1994).

of an open market economy with free competition, governed by guiding principles of stable prices, sound public finances and monetary conditions and a sustainable balance of payments.[208] Far from improving the quality of collective deliberation, such organisations actually narrow deliberation, since the only solutions that will be considered acceptable will be those that conform to the aims to which the transnational regime has been pre-committed. All in all, therefore, the efforts of Keohane, Macedo and Moravcsik to persuade us that the denationalisation of the constitution is somehow democracy-enhancing are not particularly convincing.

Another effort to extol the democratic merits of supranational governance has been made by Jürgen Habermas in his book *The Postnational Constitution*. Habermas has argued that globalisation has shaken our democratic self-confidence and that we should seek forms for the democratic process *beyond* the state.[209] Accepting that there are disempowering aspects of globalisation that can degrade the capacity for democratic self-steering within a national society,[210] Habermas has suggested that 'we will only be able to meet the challenges of globalisation in a reasonable manner if the postnational constellation can successfully develop new forms for the democratic self-steering of society' and that we should therefore take a gamble on postnational democracy.[211] This option at least promises a politics that can catch up with world markets.[212]

Habermas envisages that there can be 'at least a prospect for a world domestic policy without a world government' and that this will draw its legitimising force from 'the general accessibility of a deliberative process whose structure grounds an expectation of rationally acceptable results'.[213] Habermas openly favours reducing the importance accorded to votes and accountability and increasing the weight given to 'the procedural demands of communicative and decision-making processes'.[214] But he admits that the transnational edifice he is seeking to construct would depend on whether a cosmopolitan consciousness would arise on the part of national electorates.[215] It will be readily apparent that Habermas' hopes for democratic revival depend not only on the materialisation of this elusive consciousness but, much more importantly, on redefining democracy out of all definition.

Markets as Democracy?

Another attempt to persuade us that the new constitutional settlement is democratic promotes the idea that markets themselves provide a kind of substitute for

---

[208] Article 119 TFEU; Article 120 TFEU.
[209] Habermas (2001) 61.
[210] *Ibid*, 67.
[211] *Ibid*, 88.
[212] *Ibid*, 109.
[213] *Ibid*, 110.
[214] *Ibid*, 111.
[215] *Ibid*, 112.

accountability. Consumers can 'vote' by switching suppliers, and this constitutes a far richer form of democracy than the ballot box. Superficially, the 'markets-as-democracy' argument has its attractions. I can seemingly 'vote' on more individual issues—who will supply me with gas, who will supply me with electricity, who will provide my internet connection and so on—and I can 'vote' more often than is generally the case in a political representative democracy. And I am free to exercise my vote as public-spiritedly or as self-interestedly as I wish. At a deeper level, however, the market offers an impoverished form of democracy. There is no scope, for example, for indicating one's dissatisfaction with an economic sector as a whole. I may, for instance, want to use my vote to censure the supra-competitive prices of the British energy industry, but since its pricing structure stems from the oligopolistic nature of the market, I will not be able to express my disapproval by switching. My dissatisfaction with such an oligopoly may prompt me to support the re-establishment of public ownership and control of the industry, but once again the market provides me with no way of indicating my support for such a choice. Thus the market offers a severely limited democracy in which the most basic societal choices are removed from contestation, the ideological preference for the marketplace is cast in concrete, and corporations cannot in many cases be brought to book for their behaviour.

Moreover, corporate actions may have grave consequences that legitimately concern the wider public and not merely their customers or potential customers. For example, the public may have a legitimate case for wishing banks to be brought to book for the subprime crisis and its consequences, irrespective of whether they save with or borrow from banks. Citizens may have a legitimate interest in the safety and environmental impact of nuclear power, for example, which dwarfs the question of whether they purchase such a product, if indeed they have a choice. Thus the argument that markets provide a surrogate democratic process that remedies the lack of formal constitutional accountability of corporations is rather weak.

British Exceptionalism? Britain, France and the Ratchet Effect

This is not a comparative book: to undertake a comparative analysis would require a further volume. Nonetheless a brief comparison between Britain and its continental neighbour, France, can enhance our understanding of the effects of constitutional globalisation. Although globalisation has a strong tendency to push countries towards uniformity, each country experiences globalisation uniquely.[216] Mark Evans has noted that the degree to which globalisation conditions state, economy, society and politics, differs from state to state. Evans has highlighted the

---

[216] Martell (2008) 456.

particular strength of neoliberalism in British politics, stemming from the way in which New Labour reinforced and extended the neoliberal marketising trends of the Thatcher period.[217]

Luke Martell has characterised Britain as a particularly globalised and globalising country, both an importer and an exporter of globalising structures and processes. Martell observes that Britain was historically a strong exporter of globalisation, responding to capitalist pressures in the nineteenth century to expand the British Empire, the chief globalisation device of the period.[218] It thereby imposed free trade by force.[219] Martell accepts, however, that Britain's globalising tendencies have been punctuated by reversals. Nevertheless, the globalising policy of the Victorian era was revived by the Conservatives and New Labour governments from the 1970s onwards, making the British economy today considerably more internationalised than other G7 economies. As in its earlier phase, British globalisation has been heavily linked to neoliberalism. Although social attitudes in Britain may be no more neoliberal than in other countries, nonetheless the political and business elite are widely associated with the Anglo-Saxon model of capitalism, in contrast to continental European countries such as France, which are associated with a more social capitalist model.

France's privatisation programmes have been somewhat less extensive than that of Britain. The presidency of François Mitterand was initially characterised by the extension of public ownership, but after two exchange rate crises Mitterand abandoned hard-line dirigiste politics in favour of the pursuit of European integration. Under the conservative governments of Prime Ministers Jacques Chirac (1986–88) and Edouard Balladur (1993–95), nationalised industries were privatised. By the mid-1990s governments of both right and left became avid in their privatisation of state assets.[220] Nonetheless, there has been a more widespread resistance in France than in Britain to the legitimacy of the market as the dominant force in the economy. For this reason, although the state's direct control over the economy was reduced to core areas of public service provision, nonetheless these core areas remained in public ownership.[221] This meant that transnational liberalisation measures would have a different impact in France compared to Britain. The constitutional role of transnational liberalisation law in Britain is to constitutionalise the *pre-existing* high level of liberalisation and privatisation. In France, the same law more often provides a constitutional guarantee of the creation of a market in which corporations can start to pit themselves against the public sector provider. Irrespective of the stage of development of privatisation in a given state, transnationalisation acts as a ratchet, permitting motion only in a pro-privatisation direction.

Of course it is open to national governments to extend privatisation beyond the requirements of transnational law. Both French and British governments have

---

[217] Evans (2005) 72–73.
[218] Martell (2008) 453.
[219] Osterhammel and Petersson (2005) ch 4.
[220] Culpepper (2006) 35.
[221] *Ibid*, 45.

been eagerly pushing forward the process of liberalisation and privatisation in advance of their transnational obligations (the EDF-Suez merger, the part-privatisation of the Royal Mail). In this context it bears reiteration that trans-nationalisation is democratically problematic not because it fails to reflect national preferences at the time commitments are entered into but because of the extent to which it binds domestic policy for the future.

The Ambit of the Argument

Finally, it may be helpful to articulate the limits of the argument that this book advances. For a start, my argument focuses on the constitutional law protection of neoliberal capitalism. There are a myriad of ways other than through constitutional law by which neoliberal capitalism reproduces itself in successive generations, and these may seem to be of greater immediate significance than constitutional law changes in placing neoliberal capitalism on a more secure foundation. This is why I have characterised the present constitutional transnationalisation as an 'insurance policy'. In the long term, however, the constitutional law aspects are nonetheless important, and this book concentrates on them.

As regards the transnational constitution, I am *not* arguing that it has replaced British autonomy in every significant area. There remain important areas of policy, worthy of study and analysis by public lawyers, that fall outside the remit of the transnational regimes. I am *not* arguing that those regimes are exclusively neoliberal, merely that they are predominantly so. I am *not* arguing that the exclusive role of the legal system is to support the economic system. Transnational law may have supplementary, laudable aims, though to what extent these constitute window-dressing is open to question. And this book is *not* intended as an exhaustive encyclopaedia of transnational measures: many, such as the system of bilateral investment treaties, the system of international commercial arbitration or the use of Article 6 of the ECHR, are omitted. Nor have I space to consider domestic measures that might arguably bind the political community in an undemocratic way, such as long-term contracts under the private finance initiative. My object has been to provide sufficient evidence to advance my thesis, and I have no pretensions to comprehensiveness.

Above all, I am *not* arguing that neoliberalism has somehow been foisted on an unwilling British government. I am, however, arguing that our democratically elected and ardently neoliberal leaders have changed the constitution to make it more difficult to deviate from neoliberalism in the future, and this has been achieved in large measure through the constitutional power of the transnational regimes. This, I am convinced, has profoundly diminished our political democracy.

2

The World Trade Organisation and the Sanctity of Private Enterprise

FOR ALMOST HALF a century after the Second World War, trade policy was a matter of public indifference. It was all about 'complex technical deals between obscure negotiators', of little interest outside a tiny elite of civil servants and manufacturers.[1] Now, by contrast, world trade law excites strong feelings. In large measure this is because of its impact on the third world, a subject that falls outside the scope of this book. This chapter focuses instead on the question of whether the World Trade Organization (WTO) gives constitutional protection to the private sector. It considers the extent to which WTO membership has deprived the British political community—with its vaunted sovereign Parliament—of its freedom of choice over general economic policy. In turn this raises important issues about the contemporary relationship between the British constitution and the transnational regimes.

Some commentators have portrayed world trade law as having liberated the capitalist economy from the political restrictions formerly placed upon it.[2] Since, however, what has been privatised can always be renationalised, the WTO protection of capitalism is only worthwhile if it can constitutionally entrench the primacy of private enterprise. Some contend that this is in fact what international trade law has achieved.[3] The validity of this assertion needs to be tested from the perspective of UK constitutional law. If sound, we might regard the WTO as imposing upon Britain a very different sort of constitution from that with which we are familiar. As Peter Holmes puts it,

> Economists . . . have a tradition of using the terms 'constitution' and 'constitutionalism' to cover almost any arrangement that precommits economic policy to a fixed set of rules rather than leaving the government free to adopt any economic policy it wishes . . . Economists see constitutions as devices for pre-commitment of economic policy.[4]

It is worth examining the WTO because if it does indeed bring about such precommitment, this would appear to compromise the contestability, accountability and relative ideological neutrality that are the democratic hallmarks of the British constitution.

---

[1] Meunier (2005) 188.
[2] Hardt and Negri (2000) xi.
[3] Petersmann (1991).
[4] Holmes (2001) 60.

Assessing the WTO

Britain joined the WTO when it came into existence in 1995, having likewise been a founder member of its predecessor, the General Agreement on Tariffs and Trade (GATT) in 1947. The object of the WTO is unashamedly to restrict governments from a variety of measures that restrain the activities of the private sector. As Bernard Hoekman and Michel Kostecki put it,

> [T]he underlying philosophy of the WTO is that open markets, nondiscrimination and global competition in international trade are conducive to the national welfare in all countries. A rationale for the organization is that political constraints prevent governments from adopting more efficient trade policies, and that through the reciprocal exchange of liberalization commitments these political constraints can be overcome.[5]

The essence of the WTO then is to help national politicians escape political constraints *by imposing legal ones.*[6] This is the antithesis of the British constitutional tradition. If the WTO is indeed 'a mast to which governments can tie themselves to escape the siren-calls' of domestic pressure,[7] this should raise democratic concerns. Reaching a definitive conclusion as to whether this is the case, however, requires an examination of both the *scope* and the *enforceability* of WTO commitments. After all, every international commitment perforce involves some constraint of governmental conduct: the question is how much and how tightly?

As regards the scope of WTO obligations, accepting that not all political issues are of equal moment, one must assess the extent to which WTO lawmaking is potentially central to a governmental programme as opposed to being merely peripheral. Does the WTO concern solely 'the obscure and esoteric realms of trade policy'?[8] Or does trade seep into wider questions? José Alvarez Alvarez contends that the normative sweep of international organisations is too broad to be limited to specialised branches of law; their evolving nature is too difficult to pin down. It may therefore be misleading to regard the WTO as contributing solely to questions of trade.[9] Whilst the original GATT 1947 focused solely on trade in goods and concentrated largely on tariff barriers, the WTO enjoys a wider scope, embracing free trade in services and investment, subsidies and non-discrimination in the field of public procurement. Ostensibly the WTO exists to promote economic inter-

---

[5] Hoekman and Kostecki (2001) 1.

[6] The same philosophy underpinned the GATT 1947 system, which the WTO replaced, although GATT 1947 was concerned solely with trade in goods and had weaker enforcement machinery: 'The underlying assumption of the GATT tariff system . . . presupposes that importation and exportation are handled by private firms, stimulated by the profit motive, are guided by commercial considerations. The decisions of these firms to import and export are determined by the relation of domestic prices to foreign prices. Given this assumption, the function of the GATT is to limit the influence that governmentally imposed rules may exert upon the private calculus for decision' (Dam (1970) 318).

[7] Hoekman and Kostecki (2001) 29.

[8] Narlikar (2005) xii.

[9] Alvarez (2005) 12–13.

nationalisation: the question is whether it simultaneously constitutionalises the domination of the private sector.

As regards the enforceability of WTO obligations, the degree of bindingness inevitably affects political freedom. Britain's domestic constitution privileges our national representative democracy over international commitments since, in the event of irreconcilable conflict between statute and international law, statute prevails.[10] However, sanctions and remedies for violation might be so effective as to deter breach, especially when coupled with the natural willingness to honour Britain's international obligations. We have to consider where the WTO enforcement machinery lies on the spectrum of effectiveness. Some commentators perceive the WTO as part of a transition from traditional international law based on treaties between nations to the establishment of a global world power, and we need to consider whether this assessment is valid.[11]

For Britain, there is an additional factor that serves to enmesh us within the WTO structure: our relationship with the WTO is largely governed by European Union law. The European Economic Community, after all, constituted a customs union, encompassing not only free trade within the Community territory but a common trade policy with the rest of the world.[12] By joining in 1973, Britain agreed to be bound by the Community's common commercial policy, its trade arrangements with non-EC countries.[13] Hence it is the EU, in the form of the European Commission, that negotiates for Britain and the other EU Member States within the WTO. EU law strengthens British adhesion to the WTO. It would be difficult for the British Parliament to legislate contrary to the common commercial policy, because directly effective rules of EU law prevail over UK statute in British courts.[14] Quite apart from this, the WTO itself enjoys stronger enforcement machinery than most international organisations. The introduction of this machinery was arguably the most important difference between GATT 1947 and the WTO. The WTO's Dispute Settlement Understanding establishes Panels and an Appellate Body, which enjoy (for all practical purposes) compulsory jurisdiction to resolve disputes and build up a body of jurisprudence. Their judgments are reinforced by powerful sanctions. We will need to consider the effectiveness of this combination of EU law supremacy and WTO enforcement.

In conformity with the ethos of GATT, the European Economic Community (EEC) common commercial policy mandated free trade: Article 206 TFEU (previously Article 131 EC) describes the common commercial policy as involving

---

[10] *Mortensen v Peters* (1906) 14 SLT 227; *Cheney v Conn* [1968] 1 All ER 779, [1968] 1 WLR 242.

[11] Hardt and Negri (2000) 10.

[12] As will be described below, the very design of the European Economic Community in 1957 was dictated by the need to fit within GATT 1947.

[13] The traumatic transition from a system of 'Commonwealth preference' involving favourable trade arrangements with Commonwealth countries, to the common customs tariff was originally a stronger political objection to British membership of the Community than concerns about sovereignty, especially within the Conservative Party. See Nicol (2001a) ch 2.

[14] *R v Secretary of State for Transport, ex p Factortame Ltd (No 2)* [1991] AC 603. See Nicol (2001a) ch 7.

'the progressive abolition of restrictions on international trade and on foreign direct investment, and the lowering of customs and other barriers'. The common commercial policy undoubtedly gave the Community an exclusive competence with regard to trade in goods, but it remained uncertain whether it also gave the Community authority over the 'new subjects' covered by the enlarged ambit of the WTO. In its 1994 *Opinion on the World Trade Organization,* the European Court of Justice (ECJ) was called upon to determine whether the three main planks of the WTO—GATT, the General Agreement on Trade in Services (GATS) and the Agreement on Trade-Related Intellectual Property (TRIPS)—fell within exclusive Community competence.[15] The ECJ held that whilst GATT came squarely within the exclusive competence of the common commercial policy, both GATS and TRIPs involved 'shared competence' between Community and Member States. Competence could, however, become progressively exclusive as the Community's internal legislation regulated the treatment of non-nationals in these fields, since external competence would automatically flow from internal competence.[16] Alternatively, exclusive external competence could be expressly conferred on the Community by Treaty amendment. GATS and TRIPS were therefore 'mixed agreements' in which both the Community and the Member States enjoyed joint competence. In respect of mixed agreements, the ECJ declared that there was a duty of close cooperation between Member States and Community institutions in both their negotiation and conclusion and the fulfilment of the obligations involved.

The Amsterdam revision of the EC Treaty permitted the Council to extend the common commercial policy to services and intellectual property if it so elected, and this position was strengthened in the Nice revision of 2000 to bring services and intellectual property definitively within the common commercial policy.[17] Article 133 EC was amended to expressly authorise the Community (subject to a complex array of voting procedures) to negotiate and conclude agreements in the fields of trade in services and commercial aspects of intellectual property as part of the common commercial policy. Only certain types of agreement on services (cultural and audiovisual, educational, and social and human health) remained matters of shared competence between Community and Member States.[18] After the Lisbon revision, Article 3 TFEU now proclaims that the EU has exclusive competence with regard to the common commercial policy. Accordingly, the precise domestic effect of WTO law in Britain lies in the hands not of Parliament but of the EU institutions.[19] WTO law particularly empowers the EU judiciary, which has acted as the gatekeeper between the WTO and EU legal orders,[20]

---

[15] Opinion 1/94 [1994] ECR I-5267.
[16] Case 22/70 *Commission v Council* (European Road Transport Agreement) [1971] ECR 263, [1971] CMLR 335. See also Cremona (1999).
[17] Cremona (2000).
[18] Art 133(6) EC.
[19] Bourgeois (2000).
[20] Snyder (2003).

arguably enforcing WTO law more vigorously against the Member States than against the EU institutions.[21]

Before we consider the WTO's substantive provisions and enforcement machinery, it would be helpful to trace the evolution of GATT and the WTO through the prism of British membership. The history of the trade system and Britain's part in it furnishes valuable insights into the ideological underpinnings on which the modern WTO is based.

Britain and GATT 1947

The international entrenchment of free trade through GATT 1947 was an American initiative at a time when the United States was establishing its hegemony. In the wake of the Second World War, American statesmen saw a strong connection between freedom in international trade and the preservation of lasting peace.[22] Indeed, many US politicians and business leaders attributed the breakdown of the post-First World War peace settlement to the poor handling of economic problems.[23] They believed that the 'mistake' of protectionism had led to unemployment and economic instability, and so to war. In proposing a 'genuinely new conception of world order', they were determined to lay down an economic blueprint for a better world, as they saw it.[24] In addition, and above all, the Americans were hostile to the 'imperial preference' policy pursued by successive British governments, whereby Britain's tariff regime (its system of customs duties) discriminated in favour of products from the British Empire/Commonwealth and against products from elsewhere.[25] The American preoccupation with the British sphere indicates that GATT was conceived at the very tail-end of Britain's period as an economic and political superpower.

During the war the Americans had insisted upon including within their Lend-Lease agreement with Britain a commitment to non-discrimination in trade.[26] This bound Britain and the United States to take action, 'open to all other countries of like mind', to eliminate all forms of discrimination in international commerce. Yet despite this formal commitment, the Americans still had difficulty in persuading the British to let go of imperial preference, especially in view of the part played by the Dominions in the war.[27] In the immediate aftermath of war Britain and the United States signed a further loan agreement that prompted the British to adopt multilateralism in the currency sphere, and this was seen as a precursor to shifting

---

[21] Everling (1996).
[22] For the view of a US Secretary of State, see Hull (1937) 14.
[23] Gardner (1956) 4.
[24] 'The American Challenge' (1942) cxliii *The Economist* p 67.
[25] Gardner (1956) 18–19.
[26] Art 7, Mutual Aid Agreement 1942.
[27] Gardner (1956) ch 8.

trade policy away from imperial preference towards non-discrimination.[28] Even at this early stage, American policy seemed destined to erode the differences between the British political parties. As Ruggie has observed,

> Much of the negotiating energy expended by the United States on the creation of the postwar economic order was . . . directed toward undoing the more benign but still vexing British position. It consisted of a commitment to imperial preferences on the part of the Tories and to extensive controls on international economic transactions by Labour as part of its objective to institute systematic economic planning. Both [policies] were inherently discriminatory.[29]

When Labour came to office after its 1945 landslide victory, some in the Party already shared the American hostility to Commonwealth preference. In 1942 Labour had proposed establishing an international authority to eliminate imperialistic economic practices in an effort to raise worldwide living standards.[30] Whilst a minority in the Party opposed the liberalisation of trade (some because they wanted a socialist planned economy, others because they were mindful of the role of free trade in Britain's inter-war economic problems), Labour's mainstream appeared to support trade liberalisation, a stance that coincided with an upsurge in enthusiasm for free trade amongst the academic economists in government.[31] This did not mean, however, that Labour sought the embrace of an international 'free market'. Party opinion strongly favoured the visible hand of government rather than the invisible hand of market forces.[32] Indeed, Labour politicians viewed international economic coordination as a means of governmental intervention on a global scale. The Party shared the approach of John Maynard Keynes, who argued for the 'simultaneous pursuit' of high domestic employment 'by all countries together'.[33]

The mood in favour of state intervention in the economy had not extended as far as the United States. The Truman administration was pursuing free trade with quite the opposite aim in mind. It considered that an expansion of international trade would be essential for 'the preservation of private enterprise':

> Moreover, if this is not done, there may be a further strengthening of the tendency, already strong in many countries before the war, to eliminate private enterprise from international trade in favor of rigid control by the state.[34]

In 1946 the US administration put forward a proposal for an International Trade Organization (ITO) of the United Nations, an international body that would

---

[28] Anglo-American Financial Agreement, 6 December 1945; Gardner (1956) chs 10–12.

[29] Ruggie (1993) 25.

[30] Labour Party (1942).

[31] Gardner (1956) ch 2.

[32] D Acheson, memorandum of conversation, 28 July 1941. FRUS 1941 (Washington, DC: GPO 1959) 3:11–13.

[33] Aaronson (1996) 30. Keynes became a key figure in the ITO negotiations.

[34] Summary of the Interim Report of the Special Committee on Relaxation of Trade Barriers, US Administration inter-departmental committee (18 December 1943) id App 45, p 622.

enforce a legal code of free trade.[35] The main negotiating partners were the United States and Britain, the two major non-Communist powers in the immediate aftermath of war. Whilst both wished to prevent a return to interwar trade competition, there was disagreement as to what should replace it.[36] During the negotiations, three specific differences emerged, and these reflected divergent goals as to the extent of governmental control of economic policy: the United States tried to push the ITO in a more free market direction, whereas Britain strove to preserve the economic power of government.

First, the Attlee government was much influenced by the Beveridge Report, with its ambitious definition of full employment and widespread advocacy of central planning and controls.[37] Believing that the goal of trade policy should be full employment, it sought to commit the ITO to this aim.[38] By contrast, the American negotiators wished to avoid any such undertaking, believing it smacked of socialism. In the end, the draft included a statement that the avoidance of unemployment was not merely of domestic concern but was a necessary condition for the expansion of international trade.[39]

Secondly, the Americans sought extensive limitations on the use of quantitative restrictions, whereas the British wanted each country to be free to impose them for balance of payments purposes. The final agreement permitted quantitative restrictions, though it fell short of giving states complete freedom, by according extensive powers of review to the ITO.

Thirdly, American businessmen wanted to include a chapter on foreign investment, giving them the right to invest in other countries without the risk of nationalisation of their assets. Indeed, the issue was a sticking point for many US business associations. But they were disappointed with what was agreed.[40] The ITO acknowledged a right of governments to nationalise companies subject to 'just compensation', a compromise that many American investors found unacceptable because 'just compensation' was not defined. They viewed the ITO's provisions on investment as an unwelcome affirmation of the sovereign right of governments to expropriate.

In 1946 the Republicans won control of Congress and made it clear that the end of imperial preference was to be the precondition for Congressional approval of the ITO. This stance intensified British resistance to its elimination: indeed, both major parties became increasingly enthusiastic to maintain and even intensify economic ties with the Commonwealth. Faced with this stalemate, the ITO negotiations became protracted. Yet the negotiating states were anxious not to postpone freer trade until every last detail of the ITO had been hammered out. A temporary

---

[35] 'Its role would thus not be unlike that of a court determining whether crime has occurred' (Dam (1970) 13).

[36] Goldstein (1993) 202.

[37] Beveridge (1944).

[38] Goldstein (1993) 216.

[39] Gardner (1956) ch XIV.

[40] Aaronson (1996) 84–88.

expedient was needed to govern world trade until it came into being. In April 1947, therefore, the world's major trading nations convened in Geneva to agree the General Agreement on Tariffs and Trade (GATT 1947).

This supposedly stopgap agreement involved the creation of a negotiating forum held together by an international treaty. It lacked any organisational structure or legal personality. Paradoxically, from the American point of view, this lack of a structure was essential, for it meant that GATT fell within the grant of legislative authority bestowed upon the US President by the Reciprocal Trade Agreements Act, thereby circumventing the need for Congressional approval.[41] GATT also constituted an unprecedentedly large-scale tariff negotiation, the success of which hinged upon agreement being reached between the Commonwealth and the United States. In the end, Britain offered only modest concessions in the preferences she enjoyed in the Dominions, though the Dominions offered greater reductions in the preferences they enjoyed in Britain. Nonetheless, the US administration was still prepared to endorse GATT, since it liberalised trade overall and would in any event be swiftly superseded once the ITO came into existence.

Having endorsed GATT, the parties completed their negotiations for the ITO. Unlike GATT, the ITO was to be a formal organisation, complete with two tiers of dispute settlement machinery. It was also to enjoy an extensive substantive ambit, encompassing many issues that traditionally fell within the borders of states. Yet paradoxically this 'grotesquely complicated document'[42] was also riddled with exceptions and escape clauses, reflecting the desire of states, saddled at the time with damaged economies, to contravene the objective of freer trade.[43] Significantly, then, strong enforcement of commitments was balanced by flexibility as to the substance of those commitments.

The ITO, unlike GATT, required Congressional ratification, and from the outset it was clear that the administration would have difficulty in securing this. The White House tried to drum up support for the ITO by arguing that it would establish the rule of law in international economic relations.[44] Indeed, argued the administration, the ITO would confirm the near-universal acceptance of American economic thinking, since it would constitute an

> Amazing and unprecedented achievement [securing] agreement between the representatives of 54 nations, representing every stage of economic development and a wide variety of political philosophies, on a code of rules to guide their international trade *which embodies fundamentally the United States philosophy of the maximum amount of competition and the minimum amount of government control.*[45]

Congress, however, did not accept this argument. During the course of the ITO negotiations there had been a revival of protectionist pressure, and this coincided

[41] Aaronson (1996) 82; Winham (1998).
[42] Dam (1970) 14.
[43] Aaronson (1996) 68.
[44] Acheson (1949).
[45] Brown (1950) 132, emphasis added.

with the defection of a critical segment of the American business community that did not regard the ITO as sufficiently committed to free trade and private enterprise. The ITO, after all, permitted quantitative restrictions, and its full employment provisions were a euphemism for state intervention. Opponents subtly tainted the ITO's supporters with toleration of nationalised economies. The National Foreign Trade Council, for example, declared that the employment provisions would transform a free-enterprise America into a planned economy.[46] Similarly, the US Council of the International Chamber of Commerce criticised the Charter as a 'dangerous document' that 'jeopardizes the free enterprise system by giving priority to centralized national governmental planning of foreign trade ... in effect commit[ing] all members of the ITO to state planning for full employment'.[47] In sum, said its critics, it was an economic Munich,[48] which went too far in subordinating the international commitments of signatory countries to the requirements of national plans and policies, the paraphernalia of government regulation which would hinder the development of private enterprise.[49]

At a time of anti-communist fervour, the ITO was increasingly seen through the prism of red-baiting. An additional but related argument was that the ITO meant surrendering US sovereignty to an international organisation, for instance in the fields of employment policy and economic development—in effect an international constitution but with no bill of rights.[50] Faced with this unremitting hostility, the White House quietly announced in December 1950 that it would not resubmit the ITO Charter to Congress. Instead, the administration threw its energy into making the most of GATT.

The American controversy shows that at the heart of the debate on free trade lay the question of the private ownership of industry. Trade was merely an aspect of a bigger picture: the priority was to defend an economy based on private enterprise from the tentacles of nationalisation. At the time, the extension of public ownership was a very real threat to the private sector. Years later, some WTO supporters could see the merits of the ITO's demise from the point of view of marginalising socialism. As Kenneth Dam has put it,

> [W]hen one considers the socialist thinking, nationalizations, and central planning that were so much the vogue in the late 1940s in Paris and London and other major capitals, we are perhaps fortunate that it failed, and thus those ideas did not become part of official international trade doctrine through the ITO.[51]

Though unsuccessful, the Truman administration's attempts to persuade Congress to approve the ITO marked a watershed in US attitudes to free trade. From then on, there was a growing sense that America should always pursue trade

---

[46] National Foreign Trade Council (1950) 23.

[47] US Council of the International Chamber of Commerce, Statement of Position on the Havana Charter for an International Trade Organization, 9 May 1950.

[48] Adams Brown (1950) 366–75.

[49] Diebold (1952) 14.

[50] Aaronson (1996) 128.

[51] Dam (2005) 88.

liberalisation since it would make the country prosperous and prevent the international spread of Communism.[52] This is not to say that American politicians felt free trade should be absolute: they still considered that specific sectors merited special protection. However, the underlying assumption henceforth was always in favour of freer trade.

GATT: Evolving towards Bindingness

From modest beginnings as a temporary expedient, GATT 1947 eventually developed into a semi-permanent entity. Its de facto organisation seemingly depended upon three slender lines of the Agreement.[53] Article XXV provided that 'the Contracting Parties shall meet from time to time to give effect to those provisions which require joint action and generally to further the objectives of the Agreement'. This was not much of a legal base from which to build an institutional structure, yet perhaps this very thinness was to prove an advantage. Unlike the ITO, GATT allowed the major countries to do business with each other unencumbered by the complexities of a large organisation. Ironically though, this was precisely what GATT ultimately became.[54]

GATT's organising principle was that governments were to bundle all their trade barriers into one form alone—tariffs (customs duties). They were then voluntarily to reach deals on reductions ('tariff bindings' or 'tariff concessions') through rounds of negotiations. To this end, quantitative restrictions on imports and discriminatory internal taxes and regulatory measures were immediately prohibited (albeit with a fair number of exceptions). As for tariffs, once a state had negotiated a 'tariff binding' on a certain product, the relevant tariff could never again be raised: it could either remain the same or be further reduced in subsequent negotiations. For this reason, by the 1950s Britain was already feeling a loss of sovereignty because it was unable to raise Commonwealth preferences.[55]

However, GATT was not only a bargaining forum; it also enshrined legal principles that formed the seed from which a more law-based system could ultimately spring. In particular, it embodied the 'Most Favoured Nation' (MFN) rule, which was considered the very cornerstone of GATT.[56] The MFN rule requires states to extend to *every* GATT country the most favourable trade treatment accorded to *any* country, the most favoured nation. A product made in one member country therefore had to be treated no less favourably than a 'like' good originating in any other country (including those not in GATT). The principle that every GATT nation was to be treated as advantageously as the most favoured nation struck a

---

[52] Aaronson (1996) 121.
[53] Curzon (1965) 34.
[54] Hudec (1990) 57–8.
[55] Hudec (1993) 6.
[56] Art I, GATT 1947.

blow against discriminatory trade policies. Conversely, however, the limited scope of GATT—its exclusive focus on tariff barriers on goods—necessarily restricted the application of the principle.[57] Whilst GATT 1947 was ultimately extended to cover rules traditionally the province of national governments (for example, non-tariff measures that distort or restrict trade, a standards code and a subsidies code), it could not escape the fact that its scope was limited to trade in goods. Nonetheless, GATT survived for almost half a century with no formal constitutional rules regulating how it was organised. Instead, detailed bargaining procedures evolved over time.[58]

When the six original Member States of the European Economic Community came together to draft the Treaty of Rome in 1957, the very design of their Community was determined by GATT 1947 and its MFN rule. Article XXIV GATT 1947 permits a customs union to be treated as if it were a single contracting party. By forming a customs union, the EEC fitted itself deftly into this MFN exception, with the result that EEC Member States could avoid having to give goods from non-EEC countries the same favourable treatment that they accorded to goods from their fellow Member States. The corollary was that as part of the Community's common commercial policy vis-à-vis the rest of the world, the Community institutions assumed the role of negotiators for the Six on GATT matters. When Britain joined the Community in 1973, therefore, there was a transfer of authority for trade relations from Whitehall and Westminster to the EEC Commission and Council. Thus trade policy to a considerable extent ceased to be a matter of British politics.

Returning to the structure of GATT, the organisation, such as it was, evidently needed some form of enforcement machinery in order to encourage states to comply with its rules. Yet the legal basis for a GATT disputes settlement procedure was unpromising. The GATT texts merely sketched out a rudimentary process, permitting a state to withdraw tariff concessions as retaliation when another state 'nullified or impaired' a benefit deriving from the Agreement.[59] Few at GATT's inception could have predicted that a sophisticated disputes procedure would evolve from such a modest provision, nor how central it would become to GATT's structure. The development of the disputes procedure is all the more remarkable in view of the disagreement at the outset between those who sought a diplomacy-orientated system and those who favoured a more disciplined, impartial and law-based one.[60]

In the early days of GATT the diplomatic approach prevailed. A dispute would be settled by a Chairman's ruling or by an ad hoc working party consisting of diplomats of the contracting states. The trend towards third-party adjudication

---

[57] There were also a number of exceptions to the MFN clause. First, specified preferential arrangements were excepted, such as Commonwealth preference. Secondly, customs unions and free trade areas were excepted since they constituted movement towards freer trade (Dam (1970) 18–19.)

[58] Jackson (1998) 18.

[59] Arts XXII and XXIII, GATT 1947.

[60] Jackson (1994) 151.

was cautious and experimental.[61] In 1952 the Chairman for the first time con-vened a panel of independent members to hear all complaints referred during the session.[62] This proved an historic turning point. The transfer of adjudicative authority from the states themselves to third-party enforcement represented a striking move towards a more juridical approach.[63] In 1955 this panel procedure crystallised into formal GATT policy. GATT members appreciated the objectivity that adjudication by panels could bring and considered that this was an improve-ment on the earlier working parties, which had served as vehicles for political com-promise.[64] After a period of decline in the late 1950s and 1960s,[65] the panels procedure revived in the 1970s when the Nixon administration embarked on an aggressive campaign of litigation to enforce GATT's non-discrimination principle, part of a strategy to replace consensus political decision-making by the impartial resolution of disputes.[66] By the 1980s the disputes procedure had evolved into 'the jewel of the GATT legal system'.[67]

Thus, despite a certain 'see-sawing' between diplomacy and legalism over the decades, the historical trend of GATT procedures was markedly away from a nego-tiating model and towards a rule-orientated one.[68] The difference between a 'panel' and a 'court' would appear more formal than real: the panel members may not have been judges in the formal sense, yet they were ostensibly chosen for their expert knowledge of GATT law, and the panel system guaranteed their indepen-dence.[69] Moreover, panel rulings came to enjoy a value as precedents; whilst their precedential effect was de facto and not strict, nonetheless panels cited previous decisions to support their rulings.[70]

Whilst the enforcement system generally worked well—the letter if not the spirit of GATT was usually honoured—by the end of the 1970s it was coming under strain.[71] As the system's general efficacy increased, so its shortcomings became more apparent and ever more acute. The enforcement process could eas-ily be derailed, since at almost every stage the consent of the parties to the dispute was required in order to move things along. First of all, parties could block the request to convene a panel; secondly, they could veto the adoption of the panel report by the GATT Council; and thirdly, they could delay or fail to implement the panel recommendations back home.[72] After 1980, the number of non-adoptions of panel reports, especially in subsidies cases, increased markedly, prompting

[61] Hudec (1990) 75.
[62] *Ibid*, 75–85.
[63] Jackson (1994) 152.
[64] Hudec (1990) 91.
[65] See generally Dam (1970).
[66] House of Representatives Ways and Means Committee report No 93-571, 93rd Congress, 1st Sess (1973) 66–67; Senate Report No 93-1298, 93rd Congress, 2nd Sess (1974) 166.
[67] Hudec (1993) 9.
[68] Jackson (1994) 155.
[69] Curzon (1965) 43.
[70] Jackson (1994) 157.
[71] Hoekman and Kostecki (2001) 43.
[72] Jackson (1998) 71; Croome (1995) 144; Orrego Vicūna (2004) 88.

demands for a stronger system.[73] The weaknesses in GATT's enforcement machinery were a major factor in convincing states to replace GATT with a more binding organisation.

From GATT to WTO

Dissatisfaction with the GATT disputes machinery formed part of a wider malaise. By the early 1980s there was a growing perception that the world trade system was adrift. There were protectionist pressures, and GATT was at risk of being bypassed and undermined. National trade policies were increasingly contradictory, professing anxiety for the preservation of the GATT system whilst breaking GATT's rules in response to short-term concerns.[74] There was a growing feeling that the multilateral trading system could be preserved only if it were made to work better.[75] The GATT Secretariat commissioned an independent group, the Leutwiler group, to identify the causes of world trading problems and how they could be overcome. The group's conclusion was that the organisation's ambit could only credibly expand (for instance to cover trade in services, an area previously untouched by the multilateral system) if respect for the system as a whole could be enhanced.[76]

There was no meeting of minds, however, as to the way in which GATT should be changed. The European Community was not enthusiastic to expand its scope. By contrast, the United States, now under the Reagan presidency, was spurred on by its free market convictions and by the need to relieve protectionist pressure from Congress, to set ambitious goals for world trade, going far beyond GATT's traditional focus on tariffs. In particular, the US administration, working closely with American industry, sought to persuade the European Community to approve the inclusion of three 'new subjects' within the scope of the new organisation.[77] Specifically, the US administration wanted a framework of rules for trade in services based on principles of liberalisation of market access, transparency and national treatment; minimum standards for intellectual property rights protection and their enforcement through national law; and the elimination of controls on foreign direct investment.[78]

The involvement of private enterprise in pressing these demands was significant, for it meant that private corporations, in partnership with government, were assuming the role of constitution-builders. Indeed, arguably the very success of the negotiations was the result of the emergence of powerful corporate vested interests

---

[73] Hudec (2000).

[74] Croome (1995) 18.

[75] Nau (1987) 85.

[76] Bradley and Leutwiler (1985).

[77] Shaffer (2003) 58; Croome (1995) 16. The EC was more interested in concentrating on the completion of its own single internal market.

[78] Croome (1995) 118–38.

in globalisation.[79] Having convinced the European Community, the US administration then succeeded in isolating those developing countries that stood out
against the 'new subjects', partly through the threat of US protectionism.[80] The
American masterstroke was to request a meeting of GATT's highest body, the
Session of Contracting Parties, at which it would only have needed to muster an
absolute majority in order to secure a new round of negotiations.[81] In the event,
no such vote was necessary: since the participants realised the state of affairs,
everything proceeded by consensus.

Perhaps significantly, the US ploy had a striking contemporaneous parallel
within the European Community, where it was by a majority decision—not by
unanimity—that the EC embarked upon the negotiation of the Single European
Act 1986.[82] In both cases, profound constitutional change within an international
organisation was set in motion through the actual or threatened compulsion of
majority voting rather than through international consensus. The organising principle of state consent, traditionally central to international law, was being undermined even in formal legal terms.[83] This may be part of a more general trend in
international law whereby some states have become increasingly more equal than
others.[84] In any event it was upon this basis that GATT launched its Uruguay
Round of negotiations in 1985, aimed at creating a new international body that
would open up market access worldwide.

The World Trade Organization

The World Trade Organization negotiations proved to be a stark contrast with the
ITO ones forty years earlier. The ITO talks had been characterised by tension
between a free-market United States and a state-interventionist Britain. By the late
1980s and early 1990s, however, free-market capitalism had achieved ideological
hegemony. Capitalism was politically triumphant whilst socialist and social democratic alternatives were sinking without trace.[85] During the protracted negotiations the United States was for the most part under Republican administrations,
whilst the European Community had strengthened its commitment to the free
market through the Single European Act and Maastricht revisions of its Treaty.

GATT 1947 had represented an ideological compromise between free trade and
national autonomy, allowing governments to pursue reasonably interventionist
domestic policies.[86] By contrast, WTO 1995 embodied a private enterprise-driven

---

[79] Dunkley (2000) 4.
[80] Bhagwati (1987) 207; Croome (1995) 28.
[81] Croome (1995) 26.
[82] De Zwaan (1986); Grant (1994) 72; Nicol (2001a) 161–62.
[83] See eg Brownlie (2003) 3; Warbrick (1994).
[84] Weil (1983).
[85] Dunkley (2000) 8.
[86] Goldstein (1993) 225.

economic philosophy, reflecting the Reagan–Thatcher domination of the years during which it had been negotiated. President Reagan recognised the potential of world trade law as an 'economic constitution' that had now 'come to a turning point'.[87] In future, the WTO—this 'greatest ever achievement in institutionalized global economic cooperation'[88]—would better reflect (and entrench) Reagan's pro-private enterprise beliefs. In Britain, with both the Conservatives and (increasingly) Labour embracing the private sector, the mantra of liberalisation and privatisation was assuming ubiquitous status.[89] Thus the advent of the WTO caused little controversy. The WTO Agreements were signed using the royal prerogative, and they merited only a low-key adjournment debate in Parliament. Stuart Bell, speaking for the Labour Opposition, said that a successful conclusion to the negotiations was better than no conclusion at all and that Labour would measure the WTO by the actual fruits it bore in the years to come.[90]

In terms of the WTO's substantive ambit, there was consensus among states that tariffs, quantitative restrictions and other non-tariff distortions of trade in goods were suitable subjects for inclusion within the WTO's scope. In other areas, however, there was disagreement. The United States pressed for the inclusion of its three 'new subjects'—services, intellectual property and trade-related investment measures; Britain joined the United States in strongly pressing for services liberalisation. In the event, the 'new subjects' were approved as the basis for detailed negotiations, although many countries conceded them only with deep reluctance, considering them to be matters that ought to lie within domestic sovereignty. The comprehensiveness of the WTO's coverage made it the 'new frontier of international law',[91] biting robustly into the red meat of traditional national sovereignty. As Donald McRae put it,

> International trade law does not rest on the primary assumption of international law, that the world is composed of sovereign nation States, each surrounded by territorial borders within which it exercises plenary authority . . . Rather than focusing on the independence of States, international trade law highlights the concept of interdependence.[92]

In terms of its enforcement procedure, whilst the negotiations revealed a sense of common purpose in favour of improving the effectiveness of dispute settlement, there was disagreement over what should replace the GATT system. On one side of the argument, the United States and Canada wanted dispute settlement to establish right and wrong, to deliver legal judgments with which losing parties would have to comply. On the opposing side, the European Communities and Japan favoured dispute settlement based on conciliation, with the aim of overcoming particular trade problems rather than laying down legalised judgments.[93]

---

[87] Petersmann (1991) XXV.
[88] Sampson (2001) 5.
[89] Soederberg, Menz and Cerny (2005) 25.
[90] House of Commons debates, 14 June 1994.
[91] McRae (2000) 30.
[92] McRae (1996) 116–17.
[93] Croome (1995) 142–49.

The supporters of a more legalistic, less diplomatic approach largely got their way. The WTO Agreements contain a Dispute Settlement Understanding (DSU) which is considered the WTO's greatest achievement. It is with this machinery that we open our analysis of the WTO texts.

WTO: The Dispute Settlement Understanding

The enforcement procedure enshrined in the WTO's Dispute Settlement Understanding has been lauded as 'all-important and unique' and 'the most powerful of any international law tribunal'.[94] It is essentially this machinery that drives the world trading system towards bindingness, whilst at the same time serving as an instrument for judicial legislation and governance, since case law inevitably adds flesh to the dry bones of WTO provisions.[95] The dispute machinery exists not only to resolve individual trade disputes but, through its jurisprudence, explicitly to clarify the obligations undertaken by all the WTO Members.[96] It generates law on what the WTO Members can and cannot do: in other words it creates *constitutional* law. Furthermore, the greater the accumulation of jurisprudence, the more profound the judicialisation. In this regard the convergence between the WTO and the EU—each adopting rule-based dispute settlement by a body that acts as an undeclared constitutional court over the member nations—is striking.[97]

Why is the Dispute Settlement Understanding so effective? The fundamental difference between the DSU procedure and its predecessor lies in the inability of states to veto the judicial process at its various stages. Previously, crucial decisions—to establish a panel, to adopt its report, to authorise the remedy of suspension of concessions—had to be taken by consensus, which meant that losing states could in effect veto unfavourable decisions. Under the WTO regime, by contrast, the procedure progresses through these stages automatically *unless* there is a consensus *against* doing so. In practice this makes the adoption of all three stages automatic. Furthermore, there is a strict timeframe for all stages of dispute resolution and appellate review of panel reports on points of law by a new institution, the Appellate Body.[98] Compulsory jurisdiction goes hand in hand with effective remedies: the Panels and Appellate Body can authorise countermeasures whereby winning parties can harm the guilty Member's trade.

The Panels and Appellate Body are expressly forbidden from adding to or diminishing the rights in the WTO Agreements; but this is nonsensical since the

---

[94] Van den Bossche (2005) xiii; Jackson (2006a) 135.

[95] Trachtmann (2006) 434.

[96] Art 3.2 DSU.

[97] Holmes (2001) 79.

[98] Furthermore, if the decision comes not from a panel but from the Appellate Body, this report is final and is adopted by the Council.

interpretation required by dispute resolution necessarily affects rights.[99] It is likewise absurd that Article IX(2) WTO states that the WTO's Ministerial Conference and General Council have 'exclusive' authority to adopt interpretations of the Agreements; in actual fact the jurisprudence of the Panels and the Appellate Body plays a far greater role in giving meaning to WTO rules. To date, indeed, the WTO has not made any explicit use of Article IX (2), thereby making the WTO judiciary de facto the authoritative interpreter of the WTO Agreements. Indeed, owing to the immense difficulty of WTO Members giving definitive interpretations of WTO provisions—a three-quarters majority of WTO Members is required in order to adopt an interpretation—litigation has become the dominant form of governance. The general emphasis in the WTO Agreements towards decision-making by states on the basis of consensus means that state representatives do not achieve very much.[100] Rather like the European Court of Justice during the EEC's period of political stagnation in the 1970s, the WTO Panels and Appellate Body have filled the gap that resulted from the constitutional impasse.

Once the WTO Agreements entered into force the EU had to decide how to enable European enterprises to enforce WTO commitments. The EU's interest obviously lay in facilitating challenges to *other* WTO Members to ensure that *they* kept to their commitments. The option of making the WTO Agreements directly effective within the Community legal system was not particularly alluring, since to do so would place the focus on multinational corporations litigating *against the EU* for *its* compliance with WTO rules. The Council of the European Union stated in its 1994 decision approving the WTO Agreements that by its very nature WTO law was not capable of having direct effect, a position endorsed by the ECJ in *Dior v TUK*.[101] No doubt the Council had no wish to substitute the supremacy of Community law with the supremacy of WTO law, nor would it have sought to make WTO law more effective within the EU than it is within non-EU countries. The EU availed itself of the alternative option, namely to channel disputes through the WTO disputes machinery. To this end in 1994 the Council enacted the Trade Barriers Regulation, which enables 'Community enterprises' (and associations of such enterprises) to prompt the Commission to investigate alleged international trade violations with a view to making use of the WTO disputes procedure.[102] The effect of the Regulation is to tie the EU and its Member States tightly into the WTO disputes procedure, whilst encouraging the private sector to bypass national representatives in favour of European channels.

---

[99] Art 19.2 DSU.

[100] Jackson (2006) 113–14.

[101] Council Decision 94/800/EC, 11th recital; Joined Cases C-300/98 and C-392/98 *Parfums Christian Dior SA v TUK Consultancy BV* and *Assco Gerüste GmbH and Rob van Dijk v Wiilhelm Layher GmbH & Co KG and Layher BV* [2000] ECR I-11307, [42]–[44].

[102] Art 4, Council Regulation 3286/94/EC of 22 December 1994 laying down Community procedures in the field of the common commercial policy in order to ensure the exercise of the Community's rights under international trade rules, particularly those established under the auspices of the World Trade Organization.

It is impossible to make sense of the EU system established by the Trade Barriers Regulation without being aware that it forms part of a transatlantic network. The mechanisms in the United States are particularly important in this regard, since the United States and the European Union act as plaintiff or defendant in 84 per cent of complaints that result in judicial decision.[103] Both the European Commission and the US Trade Representative rely on industry initially to kick-start litigation by drawing attention to obstacles to free trade, and then to sustain that litigation, by providing convincing factual information and legal argument to meet the highly contextualised approach taken by Panels.[104] Cases only materialise because the private sector is moved by its own commercial interests to collect and transmit data on measures that violate WTO law and to instigate actions before a Panel or the Appellate Body through the intermediary of a WTO Member. Thus in practice both the Trade Barriers Regulation and the section 301 of the US Trade Act 1974 institutionalise collaboration between government and private companies. These systems effectively co-opt the private sector into a process of global constitutional adjudication, a practical necessity since the help of transnational corporations is indispensable to the US and EU public authorities. Without private companies there would be no litigation and therefore no generation of public law by the Panels and Appellate Body. The lack of standing of private corporations before the WTO judicial institutions therefore belies their seminal role.

The American and European machinery forms part (by far the most important part) of a global network of national procedures that induce governments to pay attention to private sector complaints of trade barriers. This network simultaneously harnesses the commercial interests of private enterprise and the politico-economic interests of governments in enforcing free trade in the teeth of state measures. Since this global system of judicial review enforces the EU's and Britain's adherence to WTO commitments—and in so doing creates a body of jurisprudence—it can convincingly be conceived as part of British public law.

Litigation by the EU and US, generated through public–private partnerships with commercial enterprises, has in fact become the most important source of WTO law. Private companies have thereby been accorded a privileged institutionalised position from which to challenge the legislation and policies of states. This represents a striking constitutional elevation of the private sector. In the past the private sector in Britain had to make do with exerting political and economic influence on lawmakers and litigating over the interpretation of domestic legislation; by contrast, the DSU procedure co-opts them into a mechanism whereby the very boundaries of legitimate national lawmaking are delineated. Moreover, the transnational character of modern enterprises should be borne in mind: it is quite

---

[103] Shaffer (2003) 9.

[104] *Ibid*, 46–47. Joseph Stiglitz, former Chief Economist of the World Bank, has emphasised the harshness of the US arrangements: 'The United States sets itself up as prosecutor, judge and jury. There is a quasi-judicial process, but the cards are stacked: both the rules and the judges favor a finding of guilty' (Stiglitz (2002) 62).

common for non-EU countries to threaten or proceed with WTO legal action, at the behest of enterprises based in the Community territory. Thus 'domestic' firms form partnerships with foreign trade authorities to challenge their own national (or EU) regulations.

Furthermore, this public–private law-generating partnership is *de facto* entrenched within the WTO system. The EU trade authorities were obliged to create their own mechanism for involving the private sector, to some extent imitating the established American procedure, in an effort to rally European enterprises against US litigative pre-eminence.[105] Now that both the US and the EU have well-established systems, neither side could countenance a unilateral discarding of their arrangements such as would hand lawmaking domination to the other side. The entrenched nature of the system is another reason why it should be regarded as constitutional. Private companies have thus been brought to the fore in the judicial process, a far cry from the era in which international law was restricted to inter-state disputes.[106] Yet the involvement of private companies remains covert; the parties to the disputes are formally the WTO Members, even though litigation is inspired and powered by companies. Indeed, the intimate participation of the private sector can be conceived as a hidden constitution, operating behind the façade of the formal arrangements.[107]

By all accounts this litigative partnership between the private sector and nation states has proven highly effective: WTO law enjoys a high rate of compliance.[108] In more than 80 per cent of cases, states have brought disputed measures or legislation into conformity with WTO law in a timely and correct manner.[109] In the rare instances when compliance does not occur, the complaining party can retaliate by 'suspension of concessions or other obligations'—normally a drastic increase in customs duties on strategically selected products of the offending party with the aim of prompting obedience to WTO judgments. The affected sector will generally lobby furiously for the WTO Member to comply with WTO law. This means of compelling compliance, which depends on the relationship between the state and private enterprise, should surely be seen as a new, alternative, channel of law enforcement, by all accounts just as effective as traditional state-centred judicial enforcement measures.[110]

Whilst the remedy of retaliation goes against the WTO's ethos of encouraging world trade, it has been invoked with increasing frequency, which suggests that WTO Members see it as an effective sanction. The potency of the remedy is well

---

[105] The procedure based on s 301 Trade Act 1974 was already well developed in the United States before the WTO came into existence.

[106] Orrego Vicūna (2004) ch 6.

[107] The nature of the system confirms that under globalisation, the relationship between the power of companies and the power of states is one of cooperation rather than antagonism. See Gowan (1999) 5.

[108] Van den Bossche (2005) 220; Yenkong (2006).

[109] Too often commentators misleadingly focus on the small number of instances of defiance, disregarding the dominant trend that 'almost all nations observe almost all of their obligations almost all of the time'. See Henkin (1979) 47.

[110] Compensation is also available as a temporary remedy.

illustrated by the *Steel Safeguards* case, in which the EU, having won an action against the United States, targeted goods made in certain politically sensitive US States, prompting the US President to withdraw the safeguard measures.[112] The EU can scarcely be blamed for pursuing an effective tactic, and yet to target industries based in key marginal states surely constitutes a profound interference in the internal democracy of another country. The system appears to invite the destabilisation of national governments unless they comply with WTO rulings.

The constitutional character of WTO law is underlined by the willingness of Panels and the Appellate Body to review not just administrative action but *legislation* of WTO Members for its compatibility with the higher law of the WTO. The WTO Panel in *US Section 301* made it clear that legislation per se can violate WTO law, independent of the question of whether and how it has been enforced, since its very existence can inhibit individual economic operators and thereby hamper world trade.[113]

A constitutional quality is also lent to WTO judicial decision-making by its mode of interpretation. Whilst the Appellate Body started life by adopting a strictly textual technique (anxious no doubt to reassure states that their nascent creation would not take liberties with issues of competence), it has gradually embraced an evolutionary approach akin to the dynamic mode of interpretation favoured by the European Court of Justice and the European Court of Human Rights.[114] By using contemporary developments in order to interpret WTO provisions, the Appellate Body has taken on a life of its own, deviating from the conception of the WTO Agreements as a contract between sovereign states and implying that the WTO Members no longer fully control their own creation. Thus the Appellate Body has made it clear that non-trade policies, for example environmental policies, fall within the scope of WTO law, enabling it and the Panels to delineate a 'line of equilibrium' between trade and non-trade policies.[115] In other words, the WTO judiciary has assumed jurisdiction to determine whether WTO members are adopting a lawful balance between free trade and other concerns such as the environment, or whether their pursuit of competing policies at the expense of free trade is unlawful. Once again this is reminiscent of ECJ jurisprudence, where fields that fall outside the ambit of the EC Treaty have nonetheless been held to be affected by Community law.[116] The Appellate Body, like the ECJ, thereby performs a function of constitutional adjudication, balancing the interests

---

[112] WTO Docs WT/DS248, 249, 251–54, 258 and 259/R, adopted 10 Nov 2003.

[113] Panel Report, *US Section 301 Trade Act*, paras 7.86–7.88. See Jackson (2006a) 178–80. The panel's decision has parallels in European human rights law, which takes the same approach of per se illegality of incompatible legislation: *Dudgeon v United Kingdom* (1981) 4 EHRR 149; *Norris v Ireland* (1988) 13 EHRR 186.

[114] *United States Import Prohibition on Certain Shrimp and Shrimp Products*, adopted 6 November 1998, WTO case nos 58 (and 61) WT/DS58/AB/R, paras 154–55.

[115] *Ibid*, 152–53.

[116] Eg, national systems of property ownership, though formally falling outside the Treaty, cannot be exercised so as to impede free movement of goods in the field of intellectual property. See Case 15/74 *Centrafarm v Sterling Drug* [1974] ECR 1147, [1974] 2 CMLR 480.

of private enterprise against social priorities. Under Britain's internal constitution, this function lies not with unaccountable bodies but with government, Parliament and the devolved authorities. The Appellate Body's adoption of this balancing role should be seen not so much as a power-grab as an inevitability; states frequently take action that impedes free trade in order to promote worthy policy objectives, and some institution has to draw a line somewhere. Thus any 'blame' for a loss of British sovereignty (and that of other states) lies not so much with the Appellate Body but rather with the decision to establish the WTO in the first place.

In any event, interpretations of WTO law by the Panels and Appellate Body have set important precedents for all to follow.[117] Whilst there is no formal doctrine of stare decisis, nonetheless the WTO judiciary itself employs a fairly powerful use of precedent. From the point of view of private companies, the body of precedent provides the rules and certainty that can lower the 'risk premium' for international transactions.[118]

To a large extent the constitutional enormity of decision-making through the WTO DSU is concealed. No doubt political leaders were anxious not to raise concerns for democracy: they would, after all, have been at pains to avoid problems over ratification. They were aided by the terminological baggage that accompanies trade policy. Thus decisions affecting the freedom of action of states are made not by courts but by 'Panels' and an Appellate 'Body'. The esoteric trade law 'spin'—the idea that complex matters are being hived off to specialist technocrats—obscures the profound centrality of WTO decision-making. The constitutional reality is that, on behalf of almost the entire world, the Panels and Appellate Body determine the permissible balance between the interests of the free market on the one hand and competing policies on the other. This role, inherent in the logic of the WTO text, has made the WTO not a mere 'specialist' trade treaty but rather an instrument for world governance.

In sum, the WTO's uniquely strong enforcement machinery substantially reduces any temptation to defy WTO norms. By closing off easy escape routes from the enforcement procedure, the overall effect of the reformed system is to make it more costly for states to evade the pressure of the enforcement process.[119] This can be seen as part of a global 'move to law' in many fields, in which growing judicialisation is accompanied by an emphasis on the importance of rule precision and a greater degree of obligation.[120] One can indeed envisage the WTO as a transitory regime that is evolving towards bindingness, since even in the absence of direct effect, WTO law exerts considerable power over national law.[121]

---

[117] Paradoxically, however, and in contrast to proceedings before the European Court of Justice, WTO Members that are not party to a case have no right to submit their observations.

[118] Jackson (2006a) 173–77.

[119] Hudec (1993) 363.

[120] Goldstein et al (2001a) 1–6.

[121] Cass (2005) 118.

The Terms of the WTO

GATT and Related Agreements

The WTO Agreements use GATT 1947 as the enduring basis for its rules on free trade in goods. GATT therefore retains the same fundamental principles but enjoys greater force by dint of the strengthened dispute settlement procedure.[122] From the point of view of the constitutional protection of capitalism, GATT's most important provisions relate to the opening-up of market access. Tariffs are subject to periodic negotiations with a view to bringing about 'tariff bindings' or 'tariff concessions', that is, commitments not to raise the customs duty on a certain product above an agreed level. Since GATT's inception in 1947, these negotiating rounds have been highly successful: in the eight rounds since the late 1940s the average duty on industrial products imposed by developed countries has been cut from 40 per cent *ad valorem* to 3.9 per cent *ad valorem*. The Uruguay Round meant that almost all customs duties imposed by developed-country Members are now 'bound'. Thus the European Union has made tariff bindings on virtually all products, and these are listed in its detailed and lengthy Schedule of Concessions. All these products, therefore, are now subject to an upper limit in respect of their customs duties.[123]

Constitutionally, the decision to make a 'tariff binding' is for all practical purposes a once-and-for-all decision. This is because the procedure for modifying or withdrawing tariff bindings is complex and punitive. If a WTO Member wishes to raise a tariff on an individual product, it must conduct negotiations with those Members with the strongest economic interest in the tariff binding.[124] It must grant these Members compensation in the form of new concessions so as to ensure the maintenance of a general level of concessions no less favourable to trade.[125] If negotiations fail, the Member may nevertheless make the modification or withdrawal, but only at the cost of empowering those Members with whom it negotiated to withdraw 'substantially equivalent concessions'.[126]

The system enshrines a remarkable loss of sovereignty, not only because it is difficult to change tariff bindings but also because of the cardinal principle (embedded

---

[122] The fundamental principles of GATT continues to include the most favoured nation rule, whereby any advantage granted by one Member to any product of another country must be extended to all like products of all other Members, thereby prohibiting both de jure and de facto discrimination between different countries (Art I, GATT 1994, Appellate Body Report *EC Tariff Preferences* WT/DS246/AB/R, adopted 20 April 2004). There is also the national treatment rule, which prevents discrimination between domestic products and products from other Members in relation to internal taxation and domestic regulations (Art III, GATT 1994).

[123] Van den Bossche (2006) 398–99.

[124] Art XXVIII:1 GATT 1994, See also *Understanding on the Implementation of Article XXVIII of the GATT 1994.*

[125] Art XXVIII:2 1994.

[126] Art XXVIII:3 1994.

in the system for modifying tariff bindings) that *there must never be an overall reduction in the level of free trade.* This is the antitithesis of the British rule that Parliament cannot be bound by its predecessors. It would prohibit the adoption of policies of planned trade that have characterised socialist economic programmes in the past. For instance in its 1945 manifesto, Labour pledged to 'give State help in any necessary form to get our export trade on its feet'.[127] This would presumably have included quantitative restrictions on imports, the possibility of which Labour carefully preserved in the ITO proposals and in GATT. Similarly in *Labour's Programme 1982*, the Party promoted the use of tariffs to ensure a controlled growth of trade in support of planning and economic expansion.[128]

As regards non-tariff barriers to trade in goods, the WTO Agreement also contains an Agreement on Technical Barriers to Trade (TBT), which binds all Members to ensure that technical barriers (requirements to which products must conform) do not create unnecessary obstacles to international trade. To this end it stipulates that technical regulations shall be no more trade-restrictive than is necessary to satisfy a legitimate objective.[129] With its language redolent of the EU landmark case *Cassis de Dijon*,[130] this prohibition has the potential (like *Cassis* in the EU context) to make deep inroads into national sovereignty. The application of such a 'least restrictive means' test involves a profound judicialisation of national politics.[131] Moreover, such rules overtly privilege free trade and correspondingly restrict the scope for implementing competing policies. The TBT Agreement is enforced through the Dispute Settlement Procedure.

Finally, the Agreement on Trade-Related Investment Measures (TRIMS) was inspired by the surge in foreign direct investment since the early 1960s, when US investors moved to Europe to take advantage of the newly formed EEC. TRIMS reflected the desire of capital-exporting countries, in particular the United States and its corporations, to subject restrictions on the flow of capital to WTO discipline.[132] TRIMS was therefore framed with the aim of facilitating investment in trade in goods across international frontiers. To that end WTO members cannot require investors to do anything that is incompatible with the GATT national treatment principle and the GATT ban on quantitative restrictions.[133] But a socialist government may choose to target transnational companies and thereby breach the national treatment principle; for example, Labour in 1972 proposed that the state, possibly through a State Holding Company, should have the power to acquire shares in the parent company of non-resident transnationals and to place a director on the board.[134] From a socialist point of view there may be

---

[127] Labour Party (1945).
[128] Labour Party (1982) 21.
[129] Art 2 TBT.
[130] Case 120/78 *Rewe-Zentrale AG v Bundesmonopopverwaltung für Branntwein* ('*Cassis de Dijon*') [1979] ECR 649, [1979] CMLR 494.
[131] Stone Sweet (2004) 244.
[132] Guisinger (1987) 217.
[133] Art 2 TRIMS.
[134] Labour Party (1972) 30.

legitimate reasons to discipline transnationalisation of the economy—in effect striking a hard bargain with transnational corporations as the price for their participation in the nation's economy—but this is now unlawful under TRIMS.

TRIMS also prohibits measures that require or encourage foreign-owned firms to use domestically produced inputs when manufacturing in the host country. This prohibition rules out measures such as the system of Planning Agreements, which formed the centrepiece of Labour Party industrial policy during the early 1970s. Under this policy selective government assistance was to be channelled to those firms that agreed to help meet the nation's planning objectives, for instance by creating a certain number of jobs in a development area.[135]

In addition, TRIMS can be seen as the genesis of a broader constitutional freedom of foreign direct investment, entrenching the liberalisation introduced by numerous countries in recent years. As things presently stand, TRIMS does not enshrine a general right of establishment. So long as members comply with the limited rules enshrined in TRIMS, they can choose their own policy on foreign direct investment. Plans to add a new Multilateral Agreement on Investment (MAI) to the WTO Agreements, guaranteeing a principle of non-discrimination against or among foreign investors in those countries signing the MAI, were halted in 1998 by a combination of developing countries and activists. Had the MAI reached a final draft, it would in all likelihood have included provisions on the protection of investment against nationalisation, in a similar manner perhaps to the North American Free Trade Agreement (NAFTA).[136] This would for all practical purposes have eliminated Parliament's power to nationalise, a power that the Labour Party planned to use extensively according to its 1945, 1973 and 1982 programmes.

GATS

If the great institutional achievement of the WTO is dispute settlement, then its great substantive breakthrough is the General Agreement on Trade in Services (GATS). In part, the inclusion of services within the WTO Agreements was attributable to privatisation in countries such as Britain, which drew attention to the opportunities for international competition. The organising principle of GATS corresponds to the system of tariff bindings in GATT. Members can enter into the free trade obligations of their choice, but once they have committed themselves, it is excessively difficult for them to abandon their commitments. To this end each Member has a Schedule of Specific Commitments containing its liberalisation obligations. These schedules are the product of successive rounds of negotiations

---

[135] Labour Party (1974).

[136] Art 1110 NAFTA prohibits nationalisation unless compensation equivalent to market value is paid without delay and is fully realisable. This provision would preclude the kind of nationalisation programme pursued by the 1945–51 Labour government whereby compensation was available in the form of non-redeemable but interest-paying bonds.

in which members commit themselves to the progressive liberalisation of services. The schedules, because they regulate market access, are considered 'the pith and substance' of GATS.[137] First, they specify the sectors within which liberalisation is to be permitted in respect of each WTO Member. Secondly, they delineate the precise extent to which, within those sectors, services are opened up to the global free market, since there are various 'modes' whereby services can be liberalised. Thirdly, the schedules govern the scope of application of the national treatment rule in each sector. Under this rule, which covers all measures affecting the supply of services, each Member must accord to services and service-suppliers of any other Member treatment no less favourable than that which it accords to its own services and service-suppliers.[138]

Negotiation on services liberalisation is similar to negotiation on tariff bindings in that it is a one-way, teleological process. The explicit purpose of the negotiating rounds is to increase the sectors covered by GATS rules and to deepen the commitments of those sectors already covered, by removing barriers to market access.[139] Once a service sector has been liberalised by its inclusion in a schedule, any attempt to 'close off' that sector through legislation will be condemned via the WTO's dispute settlement machinery. This is the case even with regard to laws that apply without distinction to domestic as well as to foreign service providers. In *US—Gambling*, for instance, a WTO Panel held that US legislation (both state and federal) that prohibited the provision of online gambling violated GATS.[140] The Panel accepted that the United States may well not have intended to include gambling services in its liberalisation commitments but held that as an objective matter of interpretation this was how the US schedule was to be construed.[141] This case underlines the way in which WTO Members lose control of their schedules once they become subject to interpretation by the Panels and Appellate Body, since little weight may be accorded to the original intent of those who negotiated them. There is, for instance, some concern that the EU schedule opens up the market as regards publicly-funded healthcare that is not also publicly provided. If it does so, this would entrench private sector access to public funds.[142] This would prevent future British governments and Parliaments from reversing the trend in favour of private sector provision within the National Health Service (NHS).

There are four 'modes' whereby services can be provided between states, and each schedule specifies the extent to which a state permits market access and

---

[137] Trebilcock and Howse (2005) 358.

[138] Art XVII GATS.

[139] Such barriers include limitations on the number of service suppliers (including the removal of monopolies); measures that require services to be provided by a specific type of legal entity or joint venture; and limitations on the participation of foreign capital, in terms of maximum percentage limits on foreign shareholding or the total value of individual or aggregate foreign investment. A definitive list is provided in Art XVI:2 (a)–(f) GATS.

[140] WT/DS285/R, 04-2687 (10 November 2004).

[141] Thankfully this decision was overturned by the Appellate Body on the specific question of the interpretation of the US schedule, but not as regards the general principle that interpretation of schedules is an objective matter for the WTO judiciary. WT/DS285/AB/R 05-1426 (7 April 2005).

[142] Pollock and Price (2003) 1074.

national treatment through each of these modes. The modes are: cross-border supply (mode 1), consumption abroad (mode 2), commercial presence (mode 3) and entry of natural persons (mode 4). It is worth dwelling on mode 3, since the concept of 'commercial presence' essentially constitutes the rights of foreign direct investment and of establishment in the sphere of services. The effect of committing Britain to allowing a 'commercial presence' of non-national service providers is to preclude policies such as those in Labour's October 1974 manifesto, which pledged the creation of a National Enterprise Board to extend public ownership and 'prevent British industries from passing into unacceptable foreign control'.[143] Moreover, it would constitutionalise privatisation. If, for example, the EU were to permit liberalisation under mode 3 in the provision of health, education, water, energy and telecommunications, this would make privatisation in those spheres irreversible. Renationalisation, after all, would by definition preclude a commercial presence in that sector by foreign corporations. From a socialist point of view, the question of whether a service is in the public sector as opposed to the private sector is far more important than the question of the identity, British or otherwise, of the private sector provider. Viewed from this perspective, therefore, services liberalisation under mode 3 can be conceived as camouflage for the entrenchment of privatisation.

The commitments made in the schedules bind national, regional and local governments, as well as non-governmental bodies exercising functions delegated by them.[144] They thereby limit the scope of Scottish, Welsh and Northern Irish devolution. If, for example, the EU annex were to liberalise health care, opening up publicly-funded health care to transnational corporations, then it would not be open to the Scottish Parliament or Welsh Assembly to opt for a publicly-run NHS, even if the British Parliament wished to accord it that freedom of choice. In one fell swoop, therefore, GATS restricts both the sovereign British Parliament's right to devolve and the right of the devolved authorities to govern.

As in the case of GATT, the cardinal principle is that a WTO Member is never permitted to reduce its general level of liberalisation. To this end a Member can modify and withdraw the commitments in its schedule only with great difficulty. It must enter into negotiations with affected Members with a view to arriving at 'compensatory adjustment'—that is, maintaining a *general* level of mutually-advantageous commitments no less favourable to trade than that provided in its schedule. In the absence of such agreement, any affected Member may refer the matter to arbitration, which will determine the compensatory adjustments to be made.[145] In the British context, the once-and-for-all relaxation of such barriers can be seen as providing the means for putting privatisation on a more secure footing, effectively binding future Parliaments.

In Britain, sectors such as rail, energy, water, telecommunications and post have already been opened up to international competition, leaving scant scope for

---

[143] Labour Party (1974).
[144] Art 1(3) GATS.
[145] Art XXI GATS.

'compensatory adjustment' and therefore ruling out widespread nationalisation. Thus far, commitments on services have not been extensive, many Members merely reflecting the status quo in their schedules.[146] Therefore, as they presently stand, the schedules do not represent any great liberalisation. Yet they do constitute a *binding* of existing liberalisation, establishing a 'liberalisation frontier' for successive negotiations to push back.[147] In constitutional terms, therefore, they represent a constitutionalisation of private ownership. The value of these bindings to businesses lies in the predictability they provide. But once again, predictability for business means lack of policymaking choice for the political community. Firms can rest assured that there will be no renationalisation, yet the very measures that secure peace of mind for private corporations represent a severe curtailment of democracy.

It might be argued that public sector services in each WTO Member are as much at liberty as the private sector to ply their trade abroad. If this were a convincing argument, one could view the WTO as neutral as between public and private ownership. To be sure, public ownership can indeed take the shape of competitive public ownership, whereby the state acts as player in a market, such as the French provider EDF in the British energy market. But equally, public ownership can be deployed to *replace* the market mechanism and thereby shelter consumers and employees from the market system. This kind of public service provision is not in the business of capturing market share and transnational expansion; its ethos is rather to provide and improve services within a given society. Such public services have been provided for the benefit of the public, reflecting the egalitarian concern that everyone, regardless of income or foresight, should have access to a decent standard of these services and that society as a whole benefits from a healthy, well-educated population with good transport, communications, utilities and so on.[148] Furthermore, any increase in funding for, say, the NHS or Royal Mail would be far more likely to be directed towards improving the national service than on an overseas expansion. The provision of public service is also intimately linked to democratic decision-making taken on national lines, such as decisions on taxation and on the internal organisation of public services. Thus it is only natural that the provision of services by the public sector generally stops at the national frontier. Insofar as the public sector can compete in international competition, it can do so only by shedding its socialised role and by adopting wholesale the characteristics of the private sector.

Defenders of the WTO might emphasise that few commitments have yet been made in the fields of health and education.[149] But this cannot diminish the monumental *constitutional* change that has been wrought: the GATS system opens up the option for each and every government of entrenching privatised provision in both these fields, with scant regard to the preservation of political choice within

---

[146] Trebilcock and Howse (2005) 349.
[147] Sauvé (1996) 142.
[148] Glyn (2006) 45.
[149] Van den Bossche (2005) 494.

their own states. In the British context, this means they may bind future Parliaments de facto. Whilst it remains true that our national courts would enforce statute that was contrary to GATS, nonetheless a government could only present such legislation to Parliament if it were prepared to defy GATS, risk the condemnation of the WTO judiciary and endure countervailing measures. This is quite apart from the problems arising from any breach of EU law, either because EU legislation is designed to embody GATS commitments or because the Commission initiates enforcement proceedings before the ECJ. Thus whilst the veneer of legislative supremacy is retained, the WTO undermines its substance by creating an alternative to national courts in order to circumvent national constitutional requirements (in Britain's case, Parliamentary sovereignty).

Through the EU, Britain and the other Member States have been committed to a particularly large number of market access commitments. Ironically, although it was the United States that originally pressed for GATS, the EU has since exerted a particularly liberalising influence on services and has actively contributed to developing the rules to open up market access.[150] In its original schedule, the EU made 392 market access commitments, a number surpassed only by Switzerland, Japan and Austria.[151]

Market access commitments also entail restrictions on the requirements that national parliaments and governments can impose on service providers. Within those service sectors in which a Member has made liberalisation commitments, it cannot apply licensing, qualifications and technical standards that nullify or impair these commitments.[152] GATS stipulates that any such rules must be based on objective and transparent criteria and must not be more burdensome than is necessary to ensure the quality of the service.[153] Once again, as is the case with trade in goods, this provision subjects to WTO oversight a vast swathe of regulations relating to services. In so doing it sets a proportionality test that gives pride of place to market access concerns over competing policies. For good measure, the WTO's Council on Trade in Services is mandated to 'develop disciplines' to ensure that national regulations are WTO-compatible.

Remarkably, and quite apart from the WTO's own enforcement machinery, GATS commits its Members to establishing a form of *domestic* judicial review in which service suppliers can obtain prompt review and appropriate remedies for administrative decisions affecting trade in services that violate GATS.[154] Article VI GATS requires Members to make available a domestic action to 'ensure that all measures of general provision affecting trade in services are administered in a reasonable, objective and impartial manner'. No definition of 'reasonable' is

---

[150] Meunier (2005) 2.

[151] It is notably *developed* countries that have made market access commitments with regard to nearly all sectors, except health and education, reflecting the current hegemony of free market capitalism in the developed world.

[152] Art VI: 5(a) GATS.

[153] Art VI: 4 and 5 GATS.

[154] Art VI (2)(a) GATS.

provided, but considerations of internal consistency would militate in favour of an interpretation whereby governmental measures should be no more burdensome on the service provider than is necessary to achieve the public-interest aim pursued. Such review must be undertaken either by a tribunal that is independent of the relevant agency or by one that is itself subject to judicial review.

The GATS approach to rule enforcement can be contrasted both with 'classical' international law and with the approach of EU law. Traditionally, international law left it to states to make their own internal arrangements for implementing international obligations. By contrast, in EU law the ECJ made it clear from *Van Gend en Loos* onwards that it would determine through its jurisprudence the precise internal effect of EU provisions within the Member States.[155] The GATS position is arguably closer to EU law in that it specifies a detailed national remedy; however, this remedy is laid down in GATS itself rather than in case law. Nonetheless, the Panels and Appellate Body will be able to embellish these domestic remedies through their interpretation of GATS, in order to make the actions and remedies effective.

Public Procurement

Public authorities need to purchase goods and services in order to perform their tasks. In most countries, indeed, government is the largest single purchaser in the economy.[156] Governments often use their purchasing power to promote various social and economic policies, such as industrial policy, regional development, protection of domestic production, and social policies, such as gender or racial equality.[157] In times of recession in particular, governments have found public procurement a useful means of boosting employment.[158] GATT 1947 initially refrained from regulating government procurement, but the WTO Agreements include a Government Procurement Agreement (GPA). This is a 'plurilateral' agreement—one that binds only the states that choose to sign it. The EU and its Member States are among the GPA's signatories. The GPA's objective is to subject government procurement of goods and services to international competition by opening up market access and by extending the GATT principles of non-discrimination (national treatment and MFN) and transparency to the tendering processes of governmental entities. These entities include not only central government but also sub-national government (which includes Britain's devolved authorities), along with public utilities.

---

[155] Case 26/62 [1963] ECR 1. Herein lies the significance of the early part of the judgment headed 'The First Question: Jurisdiction of the Court'.

[156] Trebilcock and Howse (2005) 292.

[157] Trepte (2004) 24.

[158] Meunier (2005) 128 gives the example of the US Buy American Act 1933, which was designed to help the American economy out of the Great Depression by obliging administrators to use national providers. This Act, never repealed by Congress, was effectively negated by the WTO Government Procurement Agreement.

The argument advanced for free trade in public procurement is that if numerous countries pursue discriminatory procurement practices, the worldwide impact will be inferior in welfare terms compared to a cooperative approach whereby all governments refrain from discrimination.[159] But the undesirability of discrimination is contested. Governments and parliaments may wish to regulate public procurement in a way that serves national social and economic priorities. Thus in the past British governments have sought to use public procurement to safeguard jobs, skills and fair wages. In 1972, for example, the Labour Party pledged to use the power of public purchasing to stimulate investment in chosen areas and enterprises.[160] In 2004 the Party agreed with its affiliated trade unions to encourage the giving of public procurement contracts to British firms in order to benefit British workers.[161] A more nationalistic approach to public procurement might therefore allow value-for-money considerations to be balanced against other dimensions of the country's economic welfare, such as the aim of achieving high levels of employment, not least in disadvantaged regions. Once again, the question is not whether such a policy is *desirable* but rather whether its undesirability is so incontestable that it should be made constitutionally impermissible.

The GPA has key features in common with GATS. For a start, it applies only to the extent to which Members commit themselves in the annexes to the agreement.[162] Again, the idea is that over time coverage will be extended through periodic negotiations aimed at progressive liberalisation.[163] Again, negotiation on liberalisation is intended to be a one-way, once-and-for-all process. To subject a new sector to the discipline of the GPA rules is easy; to remove a sector is exceedingly difficult. If a Member wishes to modify its annex in this way, the change must be approved by the Committee on Government Procurement (composed of representatives of all GPA states), which will consider the Member's proposal together with 'any claim for compensatory adjustment' with a view to 'maintaining a balance of rights and obligations and a comparable level of mutually agreed coverage provided in this Agreement prior to such notification'.[164] In other words, closing off public procurement in one sector must be compensated by opening up others elsewhere. This precludes a general move towards the planned use of public procurement to boost employment; where there has been widespread liberalisation, it is unlawful to have widespread economic nationalism. Once again, ongoing policy choice is therefore replaced with a once-and-for-all decision.

Also like GATS, the GPA compels the creation of a domestic remedy. It commits its signatories to place on their national statute books a 'challenge procedure',[165] enabling private parties to invoke WTO law before domestic adjudicating

[159] Hoekman and Kostecki (2001) 370.
[160] Labour Party (1972) 17.
[161] Warwick Agreement, 25 July 2004. The Agreement stated that this aim would be accomplished 'within EU law', which raises the question of whether the commitment was meaningless.
[162] Art I(1) GPA.
[163] Art XXIV(7) GPA.
[164] Art XXIV(6)(a) GPA.
[165] Art XX GPA.

bodies.[166] The challenge procedure must make available rapid interim measures to correct breaches of the GPA and to preserve commercial opportunities, in the absence of which there must be compensation for loss and damage. (Rapidity is plainly important in the field of public procurement.) The GPA also obliges government entities to provide, on request from any unsuccessful tenderer, relevant information as to why its tender was not selected, as well as the identity of the successful tenderer.[167] The challenge procedure represents a profound development in terms of effectiveness of remedies for breaches of an international agreement. It involves a considerable judicialisation, since the challenge procedure must be undertaken by a court or by an independent and impartial body with no interest in the outcome.[168]

The challenge procedure aims to correct individual administrative decisions that breach the GPA; if national legislation violates GPA rules, this would require a WTO dispute settlement panel. But it is questionable whether the UK Parliament, as the legislature of an EU Member State, could validly legislate contrary to the GPA in any event. The European Court of Justice has held that the field of public procurement (involving as it does the free movement of goods and services) falls almost entirely within the ambit of EU law.[169] Furthermore, to a large extent EC legislation embodies the GPA rules on public procurement. Thus EU law, which automatically prevails over UK statute, can enforce WTO requirements. As regards both administrative actions and legislation, therefore, Britain is thus tightly bound by the GPA, EU membership making the enforcement of the GPA particularly effective.

The GPA, as one commentator has said, 'should not be considered only as a trade issue but also as a means to smoothly accompany and prepare privatization of utilities where the latter is envisaged'.[170] Public procurement gives private companies an ever-increasing involvement in public sector service provision before a full rearrangement can be effected. At the same time it acclimatises public opinion to the prospect of private sector provision. The final stage is then the inclusion of the relevant sector in GATS, thereby precluding renationalisation. This process is arguably already well under way in the British National Health Service.

Subsidies

Subsidies have long been an important weapon in the arsenal of socialist and social democratic governments. For example, in 1966 Labour pledged a 'new system of

---

[166] Hoekman and Mavroides (1997) 21.

[167] Art XVIII(2)(c) GPA. This is reminiscent of Case 222/86 *UNECTEF v Heylens* [1987] ECR 4097, [1989] 1 CMLR 901 in which the ECJ laid down an obligation on administrative authorities seeking to impose restrictions on the mutual recognition of diplomas to furnish reasons for unfavourable decisions so that individuals can defend their rights under the best possible conditions.

[168] Art XX(6) GPA. If review is not performed by a court, the reviewing body must either itself be subject to judicial review or must have procedures akin to those of a court.

[169] Case C-324/98 *Telaustria* [2000] ECR I-10745, paras 59–63.

[170] Didier (1997) 141.

investment incentives' to 'provide direct cash grants to expanding firms' and which would 'discriminate sharply in favour of manufacturing industries, upon which the competitive strength of the economy depends'.[171] Similarly, its February 1974 manifesto again proposed direct aid to companies, in return for which the government would take a share in the firm's ownership.[172] *Labour's Programme 1982* proposed a Department of Economic and Industrial Planning with a raft of powers including powers to grant discretionary financial support and long-term credit to companies, conditional on participation in Development Plans.[173]

The WTO Agreements include a Subsidies and Countervailing Measures (SCM) Agreement, the aim of which is to restrict such state intervention. Under the SCM Agreement, only two types of subsidies are prohibited per se—export subsidies and import substitution subsidies.[174] The vast majority of subsidies, by contrast, are 'actionable':[175] they can be challenged if they cause adverse effects to the interests of another WTO Member. Such adverse effects may consist of injury to the Member's domestic industry; nullification or impairment of GATT benefits; or serious prejudice to the interests of another Member. Members have the right to use the WTO disputes settlement machinery to condemn such subsidies and oblige the culpable Member to remove the adverse effects or withdraw the subsidy.[176] From the point of view of policy, however, the whole point of subsidisation is indeed to benefit domestic industry at the expense of foreign firms, in order to boost employment.

The SCM Agreement conforms to the common pattern discussed above. Not only is it enforceable through the WTO dispute settlement machinery but also, like GATS and the GPA, it creates a domestic remedy. WTO Members that suffer adverse effects are entitled to impose 'countervailing measures' to remove the effect of any subsidy, such as a duty on the product in question.[177] To this end, each WTO Member that has national legislation authorising such measures must provide access to domestic judicial review to all interested parties.[178] This gives a remedy to a disappointed domestic-industry complainant who feels that they have been adversely affected by another country's subsidy and by their own country's reluctance to counter it. The European Union has given expression to this right through a Council Regulation.[179]

It is worth pausing to dwell on the impact of this provision on British constitutional law. The SCM Agreement aims to create a global network of judicial review.

---

[171] Labour Party (1966).
[172] Labour Party (1974).
[173] Labour Party (1982) 43.
[174] Art 3 SCM.
[175] Art 5 SCM.
[176] Art 7 SCM.
[177] Arts 10–23 SCM.
[178] Art 23 SCM.
[179] Council Regulation (EC) No 2026/97 of 8 March 2004 on protection against imports from countries not members of the European Community, as amended by Regulation (EC) No 461/2004 of 8 March 2004.

Let us suppose that the British government granted a subsidy that was, in WTO terms, unlawful. Any WTO law challenge to such a subsidy made by the British government could come from a non-EU country via its own domestic judicial review procedure. This represents a striking internationalisation of judicial review. In effect, international law is empowering foreign tribunals to rule on the constitutionality of a British subsidy and provide effective remedies (for it would only be sensible for a British government faced with countervailing measures to remove the offending subsidy). This should be considered part of our constitutional law. If the decisions of foreign tribunals delineate the limits of British governmental action, and do so effectively, the ambit of public law needs to be reconfigured accordingly.

Conclusion

Owing both to the substantive policy enshrined in the WTO Agreements and to the effectiveness of its enforcement machinery, WTO law forms the bedrock of the global constitutional protection of capitalism. Its substantive policy uncompromisingly defends the interests of the private sector by entrenching a secure business environment. In the aftermath of war, American business criticised the proposed International Trade Organization for not containing a ringing endorsement of private enterprise.[180] Nor did GATT 1947, and neither in express terms does the WTO. Yet the WTO's entrenchment of private enterprise is no less effective for being somewhat covert. The WTO aims to establish a stable basis for corporations to engage in transnational trade in goods and services. Publicly owned undertakings are likely to engage in this way only if they are managed in a manner identical to private enterprises. Whilst 'competitive public ownership' does exist, more typically the public sector works as a counterweight to market forces by providing goods and services for the benefit of a national public, reflecting egalitarian concerns for the common good of the population.[181] Normally, private enterprise benefits from WTO law at the expense of public undertakings, since the WTO facilitates its entry into new markets including those previously served by the public sector. Once a WTO Member has opened up a sector to multinational competition, it is extremely difficult to take back that same sector into public ownership. In a country like Britain, which already has a diminished public sector, it would be practically impossible. In this way the WTO and its mechanisms effectively act as the proxy for the exercise of corporate power.[182]

Some argue that the WTO is democratic because membership represents a choice within national polities.[183] However, the hallmark of democracy is *ongoing*

---

[180] Adams Brown (1950) 370–75.
[181] Glyn (2006) 44–45.
[182] Anderson (2005) 30.
[183] Howse (2000) 37.

choice. In a democracy, the making of policy involves a continuous process, not a once-and-for-all decision. By contrast, the WTO's template is characterised by the relative irreversibility of market access commitments. Negotiating the schedules to the various agreements essentially involves a series of one-way-only, once-and-for-all decisions: states can elect to 'ratchet up' their commitment to market access and therefore privatisation, but there is no scope for negotiating in the opposite direction, in favour of extending public sector provision. The WTO can thus be seen as a 'commitment device' in which states hold themselves to their initial preferences by tying the hands of government for the future. It has created a rule-orientated landscape, fashioned to reduce 'risk premium' for private enterprise.[184]

The WTO system thereby contemplates trade as a global system rather than simply as agreements between states and has effected a shift in the guiding criteria for global trade policy, prioritising commercial over other policy concerns.[185] Furthermore, like much of neoliberal globalisation, the transformation from GATT to WTO did not take place through spontaneous, organic economic change: rather it was a deliberate *political* choice. With the prompting of the private sector, the American administration—swiftly followed by the European Union—reconfigured international organisations such as the GATT/WTO to become part of their pro-private enterprise campaign.[186] Some commentators are refreshingly forthright about the constitutional aspirations of WTO law. Ernst-Ulrich Petersmann, for example, has argued that there is a relationship of interdependence between international trade law and national constitutions. WTO law can strengthen and give precision to the fundamental human right to free trade, which ought to be protected by every national constitution; it can also serve the important domestic constitutional function of restricting broad governmental discretion over trade policy. For Petersmann, international economic law rightly exists to protect the property rights of those engaged in international transactions. It is therefore preferable to the many national constitutions that afford weak protection to property rights and give too much freedom to governments to intervene in the economy. According to Petersmann, it is important to entrench WTO policy because 'liberal trade policy would not fare very well if every new generation of officials were permitted to rethink the case for free trade'.[187] He suggests that the involvement of the national courts in enforcing the 'four freedoms' in EU law might serve as a useful precedent for a global constitutionalisation of world trade law. This would better reflect his conception of 'the good constitution', a Madisonian construct in which basic rules of economic policy are constitutionalised rather than depending on the vagaries of democratic politics.[188]

This constitutional vision is at odds with the traditions of the British constitution, whereby 'every new generation' is indeed entitled to 'rethink' anything and

[184] Jackson (2006a) 205.
[185] Anderson (2005) 29.
[186] Gowan (1999) viii–ix and 84–87.
[187] Petersmann (1991) XXV.
[188] *Ibid.*

everything. Thus contestations over economic policy have traditionally formed the essence of everyday politics and elections. The party that wins such contestations, secures a working majority and forms the government, then has Parliamentary sovereignty at its service, to implement its programme as far as politics and economics allow. The Madisonian construct favoured by Petersmann would be unlikely to be adopted within our own national political community, since it represents too great a leap away from the traditions of democracy and accountability that we have learned to value. *Arguably, however, the same result has been achieved by force of international law,* not by replacing the British system of government, but rather by superimposing a more powerful constitution over it. The means of entrenchment seem innocuous and technical: they are the detailed schedules appended to the GATS, GPA, GATT and so on. Their complexity and obscurity reduces resistance to them. Petersmann has observed, indeed, that it can be easier to agree liberal trade principles through international agreements than through national law, because international solutions provide a means of escaping domestic pressures.

For British public lawyers, the enormity of the disablement of the legislature may only become apparent when we discard conventional constitutional assumptions. The doctrine of parliamentary sovereignty came into existence in the era of Westphalian autonomy, when international law was relatively weak vis-à-vis national law. This led public lawyers to focus their attention overwhelmingly on decisions of domestic courts. But we now inhabit an era of increasingly powerful international economic law. The WTO panels and Appellate Body do not merely resolve disputes: their binding interpretations determine the principles that condition the exercise of WTO power.[189] By fashioning a durable global legal system, the WTO creates an *alternative* to reliance on domestic courts, forcing British public lawyers to look to additional fora to assess the full legal limits of UK governmental decision-making.

WTO law is thus undeniably constitutional in character. It determines the economic and industrial policies that governments are allowed to pursue, and parliaments and electorates allowed to approve, and its decisions are reinforced by powerful sanctions. It redefines and delimits, indeed, the very boundaries of the political.[190] WTO membership elevates a vital array of issues of ownership and regulation above the political fray, leading inescapably to a diminution of politics.[191] In this way adhesion to the WTO constitutionalises an eminently contestable group of policies, because the fundamental right to free trade serves as a decoy for the entrenchment of the power of private enterprise.

---

[189] Sarooshi (2005) 12–13.
[190] Evans (2005) 79.
[191] The fact that WTO business is channelled through the EU, which for international trade purposes resembles a single state, adds to the sense of remoteness from British politics. See Meunier (2005) 21.

3

The European Union: A Faithful Expression of the Capitalist Ideal?

T
HE LAST CHAPTER argued that, in the case of the World Trade Organization (WTO), the distinction between the international and the constitutional has started to fall away. This is because of two developments. The first is the shift from states signing treaties to states creating transnational regimes with effective enforcement machinery. The second is the expansion of policy areas deemed suitable for transnational regulation. These changes, it has been argued, have helped to make the WTO an appropriate vehicle for the constitutional protection of capitalism. It has been contended that the WTO has constitutionalised a significant measure of business stability and business security for the benefit of transnational enterprises, at the expense of the democratic traditions of states. By contrast, the European Union is an organisation in which supranationalism is even more explicit, both in terms of the status of its rules within its Member States and in terms of the breadth of its economic policy ambit. This chapter argues that these qualities have been deployed to make the EU a particularly strong enforcer of the neoliberal cause. This in turn has had an especially corrosive effect on the British constitution's democratic attributes of contestability, relative ideological neutrality and accountability.

In contrast to the WTO, much of EU law is enforced by our national courts through doctrines fashioned by the European Court of Justice (ECJ). This makes the EU's status as part of the British constitution relatively uncontroversial.[1] Indeed, the interpenetration of EU law into the domestic legal order means that the EU is commonly regarded not so much as an international organisation but rather as supranational or quasi-federal. On these grounds the EU has been described as 'more a proto-European state in the making than an international organization'[2] and even as a 'regional state', at least in the sense of 'a regional union of nation-states in which national differentiation persists alongside regional integration'.[3]

---

[1] Thus important elements of EU constitutional law routinely feature on university syllabi in Public Law. It will be argued, however, that many British constitutional lawyers fail to take this state of affairs to its logical conclusion, by being reluctant to regard *substantive* law of the EU, in addition to EU constitutional law, as part and parcel of our domestic constitutional law.

[2] Alvarez (2005) 72.

[3] Schmidt (2006) 4.

The strength of the EU's enforcement regime throws into sharp focus the question of the EU's very nature. It might be argued that the EU simply transfers democratic decision-making from the national to the European level, and were this the case, there could be few democratic objections (unwieldiness aside) to the EU. This chapter argues, however, that such an imagining is sadly wide of the mark, and in reality EU law entrenches certain substantive policies, thereby elevating them to a higher-order, constitutional plane above the contestation of everyday politics and sheltering those who enforce them from accountability. As John Alder has noted, democracy was not regarded as the highest value in either the original European Economic Community (EEC) or today's EU; rather, these transnational regimes were based on a paternalistic concept, intended to impose a particular vision of the good life.[4] The consequence is to embed an inbuilt political partiality into the EU's 'basic constitutional charter', its Treaties.[5] The argument of this chapter is that the Treaties entrench a predominantly neoliberal programme, and this entrenched quality is incompatible with the democratic attributes of the British constitution. Furthermore, the degree of entrenchment is severe. For a start, the actual formulation of Treaty amendments is the preserve of an elite. As Carol Harlow has pointed out, the modalities of Treaty revision are situated in the realm of international affairs, responsibility for which is an executive function often reserved for the head of state or of government, and this diminishes both popular consultation and the role of national parliaments in the process of Treaty amendment.[6] Furthermore, Article 48 of the Treaty on European Union (TEU) mandates heavy entrenchment: generally speaking, the EU Treaties can only be amended by common accord, and after being ratified by all Member States in accordance with their respective constitutional requirements.

Indeed, even the secondary legislation of the EU—its regulations and directives—should, from the national perspective, be conceived as entrenched, since the government of a Member State would need to win over a qualified majority or even gain the unanimous support of the Council in order to repeal or amend such legislation, along with a measure of support in the European Parliament. The entrenching impact of EU legislation can thus serve as a trump card by which domestic policy agenda can be dictated and political accountability thereby avoided.[7]

What, then, is the policy constitutionalised by the EU Treaties? Article 3 TEU sums up the EU's overall objective as being the creation of a '*highly competitive social market economy*'.[8] Since the leaders of the Member States seemingly feel that this phrase embodies the EU's economic aims, it is fitting to dwell on it a little. Significantly, the phrase 'social market economy' was first coined by the German economist Alfred Müller-Armack in 1946 to describe his proposal for a 'third way'

[4] Alder (2007) 219.
[5] Case C-187/93 *Parti Ecologiste 'Les Verts' v Parliament* [1986] ECR 1339.
[6] Harlow (2002) 28.
[7] *Ibid*, 36.
[8] Had the Constitution for Europe been approved, the same phrase would have been part of Art I-3 of the Constitution.

between laissez-faire and socialism. This consisted of a raft of social measures subordinated to the functionality of market mechanisms. Differentiating his ideal from that of mixed economies with elements of planning, Müller-Armack maintained that social policies that threaten to distort market competition and the price mechanism, or that conflict with budgetary discipline on the part of the state, must be excluded from the socio-political agenda.[9] Perhaps Article 3 TEU tries to encapsulate this philosophy when it declares that the EU's social market economy will (merely) 'aim' to achieve full employment and social progress, rather than making these objectives absolute imperatives. In any event, and regardless of ideological pedigree, the EU's policy clearly purports to combine ideas—the 'social' and the 'highly competitive market'—that are in tension with each other. Indeed, Loïc Azoulai has pointed out that the conception of a 'social market economy' is based on a contradiction.[10] As Bruno de Witte has observed, 'depending on whether one emphasizes the word "social" or the word "market", it can provide ammunition both to those who think that the EU should act in a more market-oriented way and to those who argue that it should intervene more actively to regulate the operation of the market.'[11]

No doubt the indeterminacy of the term has the advantage of keeping everybody happy, European leaders and onlookers alike. It allows negotiators from different political traditions to think they are getting what they want, whilst taking the sting out of opposition. Yet at the same time, the indeterminacy of EU economic policy is constantly diminishing. Inevitably, its fundamental basis has become ever clearer. Martti Koskenniemi, writing of international regimes generally, has explained:

> Irrespective of indeterminacy, the system still *de facto* prefers some outcomes or choices to other outcomes or choices. That is to say, even if it is possible to justify many kinds of practices through the use of impeccable professional argument, there is a structural bias in the relevant legal institutions that makes them serve typical, deeply embedded preferences . . . In any institutional context there is always such a structural bias, a particular constellation of forces that relies on some shared understanding of how the rules and institutions should be applied. That itself is not a scandal . . . But when the bias works in favour of those who are privileged, against the disenfranchised, at that point the bias itself becomes 'part of the problem'. That is when the demonstration of the contingency of the mainstream position can be used as a prologue to a political critique of its being an apology of the dominant forces.[12]

The argument of this chapter is that when one considers the 'structural bias' of EU law as a whole, then the ambiguity largely disappears, the indeterminacy is resolved, and one is compelled to the conclusion that the Treaties predetermine a very definite economic policy—one that has increasingly privileged private over public ownership, since the free movement and competition rules have increas-

---

[9] Joerges and Rödl (2004).
[10] Azoulai (2008) 1337.
[11] de Witte (2006) 77.
[12] Koskenniemi (2005) 606–8.

ingly been deployed to consolidate and extend the power of the private sector, as well as entrench other aspects of neoliberal economic policy. For good measure, the EU system transfers considerable responsibility for economic decision-making to non-accountable institutions. Such a transfer conforms to neoliberal ideas by dressing up contestable questions of economic policy as technical problems to be resolved by an expert elite.

This chapter traces the ideological evolution of the EU from toleration of at least a wide variety of capitalisms towards a more neoliberal constitutionalisation of economic policy as part of the completion of the single European market in the 1980s and 1990s. The chapter argues that this constitutionalisation needs to be seen as part and parcel of British constitutional law. In the early years of UK membership in the rudimentary EEC (generally known simply as the Common Market), one might have been forgiven for conceiving membership as merely involving the delegation of discrete and limited chunks of policy to the European institutions. Today, however, it is more appropriate to understand the Treaties as enshrining the very essence of constitutional law. Increasingly, they supply the fundamental boundaries for legitimate national governance.

The Original Indeterminacy of the European Project: Article 345 TFEU

Successive British governments in the 1940s and 1950s rejected pressure for European integration. As we have seen in the case of the General Agreement on Tariffs and Trade (GATT) negotiations, in the 1940s Britain was a more equal partner with the United States than was subsequently the case, and this status engendered a degree of national self-confidence.[13] Quite apart from this, the 1945 Labour government was mindful that its socialist reforms could be compromised by international commitments. Thus the prevailing mood of British politicians was in favour of preserving national autonomy. To this end, they wanted the UK's international obligations to be definite, specific and none too intrusive.[14] Precise commitments—of limited scope—would be the least harmful to the maintenance of continuing policymaking discretion. These considerations compelled successive British governments to reject European supranationalism.

By contrast, for the six original Member States of the European Coal and Steel Community (ECSC) and European Economic Community, the overwhelming priority was European unity. They therefore did what British politicians were not prepared to do—they made, in the form of the Treaty of Rome, an 'agreement to agree', the details of which would be ironed out at some later stage by newly created institutions. The Treaty laid down instead a *general* statement of goals and

[13] Henig (1997) 21.
[14] *Ibid*, 29

established a set of institutions charged with achieving them. Thus the framers left much of the content of the rules vague.[15] In particular, the Treaty left unresolved the balance between market forces and state intervention that would be permissible in the new EEC. This vagueness allowed contracting parties to agree on a form of words without really agreeing as to ultimate objectives.

The early ideological ambiguity of the EEC was underlined by the heterogeneity of those seeking European integration. In continental Europe, conservatives, liberals and socialists alike had no difficulty in embracing the ideal of a united Europe. In particular, the original enthusiasts for integration included a neoliberal wing, which detested the 'totalitarian dirigisme' of the postwar period and the close connection between state and economy. To this end, they favoured the establishment of 'technocratic' or 'detached expert' institutions, which would serve to sever economic forces from the ordinary processes of government.[16] European neoliberals were supported in these efforts by their American co-ideologues, some of whom regarded the removal of trade barriers and the dilution of sovereignty—both in Europe and throughout the world—as essential for American prosperity.[17] Yet neoliberals formed only one tendency among others within the European movement; they were rubbing shoulders with socialists, social democrats and liberals, such was the motley ragbag craving European unity.

This lack of ideological clarity did not unduly faze the leaders of the Six. They took the view that European unity was an absolute priority, which must prevail over ideological differences. Erika Szyzsczak has observed:

> The EEC Treaty rules were a compromise; they . . . did not provide guidance for the complex economic and political tasks of weeding out illegitimate state intervention in the economy from legitimate forms of state intervention which were necessary and could be beneficial for European integration.'[18]

Until the mid-1980s, the EEC had 'a dull and unspectacular image',[19] partly because European institutions and Member States alike largely declined to resolve the indeterminacy of the Treaty rules. So long as the substantive scope of EEC law remained relatively modest, the need to adopt a definitive ideological position was not pressing. Indeed, to have done so would have jeopardised the very unity required for further integration.

Ideological indeterminacy was embedded in the very text of the Treaty. The exercise of the new rights of free movement of goods, services and capital were likely to be driven, primarily at least, by the private sector. Indeed, the underlying presumption of the common market was that the hand of the state must be neutered so that the individual could be left unregulated in his affairs.[20] As for the

---

[15] Lindberg (1963) 27.
[16] Haas (2004) 20–22.
[17] Hackett (1995) 109.
[18] Szyzsczak (2007) 255–56.
[19] Grant ((1994) 63.
[20] Lane (2006) 245.

competition rules, they have been described as nothing short of 'a neoliberal tract', derived from the laws bequeathed upon Germany by the Americans.[21] But at the same time, the Treaty also contained what is now Article 345 TFEU, which declared that 'this Treaty shall in no way prejudice the rules in Member States governing the system of property ownership.'

Article 345 was intended to safeguard nationalised industries in the Member States, reflecting the apparent wish of the Treaty framers to adopt a neutral stance in the debate over public and private ownership.[22] Even in the late 1960s it was still possible for commentators to claim that Article 345 enjoyed paramount importance and to argue that it removed all competence from the Community in the field of property ownership, restraining the use of all other Treaty provisions accordingly.[23] Yet from the outset there was an inherent tension between Article 345 and the logic of the common market. As one anonymous continental put it, 'there is not an article affirming a proposition that another article hidden in another corner of the Treaty would not render almost meaningless.'[24] Even from an early stage there were authors who believed that a general move towards public ownership on the part of a Member State would be incompatible with the EEC's economic constitution because of its preference for an undistorted market economy.[25] For instance, in the mid-1950s, when some industrialists were complaining of 'hyperdirigisme' by the European Coal and Steel Community, Raymond Racine emphasised that the project of European integration outlined in the Schuman plan was intended to be neither systematically liberal nor systematically dirigiste but would accord the private sector pride of place, whilst giving the public sector a subsidiary role.[26] Thus whilst at the outset the EEC Treaty permitted a wide range of capitalisms, even its bare words seemed to preclude a general move on the part of Member States towards the discarding of capitalism. At the very least, the logic of the Treaty appeared to rule out the creation of *new* publicly-owned monopolies in sectors previously subject to free competition. The free movement of goods, services and establishment, coupled with the Treaty prohibition on discrimination on grounds of nationality, meant that Member States could not 'close off' new sectors to market entrants from the private sectors of other Member States. Undertakings from other Member States were entitled to enter the relevant market on non-discriminatory terms, and in the nature of things, these would mainly be private companies. The Treaty prohibition on state aid also seemed to pull against interventionist economic policies at national level.

At the same time, however, there was material in the Treaty that could provide comfort for social democrats. Quite apart from Article 345, the Treaty seemingly permitted public services to be shielded from competition rules so as not to obstruct the

---

[21] *Ibid*, 252–53.
[22] Gardner (1995) 78.
[23] Kovar (1988) 99.
[24] Cited in Stein and Nicholson (1960).
[25] Kovar (1988) 112.
[26] Racine (1954) 224–31.

performance of their assigned tasks (Article 106 TFEU, previously Article 86 EC). It was perhaps understandable therefore why some shared the view of former UK Foreign Secretary George Brown:

> The Treaty of Rome, like the Bible, takes account of any possible sin, provides the antidote and thereby offers ways and means of obtaining sanctity afterwards . . . We found that other people bound by the Treaty of Rome had managed to provide for all their private troubles, and it was pretty obvious that we could provide for ours, even within the terms of the Treaty.[27]

Yet not all social democrats and socialists in Britain shared Brown's sense of calm. Others believed that the Treaty would obstruct progressive economic policies. During the debates on UK accession, many Labour MPs complained that the Treaty was politically biased, convinced that it would rule out traditional Labour policies on industry, taxation and the regions.[28] Indeed, even at the time of the 1975 referendum, the majority of the Parliamentary Labour Party continued to oppose UK membership of the EEC.

Resolving the Indeterminacy

From its early years, therefore, the EEC was perceived as intending to narrow the possibilities of electoral choice in Member States. The strong neoliberal trend of the 1980s and 1990s dramatically increased the extent to which this was the case. During the 1980s, Europe's national leaders increasingly embraced the neoliberal creed and started to pursue neoliberal policies in their own states. It was inevitable that this would ultimately be reflected in changes in EEC law. Essentially, a Europeanisation of neoliberalism took place, with the result that neoliberalism was *constitutionalised* at the European level vis-à-vis the Member States, and Article 345 became sidelined. Indeed, it is arguable that increasingly, neoliberalism became the predominant reason for deeper European integration. Prompted by the Commission and the European Court of Justice, the leaders of the Member States chose to embody their neoliberalism at the EEC level, enabling them to tie the hands of their successors. As things turned out in any event, these successors have essentially shared the neoliberal views of their predecessors. The strength and durability of the neoliberal consensus has thereby served to obscure the constitutional narrowing of politics.

Thus in today's EU, according to Anthony Gardner, neutrality over the system of property ownership has essentially been replaced by a presumption of illegality towards public enterprises; state intervention in the economy is now suspect.[29] The EU has thus evolved into 'a relatively faithful expression of the capitalist ideal

---

[27] Brown (1972) 221.
[28] Nicol (2001) 71–72.
[29] Gardner (1995) 79; Chalmers, Hadjemmanuil, Monti and Tomkins (2006) 1115.

which has triumphed over communism and socialism'.[30] Furthermore, the contemporary EU is not only neoliberalised but also neoliberalising, the 'principles of a market economy' being included as a standard clause on cooperation and other agreements that the Community makes with non-EU countries.[31]

The first major revision of the Treaty, the Single European Act (SEA) 1986, marked a crucial stage in this transformation. The SEA focused heavily on the aim of completing the European single market. The abandonment in March 1983 of the French government's socialistic economic programme and its conversion to the cause of European action proved to be a turning point.[32] From then on, European politicians increasingly coalesced around support for the completion of the internal market. The business sector, which was becoming frustrated by obstacles to cross-border commerce, was pressing for the same objective.[33] Despite the best efforts of the Commission to play down the fact that an ideological choice was being made,[34] the single-market focus of the SEA made it more difficult to maintain the idea that the EC could be ideologically neutral: rather, it involved 'a highly politicized choice of ethos, ideology and political culture: the culture of "the market" '.[35]

Against this backdrop, illusions about the apolitical nature of the European project struggled to survive. As Paul Craig and Gráinne de Búrca have observed, 'conceptions of market freedom are not value-free . . . [T]he appropriate limits to free markets are contestable. These are key issues that divide political parties.'[36] Joseph Weiler has made essentially the same point, arguing that the 'need for a successful market not only accentuates the pressure for uniformity, but also manifests a social (and hence ideological) choice which prizes market efficiency and Europe-wide neutrality of competition above other competing values'.[37] In this respect, the Commission, with the support of entrepreneurs, was particularly determined that the vast national public sectors should no longer be shielded from intra-EEC trade and competition.[38] In the words of Commissioner Karel van Miert,

> It is obvious that a market based on competition and free circulation of goods, services, people and capital is at odds with systems based on national monopolies. Our liberalization policy was therefore conceived as an indispensable instrument for the establishment of the internal market.[39]

It was upon these grounds that the Labour Party voted against the legislation incorporating the SEA into domestic law. The Party was concerned with the

[30] McGoldrick (1997) 212.

[31] Cremona (1999) 148.

[32] Armstrong and Bulmer (1998) 21.

[33] Gormley (2006) 17–18. In particular, Gormley draws attention to the significant influence of the Kangeroo Group, an organisation that seeks to bring together politicians and businesses in pursuit of free movement.

[34] Commission (1985).

[35] Weiler (1999a) 89.

[36] Craig and de Búrca (2008) 630.

[37] Weiler (1999a) 90.

[38] Szyszczak (2006) 88.

[39] Van Miert (2000) 1.

preservation of national sovereignty but even more with what it saw as the Thatcherite ethos of the SEA—its worship of the single market and its neglect of the social dimension. In short, Labour perceived the SEA as the triumph of 'Euro-Thatcherism'.[40] This trend was reinforced in the 1990s as the fundamental change in attitude towards the role of the state was increasingly embodied in EU law.

EU Law as British Constitutional Law

Before we consider in greater depth the neoliberalism embedded in the single market settlement, we need to take a step sideways in order to underline why, from a British constitutional point of view, it should matter whether EU law encapsulates 'Euro-Thatcherism' or anything else. It matters because of the unique effectiveness of the EU legal order. In the case of the WTO, we have seen in chapter two that the enforcement machinery operates largely (though not entirely) at the transnational level and, in spite of this, is widely seen as having achieved a high level of effectiveness. In the case of the EU, by contrast, enforcement has mainly (though not entirely) been devolved to the national courts and tribunals, and this has proven even more effective. National judiciaries have shown themselves the willing policemen of the EU system, deploying their legitimacy to compel their national executives and legislatures to comply with EU rules.[41]

The stories of the creation and development of the doctrines of direct effect and supremacy are well known. The system designed by the Treaty framers was 'inherently limited and weak. It was a system where few cases would make it to the court, and in which the largest infractions could easily and without repercussion persist until a political will to rectify the situation emerged'.[42] This state of things changed when the European Court of Justice handed down two revolutionary judgments. In 1963 in *Van Gend en Loos* the ECJ proclaimed that the EEC Treaty was more than just an agreement between states; rather, it was capable of creating rights for individuals, which the national courts and tribunals would be obliged to protect. This became known as the doctrine of direct effect. The breakthrough of *Van Gend* was that the ECJ asserted its jurisdiction to determine the precise legal effect of EU law within the domestic legal systems of the Member States. In 1964 in *Costa v ENEL* the ECJ created the supremacy doctrine, by holding that such directly effective rights prevailed over any conflicting national law 'however framed'. This doctrine serves, from a national perspective, to turn all EU law into constitutional law. The preliminary reference system, whereby any national court or tribunal can refer questions of law to the ECJ, aided the national courts in their enforcement of the two doctrines by providing a decentralised means of monitoring Member State

---

[40] Nicol (2001a) 168–69.
[41] Explanations for this willingness are advanced in Weiler (1999a) ch 5; and Barav (1994).
[42] Alter (2001) 1.

compliance with EU law.[43] But in rendering themselves accountable to the ECJ for their compliance with EU law, Member State governments and Parliaments have been made correspondingly less accountable to their electorates.[44] As Cesare Romano has pointed out,

> Preliminary rulings give national courts the possibility to transform themselves into custodians of the international, or rather supranational, regime. Moreover, by asking the regime's judicial body to rule on the direct applicability of the regime's legislation, national courts *de facto* bypass national parliaments, which ordinarily are entrusted with the mission of incorporating international law into domestic legislation.[45]

Karen Alter attributes the lack of resistance to the supremacy doctrine on the part of national politicians to the limited time horizons of politicians vis-à-vis judges. If a legal decision does not cause a problem today, she has argued, it is not worth expending political resources to mobilise against it; instead, it can be left to other politicians to deal with.[46] Whilst this insight is compelling, it is perhaps particularly valid for the years immediately following the ECJ's landmark decisions. As the neoliberal character of the EEC became increasingly pronounced, we can discern an additional, *ideological* motivation for politicians' toleration of EU law supremacy. As the pan-European—indeed global—hegemony of neoliberal ideas became established, most politicians broadly approved of the market philosophy of the EU. In consequence they developed a taste for transnational governance. They were therefore willing to sacrifice national autonomy in pursuit of their favoured policies. If this meant permanently binding future governments and Parliaments and thereby reducing democratic choice within their own states, then so much the better. The supremacy of EU law ceased to become a bugbear and became a boon.

It deserves to be emphasised that direct effect and supremacy are inextricably woven into the EU's substantive economic programme. The two doctrines give rights to individuals, but 'individuals' is a misleading term in EU law, since it embraces not only natural persons but also legal persons such as corporations. The ability of corporations to enforce the free movement of goods, services and capital, the freedom of establishment (of their branches and subsidiaries) and the competition rules was necessary in order to establish the fundamental status of these rules. This is confirmed by the ECJ's aims-driven reasoning in the two landmark cases. In *Van Gend*, it argued that the creation of direct effect was primarily necessitated by the ambitious goal of establishing the common market. Likewise in *Costa*, the ECJ justified the supremacy doctrine by appealing to the need to ensure the uniform application of the rules of the common market.[47] As Carlos Ball put it,

---

[43] Garrett and Weingast (1993) 198.

[44] Harlow (2002) 147.

[45] Romano (1998–99) 748.

[46] Alter (2001) 186.

[47] For discussion of whether the reasoning in *Costa* is convincing, see Nicol (2009) 220–23; Craig and de Búrca (2008) 344–46.

> As the Community is founded upon principles of economic integration and liberalism, the Court, through its aggressive use of the doctrines of direct effect and supremacy, has seen itself as the guarantor of the integration process. Thus, Community law has had a vast impact in transforming and integrating the economies of the Member States in a manner that is consistent with those principles.[48]

Increasingly, therefore, supremacy and direct effect have become the means through which neoliberal ideology is made to stick.

In the context of the world trading system, we have seen that as GATT was replaced by the more determinedly neoliberal WTO, this went hand-in-hand with the creation of a powerful enforcement system. In the case of the EU, this system was for the most part already in place. Nonetheless, the neoliberalism of the single market project formed the backdrop for its further strengthening. Thus the ECJ developed its jurisprudence on the requirement for effective remedies in the national courts (eroding the traditional respect for national procedural autonomy)[49] and created an EU-wide remedy of state liability, enabling individuals to seek compensation when states violated EU law.[50] Similarly, the Treaty was amended to empower the ECJ to fine Member States that fail to comply with its judgments in enforcement proceedings.[51]

We dwelt in chapter one on the centrality of the legislative supremacy of Parliament in the British constitution and the way in which it protects the democratic attributes of contestability, relative ideological neutrality and accountability. Against this backdrop, acceptance of the supremacy and direct effect of EU law in Britain would entail a very profound constitutional change. If the British judiciary chose to embrace the ECJ's doctrines, then far from having to enforce each and every Act of Parliament, British courts and tribunals (whatever their rank in the legal hierarchy) would be empowered—indeed, obliged—to disregard any statute that in their opinion contravened EU law. The traditional loyalty of the courts to the latest expression of the will of Parliament would be seriously undermined. Nonetheless, in 1991 in *Factortame* the House of Lords made it clear that EU law prevailed over British Acts of Parliament, Lord Bridge holding that whatever limitation of its sovereignty Parliament accepted when it enacted the European Communities Act 1972 was 'entirely voluntary'.[52] In fact, the evidence suggests that British MPs did not realise that EU membership would result in British courts setting aside statute law.[53] With this in mind, perhaps a more

---

[48] Ball (1996) 308–9.

[49] See eg Case 222/84 *Johnston v. Chief Constable of the RUC* [1986] ECR 1651; Case C-213/89 *R v Secretary of State for Transport, ex parte Factortame Ltd and Others* [1990] ECR I-2433; Case C-271/91 *Marshall v Southampton and South West Hampshire Health Authority II* [1993] ECR I-4367; Case C-430–431/93 *Van Schinjdel and Van Veen v Stichting Pensioenfonds vooor Fysiotherapeuten* [1995] ECR I-4705.

[50] Cases C-6 and 9/90 *Francovich and Bonifaci v Italy* [1991] ECR I-5357; Cases C-46/93 and 48/93 *Brasserie du Pêcheur SA v Germany, and R v Secretary of State for Transport, ex parte Factortame Ltd and Others* [1996] ECR I-1029.

[51] Art 228(2) EC.

[52] For criticism, see Nicol (2001a) ch 7.

[53] *Ibid*, chs 2–4.

convincing explanation for their Lordships' holding in *Factortame* is that put forward by Paul Craig:

> That . . . disagreements [over the EU] continue to exist should not . . . serve to mask the fact that the United Kingdom has been in the Community for over twenty years; that within this period Community law has become an increasingly accepted part of national law; and that the majority of the population accept, in general terms, the United Kingdom's membership of the Community as a political norm . . . Viewed against this backdrop the legal reasoning and result in Factortame can be seen as an attempt by the judiciary to bring constitutional doctrine up to date with political reality.[54]

In any event, *Factortame* clearly evinces a general rule that British courts rank EU law above Acts of Parliament. Nonetheless, there remains an ongoing debate as to whether Parliament could validly legislate contrary to EU law *by evincing an express intention so to do*. It should be emphasised that this argument remains hypothetical: Parliament does not do this, so the daily reality is that British courts and tribunals give priority to EU law over statute as a matter of routine.[55] Nevertheless, in the 1979 case of *Macarthys v Smith*, Lord Denning MR flagged up the possibility of express parliamentary defiance, asserting that in such circumstances it would be the duty of the English judge to ignore EC law and to give effect to the Act of Parliament.[56] In the same vein, Alison Young has proposed that the most appropriate way of viewing the European Communities Act is to regard Parliament in 1972 as having issued an instruction to the courts to accord primacy to EU law until further notice, so that it would always be open to Parliament to countermand this instruction in whole or in part.[57] By contrast, David Feldman has argued:

> Accepting that both Acts of Parliament and directly effective Community law are judiciable in courts in the United Kingdom entails accepting the need for some hierarchically superior judicial body to have the last word on such questions of law, and the combined effect of the European Communities Act 1972 and the EU Treaty is to make it clear that the Court of Justice of the European Communities is that body. If anyone fails to recognise this it can only be because of an inability to take account of all the perspectives from which the United Kingdom's constitution must now be viewed.[58]

Young's suggestion constitutes the more normatively attractive interpretation of the European Communities Act from the democratic perspective and serves as a valiant attempt to reconcile the supremacy of EU law with parliamentary sovereignty. Conversely, however, Feldman perhaps provides the more likely prediction of what would happen in the event of express Parliamentary defiance of an EU rule, especially in view of the inevitable making of a preliminary reference to the

---

[54] Craig (1997b) 211.

[55] Nicol (1996).

[56] [1979] 3 All ER 325, 329 c–e.

[57] For this reason, she has contended, there is in reality no incompatibility as such between the 1972 Act and a later Act that merely contains provisions which are incompatible with EU law (Young (2008) 43–44).

[58] Feldman (2005).

ECJ on the matter, which would undoubtedly reiterate its position that EU law prevails over any national law 'however framed'.

It is also conceivable that UK courts would take into account the *kind* of defiance of EU law that Government and Parliament were pursuing. Our judiciary might be more likely to tolerate defiance on a single, isolated issue than the implementation of an entire political or economic programme that conflicts with EU law. If it were clear that a Parliamentary flouting of EU law were not simply a 'one-off' but rather part of a comprehensive project that contravened EU rules in multiple respects, this might well prompt the judiciary to compel Government and Parliament to make a straight choice between membership with its obligations or withdrawal from the EU. In so doing, the judiciary would in all likelihood merely be joining the chorus of an outraged Commission and other Member States. For in this context it is misguided to view judicial decision-making as existing in a hermetically sealed container unaffected by politics. We can therefore largely discount the idea of wide-ranging British defiance of EU law whilst remaining a Member State.[59]

The Free Movement of Goods: Control of Imports

The aim of the previous section was to underline the status of EU law as part of British constitutional law. We can now consider the substance of EU law and its connection to neoliberalism. The common market was intended to be based on the free movement of goods, services, persons and capital. Of these 'fundamental freedoms', the free movement of goods was particularly controversial at the time of UK accession. There were two reasons for this. First, both Labour and the Conservatives had long been strongly committed to the system of Commonwealth preference, whereby Britain gave largely free entry to raw materials and manufactured goods from Commonwealth countries and in return received favourable trade treatment from them.[60] GATT had already eroded Commonwealth preference to some extent; the EEC would finish it off. EEC rules subjected Commonwealth imports to the tariff barriers of the common commercial policy, whilst EEC goods could enter the UK free. Secondly, the Labour Party's commitments to economic expansion and full employment always involved some control of trade. In 1950, for instance, the Labour manifesto argued that 'there can be no advance without planning. Exports must be sold in the right markets at the right price, and imports arranged according to our needs.'[61] In 1966, the Party manifesto commended the government's imposition of a surcharge on imports to curb

---

[59] Indeed, it is possible to conceive the purely theoretical possibility of express, intentional defiance as merely serving as a safety-valve to make the supremacy of EU law more tolerable.

[60] Nicol (2001a) 25.

[61] Labour Party (1950).

a 'disastrous increase in imports in 1964' and promised intense efforts to ensure that imported products were replaced by British products.[62]

Even after Britain joined the EEC, Labour rather bizarrely seemed to think it could control trade. In 1979, for instance, the Party promised to 'ensure that imports enter our market only within acceptable limits'.[63] In the early 1980s, Labour was committed to withdrawal from the EEC, and this allowed the Party with greater legitimacy to propose in its 1982 programme that imports in certain sectors would have to be held back or even cut where this was necessary for particular industries to develop.[64] In 1983, Labour pledged to introduce import controls, including tariffs and quotas, to achieve the objective of trade balance upon which the Party believed sustained expansion depended; the expansion of imports needed to be 'orderly'.[65]

The question of planned trade was connected to issues of public and private ownership, since public ownership in some form or other was often envisaged as the spearhead of manufacturing investment.[66] This reflected wariness in Labour ranks as to the private sector's willingness to invest. The ability to impose selective import controls on the types of products manufactured by these nationalised industries would have been a valuable weapon in ensuring their viability. In the words of Labour's 1983 manifesto, 'we must therefore be ready to act on imports *directly* . . . so as to check the growth of imports should they threaten to outstrip our exports and thus our plans for expansion'.[67] EU membership would appear to be incompatible with this stance. Thus free trade has long been an eminently contestable policy—yet the EU Treaties constitutionalise it.

Cassis de Dijon

Goods, Regulation and the Corporate Role in Constitution-Building

If the EU is to be a genuine single market, it needs to confront not only straightforward obstacles to trade such as quotas and customs duties but also the myriad

---

[62] Labour Party (1966).

[63] Labour Party (1979).

[64] Labour Party (1982) 21.

[65] Labour Party (1983).

[66] Thus Labour's nationalisation commitments were never limited to the provision of services: the Party often intended to extend public ownership to manufacturing. Labour in 1945 pledged to nationalise a number of key goods-producing industries, as well as those providing a combination of goods and services, such as coal, gas, electricity, iron and steel. In 1950, Labour repeated its commitment to coal and steel nationalisation and wanted to bring sugar beet manufacture and refining and cement into the public sector, along with sections of the chemicals and minerals industries. In the 1955 manifesto, machine tools industries were added to the list. The (unimplemented) *Labour's Programme 1973* contained a more ambitious commitment, aimed at tackling the trend towards domination of the economy by transnational corporations. Specifically, it pledged nationalisation of at least one top company in each of the major manufacturing sectors of the economy.

[67] Labour Party (1983), original emphasis.

of regulatory rules governing the marketing of goods in the Member States. In the past, although product standards might not have been the stuff of party manifestos, they nonetheless remained a matter of legitimate political contestation. This situation was profoundly altered by the European Court of Justice's 1979 judgment in *Cassis de Dijon*.[68] The case is of seminal importance for the British constitution, no less for the national constitutions of all the other Member States, because of its revolutionary consequences for the division of competences between the EU and its Member States.

Article 34 TFEU (previously Article 28 EC) prohibits between the Member States 'quantitative restrictions on imports and all measures having equivalent effect'. In *Cassis de Dijon*, the ECJ resolved a longstanding controversy as to whether the Treaty prohibition on measures having equivalent effect to quantitative restrictions between Member States could apply to 'indistinctly applicable measures', that is, measures that apply both to domestic products and those from other Member States but are nonetheless capable of hindering free movement. The ECJ held that Article 34 could indeed prohibit such measures. In a bold act of Treaty interpretation, it declared that there was a presumption that if products have been lawfully produced and marketed in one Member State, they should be capable of being marketed in all other Member States (the 'mutual recognition principle'). In the absence of EU legislation, this presumption could be rebutted only if the Member State could justify the measure by reference to an overriding requirement of the public interest (such as public health, consumer or environmental protection, etc).[69] In so doing, the national measure must meet an exacting standard of proportionality: if there are alternative means of achieving the same overriding requirement that would be less of a hindrance on the free movement of goods, then the Member State will fail to justify the measure.[70]

The *Cassis* principle revolutionised not only the law on the free movement of goods but arguably the evolution of the entire European project. It has been extended so as to apply to freedom to provide services, freedom of establishment and the free movement of persons.[71] Above all, however, it has provided the conceptual basis for the legislation of the internal market. The decision has rightly been the subject of extensive scholarship,[72] but for our purposes, two main observations need to be made. First, *Cassis* has received remarkably little attention from British constitutional lawyers (and national constitutional lawyers generally), despite its profound expansion of EU competence and its corresponding diminution of

---

[68] Case 120/78 *Rewe-Zentrale AG v Bundesmonopolverwaltung für Branntwein* ('*Cassis de Dijon*') [1979] ECR 649.

[69] Para 8. The judgment uses the phrase 'mandatory requirement', but 'overriding' or 'imperative' requirement is a better translation.

[70] Para 13.

[71] Services: Case 33/74 *Van Binsbergen v Bestuur van de Bedrijfsvereniging voor de Metaallnijverheid* [1974] ECR 1299; Establishment: Case C-55/94 *Gebhard v Consiglio dell'Ordine degli Avvocati e Procuratori di Milano* [1995] ECR I-4165; Persons: Case C-281/98 *Angonese v Cassa di Riparmio di Bolzano SpA* [2000] ECR I-4139.

[72] See, eg, the authors discussed in Stone Sweet (2004) 127–39.

national autonomy. Far from looming large in British constitutional law textbooks, it tends not to be mentioned at all. This owes much to orthodox ideas of the academic division of labour, whereby constitutional law and EU law are to some extent still considered to be separate. In particular, there is scant recognition of the connection between British public law and the substantive law of the EU. Yet these disciplinary distinctions, however deeply engrained in academic tradition, are nonetheless suspect. All directly effective EU law prevails over conflicting national law; therefore all EU law is constitutional law. The substantive law of the EU determines the residual legislative competence of the Member States. By extending the protection of EU law to all trading arrangements, even those that do not actually discriminate against the products of other Member States, *Cassis* vastly enlarged the substantive scope of EU law and, with it, the power of the national courts and ECJ to supervise governmental and parliamentary regulation in the Member States. Post-*Cassis*, 'no aspect of national regulatory policy touching on the market for goods could be considered, a priori, to be exempt from judicial scrutiny'.[73] For this reason, *Cassis* deserves to rank with *Van Gend en Loos*, *Costa v ENEL* and *Francovich* as one of the landmark cases of British constitutional law.[74]

Secondly, whilst *Cassis* plainly promotes European integration, the way in which it does so is by no means ideologically neutral. Indeed, the ideological underpinnings of *Cassis* conform strikingly to neoliberal policy, in that the decision seriously compromises the ability of governments to favour competing considerations over those of free trade. By explicitly privileging free trade above other public concerns, *Cassis* creates a hierarchy of values. This hierarchy to some extent acts as a substitute for the outcomes of democratic politics. Thus it is no longer open to a government, as a matter of policy, to prioritise health or environmental protection over free trade. Under *Cassis*, competing public interests will not be permitted to 'trump' free trade unless (a) they are interests that the ECJ recognises as sufficiently compelling; and (b) the national measures advancing those interests satisfy the rigours of the proportionality test.

In the wake of the *Cassis de Dijon* judgment, the Commission addressed a 'communication' to the Member States, declaring that the ECJ decision meant that mutual recognition was now a 'constitutional principle' and that 'only under very strict conditions does the Court allow exceptions' to it.[75] Thereafter, the Commission formed an alliance with transnational business coalitions, with the aim of convincing the governments of the Member States to make *Cassis* their legislative model. Corporations, as well as the Commission, wanted mutual recognition to

---

[73] *Ibid*, 128.

[74] Since the *Cassis* principle is based on the interpretation of a Treaty article, it could only be altered by Treaty revision or by further jurisprudence. In respect of 'certain selling arrangements' which do not affect, in fact or in law, market access, *Cassis* has been limited by *Keck* (Cases C-267 and 268/91 *Criminal Proceedings against Keck and Mithouard* [1993] ECR I-6097). The post-*Keck* case law however shows that it is rare for contested measures not to fall within the free movement of goods, since the ECJ places considerable emphasis on whether the effect in fact of such measures creates a distinction between domestic and imported goods.

[75] Commission (1980).

become the fundamental strategy of the Community for the purposes of the SEA and for the completion of the single market.[76]

It is noteworthy that the business community was intimately involved in fashioning this template for the European internal market at the very time that they were also advancing the design for the WTO Agreements: national leaders were plainly in a receptive mood towards corporate demands and seemingly had no objection to 'corporation creep' into their supranational arrangements. It is unsurprising, therefore, that transnational corporations were heavily implicated in this reshaping of EEC legislative strategy. The Roundtable of European Industrialists, a grouping that included such companies as Philips, Siemens, Olivetti, GEC, Daimler Benz, Volvo, Fiat, Bosch, ASEA and Ciba-Geigy, gave substantial support to the Commission's initiative. Somewhat ironically, the Roundtable, consisting as it did of the most powerful industrialists in Europe, was able to put considerable pressure on national governments, with the ultimate objective of creating a system whereby business could bypass national governmental processes.[77] As Sandholtz and Zysman put it,

> The third actor in the story [of the SEA], besides the governments and the Commission, is the leadership of the European multinational corporations. The White Paper and the Single European Act gave the appearance that changes in the EC market were irreversible and politically unstoppable. Businesses have been acting on that belief. Politically, they have taken up the banner of 1992, collaborating with the Commission and exerting substantial influence on their governments. The significance of the role of business, and of its collaboration with the Commission, must not be underestimated.[78]

To corporations, this apparent irreversibility of the single market reforms must have been attractive, since it dovetailed with the advancement of the perennial business demands of stability and security. Corporate rights would essentially be enshrined in constitutional law.

Thus corporate pressure provided much of the impetus for a 'New Approach' to EEC legislation in the mid-1980s. The traditional strategy of 'harmonisation' had involved the painstaking negotiation of uniform European norms. This had barely succeeded in slowing down the rate of increase of trade barriers. The Commission took the view that 'a strategy based totally on harmonisation would be over-regulatory, would take a long time to implement, would be inflexible and could stifle innovation'.[79] It pressed instead for a new strategy, based on the template of *Cassis*, which would place the emphasis firmly on mutual recognition. Weiler has explained:

> The key to the success of the New Approach was the shift in presumption; goods certified by a national body as complying with specifications established pursuant to a Community standard would be allowed to circulate freely without having to prove on a case-by-case basis their equivalence—simply, but with profound market implications.

[76] Stone Sweet (2001) 181.
[77] Sandholtz and Zysman (1989) 116–18.
[78] *Ibid*, 111–12.
[79] Commission (1985) para 64.

This coupled with the shift to majority voting, which made it possible to set standards at the Community level, meant a veritable sea change in the evolution of the marketplace.[80]

Sure enough, once the Single European Act came into force in 1987, the New Approach combined with the advent of qualified majority voting to enact internal market measures broke the perennial legislative logjam. This meant, in turn, that the supremacy of EEC law was no longer merely of peripheral importance: rather, completion of the single market gave the supremacy doctrine a new lease of life. The EEC was now generating a burgeoning volume of important legislation that enjoyed a higher legal status than national law. Moreover, the kind of EEC legislation being produced inevitably enhanced the commercial freedom of the private sector at the expense of the policymaking discretion of Member States.

Standardisation: A Privatisation of Governance?

A crucial aspect of the new legislative technique, again influenced by the pervasive sway of *Cassis,* was a change in approach to product standards. Earlier attempts by the Commission to harmonise standards through Community legislation had proven inefficient and ineffective.[81] Rather than continuing to hammer out detailed agreement within the EEC's political institutions, the EEC handed over the task of setting technical standards to three private organisations, the European Committee for Standardisation (*Comité Européen de Normalisation* or CEN), the European Committee for Electrotechnical Standardisation (*Comité Européen de Normalisation Électrotechnique* or Cenelec) and the European Telecommunications Standards Institute (ETSI). From then on, EC legislation limited itself to laying down in very general terms only the 'essential requirements' imposed on products for free circulation in the EU.

The New Approach obliges Member States to recognise that products manufactured in compliance with CEN, Cenelec and ETSI standards are presumed to be in conformity with the 'essential requirements' laid down in directives. The standards can also be said to be de facto binding on economic operators, if they wish to take advantage of this presumption in order to avail themselves of their EU rights to free trade. In a revision of its General Product Safety Directive in 2001, the Council and European Parliament effectively endowed European standards with the same status as EU law, by enacting that products manufactured according to national standards that transpose European standards are now presumed to be in conformity with the general safety requirement. In this way, the EU's political institutions have used reliance on standards as a means of avoiding the need for legislation. Standardisation has, in other words, become an established alternative to the enactment of EU legislation.[82]

---

[80] Weiler (2000) 224.

[81] Pelkmans (1987) 251–53.

[82] Schepel (2005) ch 2.

Furthermore, it bears emphasis that the standardisation bodies are private organisations. They were not established by the EU at all. They were formed by national standardisation bodies eager to colonise the European market. In turn, national standardisation bodies also tend to be private organisations, originally established by industries that needed to indicate to buyers that their goods were 'up to standard'. In Britain, for instance, the British Standards Institution was established in 1931, having evolved from an organisation set up by the civil engineering industry in the Edwardian era. The UK government recognised it in 1942 as the sole organisation for the issuing of national standards, and since the 1990s it has grown into a global corporation, the BSI Group, having acquired major American and Asian interests. BSI's main task, however, is to reassure consumers. As Harm Schepel has put it, 'standard-setters get together to write standards not moved by a civic duty but because they hope to use these standards as marketing tools and hence sell more products'.[83]

Both national and European standardisation bodies are generally financed by industry as well as by governments. Andrew McGee and Stephen Weatherill discern 'broad issues of democratic accountability' that are raised by the privatisation of the standardisation process. In particular, they have identified a structural imbalance in the standardisation bodies that guarantees that they are dominated by corporate interests: 'for financial reasons it is likely that business will capture the standardisation process within CEN. Consumer organisations lack resources to participate fully in CEN committee work.'[84] With standards-making becoming the province of business alone, they have argued, the regulated become the regulators.[85] To be sure, in the wake of the Maastricht Treaty, the Commission presented the transfer of power to CEN, Cenelec and ETSI as guaranteeing 'light touch' regulation, on all fours with the subsidiarity principle. It would 'contribute to the European economy while avoiding the unnecessary stifling of economic initiative due to excessive regulation'.[86] Complaints that governance by standardisation bodies favours corporate interests has not been dispelled by the creation of an organisation to represent the consumer interest, the European Association for the Co-ordination of Consumer Representation (ANEC), since the inherent imbalance of resources remains endemic.[87]

It has been argued by Craig and de Búrca that

> Tensions which result from the imbalance in power between consumer and commercial interests are not *created* because harmonisation measures are passed at Community rather than national level. They are endemic in most Western-style market economies. Whether consumer interests fare better in the regulatory process at national or Community level will therefore depend, inter alia, on the relative capacities of commer-

[83] *Ibid*, 414.
[84] McGee and Weatherill (1990) 582.
[85] *Ibid*, 585.
[86] Commission (1995) 4.
[87] Armstrong and Bulmer (1998) 165.

cial and consumer interests to influence the legislative process within the Community and the nation state, and the relative costs involved in operating within these differing polities.[88]

Whilst this argument is perfectly valid on its own terms, there *is* a difference between harmonising at EU level as opposed to national level: in a nutshell, Europeanisation almost inevitably involves constitutionalisation. Now that the EU system has been firmly established, it has essentially become entrenched. The New Approach resulted from a consensus in the mid-1980s on the part of the Council at a time when its members were receptive to corporate demands for constitutional change. In all likelihood, a similar consensus would be required in order to alter the legislative strategy once again. Legislative strategy is unlikely to change merely because of a political shift in one or even several Member States. Consequently, a shift of competence from national to Community level has the constitutional effect of *consolidating* the power of the private standardisation bodies vis-à-vis those national political institutions that are democratically accountable.

Free Movement Rights versus Social Rights

It took until a series of decisions in 2007 and 2008 to confirm what should have been reasonably obvious from the general tenor of the free movement case law, namely that the European Court of Justice privileges the free movement rights of corporations over social and labour rights.[89] In so doing, the ECJ has further reinforced the fundamentality of these free movement rights by indicating that they enjoy 'horizontal direct effect'—allowing one private party (the corporation) to enforce them against another private party (the trade union). In *Viking*, the ECJ held that corporations could rely on their free movement rights against trade unions when industrial action threatened employers' exercise of those rights.[90] In *Laval*, the ECJ held that free movement rights precluded a trade union from using a blockade of sites to force an employer from another Member State to sign a collective agreement containing terms that were more favourable than those laid down in the relevant legislation.[91] In *Rüffert* the ECJ made it clear that national public authorities could not require public works contractors to comply with prevailing collective agreements that had not been declared universally applicable.[92] In *Commission v Luxembourg*, the ECJ declared that Member States lack the power

---

[88] Craig and de Búrca (2008) 628.

[89] Stone-Sweet (2000) 99.

[90] Case C-438/05*International Transport Workers' Federation v Viking Line ABP* [2007] ECR I-10779, [2008] 1 CMLR 51.

[91] Case C-341/05*Laval un Partneri Ltd v Svenska Byggnadsarbetareförbundet* [2007] ECR I-11767, [2008] 2 CMLR 9.

[92] Case C-346/06 *Rüffert v Land Niedersachsen* [2008] 2 CMLR 39.

to require all employers posting workers to comply with relevant collective agree-ments, notably those not declared universally applicable.[93]

It should be emphasised that in all these cases the ECJ was essentially interpreting Treaty provisions: Article 49 TFEU (previously Article 43 EC) on freedom of estab-lishment in *Viking*, and Article 56 TFEU (previously Article 49 EC) on freedom to provide services in *Laval, Rüffert* and *Commission v Luxembourg*. Accordingly, the only guaranteed way to override the ECJ's prioritisation of corporate interests over social interests would be for all 27 Member States to amend the Treaty in accordance with the procedure laid down in Article 48 TEU. The European Trades Union Congress appears to have recognised that only Treaty revision will change the situ-ation, proposing a draft protocol to the Treaty on European Union to the effect that 'nothing in the Treaties, and in particular neither economic freedoms nor competi-tion rules, shall have priority over fundamental social rights and social progress . . . In case of conflict fundamental social rights shall take precedence'. Yet if Treaty amendment is the solution, it would only require a single Member State to veto such a reprioritisation of EU values.[94] Therefore, the ECJ's interpretation of the relevant Treaty provisions enjoys a high degree of entrenchment.

The ECJ's methodology also highlights the extent to which the free movement rights are accorded a supreme status over competing concerns. In *Viking* and *Laval*, the ECJ accepted that the right to take collective action, including the right to strike, was a fundamental right, forming an integral part of the general principles of EU law.[95] The ECJ was confronted, therefore, with a conflict between two rights, both ostensibly of a fundamental nature—free movement on the one hand, the right to collective action on the other. Normally, the effect of such a conflict would be to expand the margin of appreciation enjoyed by the state authorities. The European Court of Human Rights (ECtHR) so held in *Otto-Preminger Institut v Austria*,[96] and the ECJ appeared to take the same position in *Schmidberger*[97] and in *Omega*,[98] the thinking being that when a state is faced with a conflict between two fundamental rights, the scales are evenly balanced and a difficult choice has to be made, so it makes sense to give the state considerable leeway. The ECJ, however, took a strikingly dif-ferent approach in *Viking* and *Laval*, adopting its normal test that a restriction on free movement could only be accepted if it pursued a legitimate aim compatible with the

---

[93] Case C-319/06 *Commission of the European Communities v Grand Duchy of Luxembourg* [2008] ECR I-04323.

[94] It is true that three of the cases also involved the interpretation of the Posted Workers' Directive (Directive 96/71/EC). However, in para 48 of *Laval* the ECJ appeared to endorse the Advocate General's view that the sole relevance of the directive was that it might shed light on the interpretation of the Treaty article. Yet there can be no certainty that the ECJ would change its interpretation of Arts 43 and 49 EC if the Council and European Parliament changed the secondary legislation. Whilst the ECJ is not bound by its previous decisions, it reverses them relatively rarely. Furthermore the ECJ traditionally accords a wide interpretation to the four freedoms and a narrow interpretation to per-missible limitations on them.

[95] *Viking* [44]; *Laval* [91].

[96] *Otto-Preminger Institut v Austria* (1994) 19 ENRR 34, E Com HR.

[97] Case C-112/00 *Schmidberger v Austria* [2003] ECR I-5659.

[98] Case C-36/02 *Omega Spielhallen- und Automatenaufstellungs-GmbH v Oberbürgermeisterin der Bundesstadt Bonn* [2004] ECR I-9609.

Treaty and was justified by overriding reasons of public interest. The ECJ went on to hold that even if this was the case, the restriction would still have to be suitable for securing the attainment of the objective pursued, and—crucially—must not go beyond what is necessary in order to attain that objective.[99] It was on that final limb of the proportionality test that the trade unions' case collapsed.

As Anne Davies has observed, the proportionality test is commonly used as a way of assessing the state's limitations on the right to strike, whereas in *Viking* and *Laval*, the right to strike was not the starting point for analysis.[100] Rather, the ECJ's reasoning began with the employer's assertion of its free movement rights under Article 49 or Article 56, against, not the state, but a trade union. The union's industrial action then had to be tested for proportionality in relation to the employer's fundamental freedom of movement. The ECJ's recognition of the right to strike is therefore *conditional* on the satisfaction of the proportionality test. Furthermore, in *Viking* in particular, the Court emphasised the 'least restrictive alternative' version of the proportionality test. This directs courts to consider whether there was any other form of action open to the unions which would have been less restrictive of the employer's free movement rights. Yet industrial action is *intended* to cause harm to the employer: the more harm it causes, the more effective it is likely to be in persuading the employer to make concessions.[101] To put it crudely: the more disproportionate it is, the better.

Davies has observed that for an English lawyer, the introduction of proportionality is a remarkable new development. UK domestic law seeks to avoid 'politicising' the courts by preventing them from considering the merits of a dispute and the harm caused to the employer. By contrast, the EU law approach involves the courts in a much more politically sensitive analysis involving the application of the proportionality test to industrial disputes.[102] Jonas Malmberg and Tore Sigeman have pointed out that the rulings compromise the freedom of Member States such as Denmark, Finland and Sweden to preserve their favoured 'variety of capitalism', whereby it is almost entirely the responsibility of trade unions to safeguard high levels of wages and conditions of employment.[103] Thus the ECJ's profession of a commitment to a fundamental right to collective action cannot be taken at face value. In practice, it emphatically subordinates this right to its 'right of rights'— the free movement of economic actors.

This conclusion is confirmed by the ECJ's holding in *Zaera* that although Article 3 TEU (previously Article 2 EC) commits the EU to 'the raising of the standard of living', this commitment did not create a directly effective right but was rather an expected consequence of the creation of the common market.[104] In other words, the expectation was that the economic benefits of integration would automatically

---

[99] *Viking* [75]; *Laval* [101].
[100] Davies (2008) 141.
[101] *Ibid*, 141–43.
[102] *Ibid*, 146.
[103] Malmberg and Sigemann (2008) 1117.
[104] Case 126/86 *Zaera v Institutio Nacional de la Seguridad* [1987] ECR 3697.

prompt a rise in living standards. By and large, EU law appears to accept that to require Member States to attempt to raise living standards and improve working conditions beyond the levels that would 'naturally' occur through the operation of the free market would be inconsistent with liberal economic principles.[105] For this reason, measures advanced by the EU in the social field have to be compatible with the liberal order of the EU 'economic constitution'.[106] Indeed it has been argued that 'market making'—creating an efficient, integrated European labour market—rather than correcting market outcomes in pursuit of social justice, has been the primary influence on the shape of EU social policy, such as it is.[107]

From Free Movement to a European Economic Policy

In the early years of its existence, there was a belief that the EEC would concern itself mainly with trade matters whilst other aspects of economic policy would remain the preserve of the Member States. This distinction could not be sustained, and ultimately Member States came to appreciate that the creation of a single internal market would be only one element of an economic policy for the EU. Indeed, by the late 1980s it was becoming clear that a convergence of economic policies was inconceivable without a consensus among the Member States on economic fundamentals.[108] The decade had seen both France and Greece go through periods of socialisation of their economies, and such divergences stood in the way of a common policy. Increasingly, the very existence of national economic policies was seen as presenting an obstacle to the European project itself.

Of course, the idea of transferring control of economic policy—as opposed to 'merely' trade policy—from national to European level connotes a fundamental loss of national sovereignty. For this reason, at the time of the SEA, the UK government was wary of talk of a European economic policy and insisted that the Treaty should continue to refer merely to 'co-operation in economic and monetary policy'.[109] A few years later, during the negotiations on the Maastricht revision of the Treaty, however, any British determination to resist a common economic policy was eclipsed by the overriding priority of securing an opt-out from the single currency.[110] In fact, British ministers accepted the need to ensure that the single currency, even if the UK did not join it, was financially sound; and this would require some collective discipline in the field of economic policy.[111] After all, earlier attempts at monetary union had foundered on the rock of diver-

---

[105] Ball (1996) 325.
[106] Majone (1993) 156.
[107] Barnard (1999) 497.
[108] Wulff (1988) 16.
[109] Thatcher (1995) 555.
[110] See generally Major (1999) ch 12.
[111] Lamont (1999) 118–20.

gent national economic policies.[112] As regards monetary policy, the so-called UK opt-out recognises that Britain would not be obliged to adopt the Euro without a separate decision to do so by its government and Parliament.[113] But exemption from the Euro does not exempt the UK from many of the norms of EU economic policy.

Thus Article 119 TFEU (previously Article 4 EC) commits the Member States to 'the adoption of an economic policy . . . conducted in accordance with an open market economy with free competition'. Article 119 goes on to prioritise as 'guiding principles' for this economic policy 'stable prices, sound public finances and monetary conditions and a sustainable balance of payments'. In the Treaty Chapter on 'Economic Policy', Article 120 reiterates that 'the Member States and the Community shall act in accordance with the principle of an open market economy with free competition, favouring an efficient allocation of resources and in compliance with the principles set up in Article 119.' Article 121 mandates Member States to regard their economic policies as matters of common concern and to coordinate them in the Council.

Article 121 TFEU also establishes a multinational surveillance procedure. This authorises the Council to issue broad guidelines for the economic policies of each of the Member States, as well as for the EU as a whole. If a Member State deviates from these guidelines, the Council may, on a qualified majority following a recommendation from the Commission, make the necessary recommendation to the Member State concerned. It might be thought that this is rather a toothless system, since the Council's recommendations ostensibly have no sanction. If, however, one accepts the wider conception of 'the constitutional' proposed in chapter one above, the system can be conceptualised as a way of making government more accountable to transnational corporations. It could be argued that such public naming-and-shaming would have an adverse effect on markets and investment, and against this backdrop it might be considered a more effective, if informal, sanction.

By contrast, the Treaty lays down formal sanctions for breach of the excessive deficit procedure embodied in Article 126 TFEU (previously Article 104 EC), under which 'Member States shall avoid excessive government deficits.' The Commission is authorised to examine compliance with budgetary discipline and to report to the Council those Member States that fail to keep their government deficits and debts in a specified ratio to their gross domestic product. On the basis of the Commission's report, the Council may decide that an excessive deficit exists. If a Member State persists in failing to put into practice the recommendations of the Council, the Council may apply various sanctions, including inviting the European Investment Bank to reconsider its lending policy towards the Member State concerned, and imposing fines. At present, the UK is sheltered from the sanctions attached to the excessive deficit procedure by its 'opt-out' from the

---

[112] Swann (2000) 204–5.
[113] Protocol on Certain Provisions Relating to the United Kingdom of Great Britain and Northern Ireland.

Euro.[114] It is not, however, protected from scrutiny and censure under the procedure, and in June 2008 the Commission instituted proceedings against the UK for its excessive spending during the credit crunch.

Whilst not wishing the system in its entirety to apply to the UK, the Major government indicated that it had no objection in principle to the excessive deficit procedure, believing that it represented 'good Conservative aims' of keeping down national debt and running low deficits.[115] If the protection afforded by the opt-out were to be lifted, there would therefore be a danger of the country being saddled with such 'good Conservative aims' irrespective of the electorate's choice of government.[116] In any event, the system illustrates how tightly adoption of the Euro is tied to orthodox attitudes to state spending.

Although the UK has not adopted the Euro, a brief discussion will be valuable because the constitutional architecture of economic and monetary union (EMU) may provide insights into the nature of the EU as a whole. Constitutionally, EMU is no dry, technical matter. As Francis Snyder has pointed out, it intimately involves 'essentially political questions, concerning the use of power, the choice of values, and the determination of the basic features of polity, society and identity'.[117] In these respects, the constitutional arrangements are striking in their conformity to neoliberal dogma. The negotiations on the European Central Bank (ECB) and European System of Central Banks (ESCB) were somewhat depoliticised by dint of the fact that the key players were not Europe's political leaders but rather the central bankers themselves. In consequence, the outcome has been a transfer of power that has given central banks a significant degree of autonomy from their former political masters.[118]

Moreover, unlike in Britain, this autonomy is entrenched at the constitutional level through the Treaty. Article 127 TFEU (previously Article 105 EC) gives the ESCB (consisting of the ECB and the national central banks) its normative mandate. Its primary objective in defining monetary policy is to maintain price stability. In so doing it is to act in accordance with the principle of an open market economy with free competition. Article 130 ordains that neither the ECB *nor any national central bank* shall take instructions from any national government or EU institution, a striking inroad into the internal constitutions of the Member States. Article 283 provides that the members of the ECB shall be chosen by common accord of the Member States for non-renewable eight-year terms, again guaranteeing their non-accountability. Commentators have discerned a lack of democratic accountability even compared to other independent central banks.[119] For

---

[114] *Ibid*, Art 5.

[115] Lamont (1999) 134.

[116] To be sure, it might be argued that in the wake of the 2002–03 debacle in which France and Germany flouted the Stability and Growth Pact, the Council changed the relevant Regulations to soften both multilateral surveillance and the excessive deficit procedure. But by the same token, it remains open to the Council to harden its stance again.

[117] Snyder (1999) 471.

[118] Daintith (1997).

[119] De Haan and Gormley (1997).

example, whilst Britain itself has now transferred responsibility for control of interest rates from the Chancellor of the Exchequer to its own central bank, the Bank of England Act 1998 can nonetheless be amended or repealed by Parliament, and even within the terms of the Act, the Treasury can to some extent modify the Bank's monetary policy objectives.[120] By contrast, national governments and parliaments have no direct control over the arrangements entrenched in the EC Treaty.

Public Monopolies and Privatisation

Article 106 TFEU

The constitutional architecture of EMU illustrates one aspect of neoliberal ideology: the 'cult of the expert', leading to the transfer of power from accountable ministers to unaccountable technocrats. EU industrial policy brings in two other key elements of neoliberalism. *Liberalisation* has been the fundamental policy of the EU, and this has brought in its wake an inevitable degree of *privatisation*. To a considerable extent, the degree of privatisation will depend on how much has already taken place at national level. In the British context, where widespread privatisation preceded EU liberalisation, the effect has been a constitutional entrenchment of the privatisation already undertaken.

The main moves towards liberalisation were enacted by the Council and the European Parliament, as the political climate became increasingly favourable to discarding state monopolies. Once again, however, the EU's unelected and unaccountable institutions—the Commission and the European Court of Justice—formed a vanguard. They initiated the liberalisation campaign through the application of the Treaty's competition rules before the legislative programme started in earnest. According to Commissioner van Miert, 'competition law has acted as a "can opener" in prompting liberalisation in many sectors'. He has described the applicability of the competition rules, as proposed by the Commission and supported and confirmed by the ECJ, as having acted as a fuse to the subsequent process of liberalisation.[121]

The relationship between public undertakings and EU competition law goes to the heart of the constitutional power of the EU to control the economic, social and political choices of Member States.[122] Essentially, do the Member States any longer have the power to reserve certain activities to their public sectors?[123] The question of whether Member States retain choice in these matters or whether the Community legal order enshrines a judicially-enforced EU regime is of an intensely constitutional character.[124] Article 106 TFEU (previously Article 86 EC) states:

---

[120] S 12 Bank of England Act 1998.
[121] Van Miert (2000) 1–2.
[122] Edward and Hoskins (1995).
[123] Hancher (1999).
[124] Baquero Cruz (2005) 170.

1. In the case of public undertakings and undertakings to which Member States grant special or exclusive rights, Member States shall neither enact nor maintain in force any measure contrary to the rules enacted in this Treaty, in particular to those rules provided for in Article 18 and Articles 101 to 109.
2. Undertakings entrusted with the operations of services of general economic interest or having the character of a revenue-producing monopoly shall be subject to the rules contained in this Treaty, in particular to the rules on competition, insofar as the application of such rules does not obstruct the performance, in law or in fact, of the particular tasks assigned to them. The development of trade must not be affected to such an extent as would be contrary to the interests of the Union.
3. The Commission shall ensure the application of the provisions of this Article and shall, where necessary, address appropriate directives or decisions to Member States.

The power to interpret Article 106 has enabled the ECJ to determine how far it will maintain the original EEC toleration of Member State choice between public and private ownership, which Article 345 appeared to guarantee. In this respect, the case law shows that the interpretation of Article 106 has moved discernibly in the direction of a presumption of illegality of special or exclusive rights, unless the Member State can show that these are indispensable. In fact, it can be argued that over the last two decades the ECJ has through its jurisprudence encouraged private companies to take advantage of the direct effect of Article 106 in order to undermine, if not destroy, state reservations of exclusivity.[125] The ECJ has held, indeed, that there may be situations in which a public monopoly, simply by exercising its exclusive rights, cannot avoid abusing its dominant position and will therefore fall foul of Article 106.

In *Höfner and Elster v Macrotron GmbH*, 'a case seen as the turning-point in the Court's attitude towards public monopolies',[126] the ECJ held that a Member State violates Article 106 when it grants an exclusive right to carry on an activity that creates a situation in which the undertaking cannot avoid abusing a dominant position in the relevant market.[127] It seemed to weigh heavily with the ECJ that the undertaking (here a public employment agency) was manifestly incapable of satisfying demand prevailing on the relevant market. Yet in the context of public services, it is contestable whether one should equate 'demand' with the operation of market forces, since to do so conflates demand with ability to pay: there may be considerable demand for a public service on the part of those unable to bear its costs. Breaking up a public monopoly by allowing private firms to participate in a certain sphere may in some contexts restructure the market in a way that leads to the development of two-tier provision, whereby prosperous individuals opt for private provision, deserting the public service as a mediocre safety net for the disadvantaged. Destruction of public monopolies may also prevent the state from legitimately sheltering employees from the harshness of market conditions.

---

[125] Szyszczak (2007) 109.
[126] *Ibid*, 122.
[127] Case C-41/90 *Höfner and Elser v Macrotron GmbH* [1991] ECR I-1979, [1993] 4 CMLR 306.

In *Höfner and Elster* both parties to the case were German, and the ECJ underlined that Article 106 does not require the litigant to show an actual effect on trade between Member States, merely a potential effect. It is therefore open for EU corporations to use Article 106(2) in conjunction with Article 102 TFEU (previously Article 82 EC) (prohibiting abuse of a dominant position) against their own state. The ECJ's stance in *Höfner and Elster* was confirmed in *Job Centre*, in which the ECJ held that when an economic sector (here again job placements) was subject to enormous changes as a result of economic and social developments, the public sector may well be unable to satisfy a significant portion of all requests for services, and in such circumstances it is contrary to Article 106 for a Member State to prohibit rival undertakings from operating in the relevant market.[128]

It is readily apparent that the dominant trend in the case law compels the courts (the ECJ or national courts) to adopt a balancing role with regard to Article 106(2).[129] They must weigh the requirement to comply with competition rules against the need for the undertaking to carry out the particular tasks mandated by the state. Yet this may oblige courts to make decisions that are central to the public/private ownership divide. Indeed, the ECJ seems to invite national judiciaries to usurp the role of states by rewriting and restricting the 'particular tasks assigned' to monopoly-holders. Thus in *Corbeau* the ECJ considered whether private sector provision of high-speed mail services would compromise the Belgian postal service:

> The starting point of such an examination must be the premise that the obligation on the part of the undertaking entrusted with that task to perform its services in conditions of economic equilibrium presupposes that it will be possible to offset less profitable sectors against the profitable sectors and hence justifies a restriction of competition from individual undertakings where the economically profitable sectors are concerned.
>
> Indeed, to authorize individual undertakings to compete with the holder of the exclusive rights in the sectors of their choice corresponding to those rights would make it possible for them to concentrate on the economically profitable operations and to offer more advantageous tariffs than those adopted by the holders of the exclusive rights since, unlike the latter, they are not bound for economic reasons to offset losses in the unprofitable sectors against profits in the more profitable sectors.
>
> However, the exclusion of competition is not justified as regards specific services dissociable from the service of general interest which meet special needs of economic operators and which call for certain additional services not offered by the traditional postal service, such as collection from the senders' address, greater speed or reliability of distribution or the possibility of changing the destination in the course of transit, insofar as such specific services, by their nature and the conditions in which they are offered, such as the geographical area in which they are provided, do not compromise the economic equilibrium of the service of general economic interest performed by the holder of the exclusive right.
>
> It is for the national court to consider whether the services at issue in the dispute before it meet those criteria.[130]

---

[128] Case C-55/96 *Job Centre coop arl* [1997] ECR I-7119.
[129] Edward and Hoskins (1995) 166.
[130] Case C-320/91 P *Procureur du Roi v Paul Corbeau* [1993] ECR I-2533 paras 17–20.

The ECJ thereby bestowed upon the national courts the power to decide whether severing specific services from a general service compromises the latter's economic equilibrium. Yet this is not some objective, technical decision that can be isolated from a court's general stance as to whether it should encourage private or public ownership. If, for example, a court were to hold that an 'additional service' should be open to private-sector competition, this would appear permanently to preclude nationalisation of that additional service through its incorporation into the general postal service at any later date. In the ECJ's eyes, such incorporation would illegitimately stifle free trade and competition in services between Member States. Conversely, however, the ECJ made it clear in *Corbeau* that the application of its test can vary over time. As the 'special needs of economic operators' evolve, so the courts must be vigilant of governments that fail to allow the private sector to fill new gaps. The ECJ thus appears to have constructed a one-way street in favour of private-sector service provision: nationalised services are prima facie suspect and must be analysed for their necessity. This is patently not a neutral stance but a pro-private enterprise one.

Commentators have observed that attempts at even-handedness have gone by the board. As Craig and de Búrca have put it, 'agnosticism as to forms of economic organisation has been replaced by a more strident belief in the operation of free markets, unless the State can provide special justification for the privileges accorded.'[131] Gardner has characterised the case law as revolutionary, since it 'has reversed the decades-old presumption—reflected in the very text of Article 86— that public monopolies and privileged undertakings are compatible with the EC Treaty and that Member States are free in principle to determine their preferred system of property ownership'.[132]

Malcolm Ross has suggested that the pro-market ideology of Article 106 jurisprudence could be countered by deploying 'solidarity' as a pre-eminent core value of the EU. But Ross himself has admitted that 'thus far, incoherent appeals to solidarity in the EU context have failed to provide a social paradigm, hence the prevailing dominance of the market when considering public services.'[133] Against this backdrop, it would appear wise not to expect too much from Article 14 TFEU (previously Article 16 EC), which mandates both EU institutions and Member States to take care that services of general economic interest operate on the basis of principles and conditions that enable them to fulfil their missions. This provision has received scant attention in ECJ judgments since its incorporation into the Treaty at Amsterdam in 1997. Moreover, Article 14 explicitly states that the obligation that it contains is 'without prejudice to Article 106'.

---

[131] Craig and de Búrca (2008) 1079.
[132] Gardner (1995) 85.
[133] Ross (2007) 1079.

EU Legislation

The Article 106 jurisprudence was merely a prelude: by eroding the legal legitimacy of public monopolies, the ECJ prepared the ground for a far more comprehensive assault on public ownership. The 1990s witnessed a wave of liberalisation through legislative intervention at EU level.[134] EU legislation has made a far more comprehensive contribution than ECJ jurisprudence to opening up the public monopolies, because legislation is general rather than piecemeal.[135] All the same, we should not discount the vital ideological role played by the ECJ and the Commission in preparing the ground for such legislation.

It might be argued that the liberalisation legislation is the product of democracy, since it has been enacted after due deliberation by the Council and the European Parliament, and so there can be little objection to its legitimacy. True enough, no one forced them to pass this legislation. Yet at the same time, the Council and Parliament do not operate in an ideologically impartial constitutional environment. Since the Treaty entrenches free movement rights, it is far easier for the EU institutions to liberalise sectors than for them to permit Member States to renationalise them. A hypothetical scenario may help to prove the point. Imagine that a national government seeks the introduction of EU legislation to permit Member States to renationalise in their totality their postal, gas and electricity services. The state in question would have to depend on the Commission putting forward such a proposal to the Council and European Parliament. It would also require a convincing legal base in the Treaties—an article authorising the creation of such legislation. The most obvious possibility would be Article 352 TFEU (previously Article 308 EC), which requires the Council to act unanimously.[136] However, any Member State could veto the legislation (perhaps, for example, at the prompting of a transnational corporation providing public services on its territory and in other Member States). Even if legislation were to emerge, it might well be struck down by the EU judiciary for its incompatibility with the fundamental freedom to provide services between Member States.[137] If this were the case, then only Treaty amendment, requiring the common accord of all Member States, could guarantee the constitutionality of such legislation. By contrast, when the EU legislates to liberalise public utilities, this is subject to a lower hurdle, the approval of a qualified majority of the Council.[138]

[134] Geradin and Humpe (2004) 91.

[135] Baquero Cruz (2005) 211.

[136] 'If action by the Union should prove necessary within the framework of the policies defined in the Treaties, to attain one of the objectives set out in the Treaties, and the Treaties have not provided the necessary powers, the Council, acting unanimously on a proposal from the Commission and after obtaining the consent of the European Parliament, shall adopt the appropriate measures.'

[137] It might be argued that in this context the EU Charter of Fundamental Rights 2000 might prevail over the freedom to provide services. In fact, Art 36 of the Charter protects access to services of general interest only 'in accordance with the Treaties'. Art 16 of the Charter protects the freedom to conduct a business in accordance with Union Law.

[138] Art 114 TFEU, previously Art 95 EC.

Article 56 TFEU (previously Article 49 EC) guarantees the free movement of services within the EU, prohibiting restrictions on freedom to provide services between Member States. Article 59 TFEU enables the Council, by qualified majority, and the European Parliament to issue directives in order to liberalise specific services. Initially, since these obligations sat side by side with Article 345 TFEU, which reserves the system of property ownership to the Member States, it seemed uncertain whether freedom to provide services could legitimately be extended to the 'classical' public services—energy, transport, postal services, telecommunications, education and health. The EU institutions might have interpreted Article 345 as preserving an ongoing choice to Member States over whether to preserve their national state-owned monopolies in these fields. However, in the early and mid-1980s the Commission started to press for the opening-up of markets in telecommunications and energy, a stance that some commentators perceived as 'uploading' the British liberal model to the EU and 'downloading' it to the other Member States.[139] The Commission initiated its single-market programme in both telecommunications and energy soon after the Single European Act came into force, with Green Papers on telecommunications in 1987 and energy in 1988.

Although liberalisation appears to be conceptually distinct from privatisation, in practice it is difficult to distinguish them.[140] The Commission itself has readily conceded as much. In its *23rd Competition Report* in 1993, it accepted that the entry of new competitors into a public services market would probably result in some privatisation in the sector, especially if private enterprise could hope to benefit from an open environment.[141] As Wolf Sauter has observed, the increasing constraints on Member States' freedom of action imposed by EU law have de facto promoted not only liberalisation but privatisation, and this has severely reduced the practical meaning of Article 345 TFEU.[142]

The two directives on the internal market in gas and electricity are explicitly premised on a conception of free movement rights linked to services liberalisation, their preambles proclaiming that 'the freedoms which the Treaty guarantees European citizens—free movement of goods, freedom to provide services and freedom of establishment—are only possible in a fully open market, which enables all consumers freely to choose their suppliers and all suppliers freely to deliver to their customers.'[143] The directives envisage 'the gradual and controlled liberalisation of the market'. They identify as the prime obstacle to liberalisation the different degrees of market opening between the Member States. Accordingly, they commit the Member States to opening up network access to third parties on non-

---

[139] Bartle (2005) 31–32.
[140] *Ibid*, 63.
[141] Commission of the European Communities (1994).
[142] Sauter (1998) 128.
[143] Directive 2003/55/EC of the European Parliament and of the Council of 28 June 2003 concerning common rules for the internal market in natural gas and repealing Directive 98/30/EC, OJ L 176, 15.7.2003, p 57, recital (4); Directive 2003/54/EC of the European Parliament and of the Council of 26 June 2003 concerning common rules for the internal market in electricity and repealing Directive 96/92/EC, OJ L176, 15.7.2003, p 37, recital (4).

discriminatory and fairly priced terms. As regards both gas and electricity, they oblige Member States to designate systems operators to take responsibility for the systems of transmission, distribution and so on. Third parties are then to be given access to these systems on the basis of published tariffs.[144]

The case of postal services provides a good example of what is meant by 'gradual and controlled' liberalisation. Initially, the Postal Services Directive 1997 represented a compromise between Member States that had already undertaken a degree of liberalisation and those that were anxious to protect their own postal operators.[145] To this end it authorised liberalisation whilst at the same time permitting Member States to retain a 'reserved sector' of activity for their public postal operators. Yet at the same time it created a dynamic in favour of an ever greater erosion of the postal monopoly.[146] Thus Member States were obliged to provide a 'universal service', a basic service for domestic correspondence below a certain weight and at a standard speed.[147] Some or all of this universal service could be provided by the public postal operator ('the reserved sector'). Everything else ('non-reserved services') had to be opened to commercial competition.[148] For good measure, new services—those prompted by technological development— could not be 'reserved'.[149]

To achieve the desired 'gradual and controlled' liberalisation, the Council and European Parliament would progressively erode the 'reserved sector' (by amending its weight and price criteria), thereby ensuring greater market opening.[150] To this end, the directive committed the Council and European Parliament to a deadline by which they had to consider further liberalisation.[151] Sure enough, in 2002 they legislated again to reduce the permissible scope of the 'reserved services'.[152] They trimmed down the market share of the public postal operators by reducing the weight limit of the letter services that could be reserved. In 2008 the Council and European Parliament legislated to do away with the reserved area altogether, proclaiming the need for a 'complete market opening' in which 'the reserved area should no longer be the preferred solution for the financing of the universal service.'[153] Thus Article 7 provides that 'Member States shall not grant or maintain in force exclusive or special rights for the establishment and provision of postal services.' Any element of universal service provision must now be provided on the basis of competitive tendering.

[144] Art 18, Directive 2003/55/EC; Art 20, Directive 2003/54/EC.
[145] Directive 97/67/EC.
[146] Geradin and Humpte (2004) 119.
[147] Art 7, Directive 97/67/EC.
[148] Arts 9–10, Directive 97/67/EC.
[149] Geradin and Humpte (2004) 100.
[150] *Ibid*, 101.
[151] Art 7(3), Directive 97/67/EC.
[152] Directive 2002/39/EC of the European Parliament and of the Council of 10 June 2002 amending Directive 97/67/EC with regard to the further opening to competition of Community postal services. OJ L 175, 5.7.2002, p 21.
[153] Directive 2008/6/EC of the European Parliament and the Council of 20 February 2008 amending Directive 97/67/EC with regard to the full accomplishment of the internal market of Community postal services OJ L 52/4 27.2.2008.

It is intriguing to observe the way in which EU secondary legislation expands the interpretation of the freedoms enshrined in EU primary legislation, the Treaties. One can discern a process whereby secondary legislation upgrades and ratchets up the Treaty rights of freedom of establishment and freedom to provide services. Once the political institutions have legislated, entrepreneurs can then invoke their expanded Treaty rights in order to prevent their exclusion from the relevant markets. Yet it is seemingly not open to the political institutions to do the opposite. Having enlarged the scope of the free movement rights through secondary legislation, it would seem unlikely that they could validly use secondary legislation to contract the scope of these rights once again, to the point of permitting Member States to reintroduce state-owned monopolies. The ECJ would be unlikely to countenance such a diminution of the Treaty's fundamental freedoms. It would appear that nothing short of Treaty amendment could authorise this. In this way, transnational provision acts as the Trojan horse for a constitutionalisation of private enterprise.[154]

Some have praised the EU for imposing public service obligations (the concept of the 'universal service') on liberalised utilities, welcoming this as a laudable switch from a harsh, pro-competition stance to a more progressive, public-service-orientated ethos. Yet the only reason for the EU's imposition of public service obligations is liberalisation itself. As Sauter has observed

> Arguably, the concept of universal telecommunications service might today be practically meaningless if it had not been for liberalization. Vice versa, defining and implementing universal services has been the key to resolving an apparent stalemate on telecommunications liberalization in the Community.[155]

Had Member States retained their freedom of choice to maintain provision of public services through publicly owned monopolies, there would have been no call for the EU to bother with public service obligations. After all, the raison d'être of public-sector monopolies was to provide a public service, and the extent to which they did so was largely a matter of democratic accountability. By contrast, universal service obligations were arguably the necessary accompaniment to privatisation. Once the EU was well on the way to realising the single market, it needed bases for self-legitimisation other than free trade alone.[156] More urgently, the Commission needed to win over to the cause of liberalisation those Member States with strong traditions of public service, which were hostile to the forward march of competition.[157] The Commission's solution was to create the concept of the

---

[154] See likewise Case C-372/04 *R (Watts) v Bedford Primary Care Trust* [2006] ECR I-4325, in which the ECJ interpreted Art 56 TFEU on freedom to provide services as meaning that a British patient could be entitled to reimbursement from the NHS for the difference between the cost of treatment in an NHS hospital and the cost of treatment in another Member State along with reimbursement of the ancillary costs associated with cross-border movement. This decision disadvantages those patients who cannot afford the up-front costs of such movement.

[155] Sauter (1998) 118.

[156] Freedland (1998) 14

[157] Geradin (2000a) 195.

'universal service', which it would deploy to minimise opposition to liberalisation. It is therefore misconceived to present public service obligations as some change of heart in favour of social justice or public service.

Once in force, the liberalisation directives fell to be interpreted by the ECJ. Taking its cue from *Höfner and Elsner* and *Corbeau*, the ECJ has tended to construe the directives in such a way as to maximise the opening-up of markets. For instance, in *Deutsche Post* the ECJ interpreted Article 12(5) of Directive 97/67/EC (as amended by Directive 2002/39/EC) as meaning that national post services must help their competitors to break into the market for pre-sorting of mail by extending to them the special tariffs normally granted to business customers who deposit pre-sorted mail at sorting offices.[158] ECJ interpretation has therefore served to reinforce 'the relentless march of the legislation towards full competition'.[159]

Public Procurement

One of the Commission's aims in creating the single market was to open up public procurement to ensure that the purchasing activities of public-sector bodies would be open to cross-border competition comparable to that of the private sector. In the past, public procurement has been a valuable tool of economic intervention. Governments have deployed their procurement powers for a variety of social purposes: to stimulate economic activity; to protect national industry against foreign competition; to improve the competitiveness of certain industrial sectors; to remedy regional disparities; and to help to realise particular social policy goals.[160] To this end, in 2004, the UK Labour Party struck a deal with its affiliated trade unions (the Warwick Agreement) with the aim of enlisting their support for the 2005 general election. The policies enshrined in the Warwick Agreement included a commitment to 'promote a public procurement programme which encourages contracts to be given to UK firms for UK workers *within EU law*'.[161] Such a policy, however, would appear to be a contradiction in terms. In *Telaustria*, the ECJ ruled that irrespective of whether instances of public procurement fall within the scope of EU legislation, contracting entities are bound to comply with the fundamental rules of the Treaty, in particular the principle of non-discrimination on grounds of nationality. It is therefore the duty of national courts to review the impartiality of procurement procedures. The non-discrimination principle also obliges public authorities to ensure a sufficient degree of advertising to enable the market to be

---

[158] Joined Cases C-287/06 to C-292/06 *Deutsche Post AG, Magdeburger Dienstleistungs- und Verwaltungs GmbH (MDG), Marketing Service Magdeburg GmbH, Vedat Deniz v Bundesrepublik Deutschland* [2008] ECR I-1243.

[159] Baquero Cruz (2005) 206.

[160] McCrudden (2007) ch 2.

[161] Emphasis added.

opened up to competition from providers in other Member States.[162] The fact that the ECJ derives these obligations from 'fundamental rules of the Treaty' itself—and not merely from secondary legislation—surely constitutes a profound entrenchment of public procurement policy.[163]

For good measure, in 2004 the European Parliament and Council issued two major directives to govern procurement procedures in the EU.[164] These specify that only two criteria for the award of contracts are lawful. The first—'lowest price only'—is straightforward. The second is 'most economically advantageous tender'. This obliges the contracting authority to specify various factors linked to the subject matter of the contract in question, such as delivery or completion date, running costs, cost-effectiveness, quality, aesthetic and functional characteristics, environmental characteristics, technical merit and so on. The application of either criteria would plainly rule out a policy based on supporting British industry.

Christopher McCrudden in his book *Buying Social Justice* has argued that EU law can nonetheless be interpreted in such a way as to permit national authorities to use public procurement to promote 'status-equality'.[165] By this, he means the association between a limited number of particular characteristics, such as race and gender, and the discrimination suffered by those who have or who are perceived to have those characteristics. He concedes that this vision of equality is 'less concerned with the importance of the good being allocated, and more concerned with the use of actual or imputed identity in a wide range of situations'.[166] In McCrudden's scheme of things, the ECJ's prohibition on nationality discrimination reflects a general principle of rationality whereby 'prized public goods' are distributed without arbitrary distinction, whereas measures to prevent 'status-harms' arising from discriminations on particular grounds are lawful. Yet the normative merit of this limited vision of equality is contestable. In privileging the elimination of discriminations based on status such as gender and race, it deprioritises harms based on the more general characteristics of class, income and wealth, which are no doubt better tackled by UK governments having the freedom to use public procurement in the general interests of British employees. If ideas of equality are contestable, then the entrenchment in the Treaties of a single conception of equality is of questionable legitimacy. Disagreements over the most desirable notion of equality have after all long been the essence of inter-party (and intra-party) differences. In a democracy, such questions, rather than being authoritatively settled by constitutional entrenchment, should remain open to political contestation.

---

[162] Case C-324/98 *Telaustria Verlags GmbH and Telefonadress GmbH v Telekom Austria AG* [2000] ECR I-10745.

[163] Arrowsmith (2004) 1278.

[164] Directive 2004/18/EC of the European Parliament and of the Council of 31 March 2004 on the coordination of procedures for the award of public works contracts, public supply contracts and public service contracts OJ 2004, L 134/114 and Directive 2004/17/EC of the European Parliament and the Council of 31 March 2004 coordinating the procurement procedures of entities operating in the water, energy, transport and postal services sectors OJ 2004, L 134/1.

[165] McCrudden (2007) ch 16.

[166] *Ibid*, 514.

State Aid

Since 1957 the Treaty has sought to control subsidies from Member States to industry. Yet EU state aid law has been a comparative latecomer in terms of legal development, shadowing perhaps the rise of neoliberalism. Only in the last two decades has it emerged from a legal backwater to form a strong system of enforcement driven by the Commission.[167] It is the Commission that enforces the regime, generates jurisprudence and produces legislation. In all these spheres it has become increasingly active. The system of the Treaty thereby entrusts the Commission with the power to balance the interests of the market against those of competing social concerns, inviting it to create a constitutional hierarchy of EU values.[168] The Commission is the least accountable of the three 'political' institutions and no doubt deliberately so: its function (like that of the EU judiciary) is to pursue the EU's goals unencumbered by too much popular pressure. The institutional structure of the state aid regime thereby conforms to neoliberal ideals of sheltering economic decision-making from the vagaries of democratic politics. Commentators tend to agonise over whether the Commission strikes the 'right balance' in its state aid jurisprudence, but the more basic question is whether an unaccountable body should be charged with this role in the first place. It could be argued that there is no such thing as a 'right' balance between market liberalism and state intervention, in the sense that it is not a technical question that can elicit a right or wrong answer. Rather, different people legitimately hold different views on the appropriate extent of state intervention, according to the kind of society they wish to see emerge. The question, indeed, goes to the heart of the divide between Right and Left in democratic, contestable politics. Substituting decision-making by the Commission for this disagreement assumes that a technocratic institution can divine some kind of rational consensus that can replace the antagonism of democracy.[169]

Supranational control of state aid has the potential to close off two democratic possibilities. First, state subsidies have long been seen as a key tool of social democratic economic policy. Thus they have generally formed an important part of the economic proposals of the UK Labour Party. In Labour's 1945 manifesto, for instance, the Party pledged to give 'state help in any necessary form to get our export trade on its feet . . . but state help on conditions—conditions that industry is efficient and go-ahead'. In 1964 Labour promised 'help for small exporters, particularly on a group basis' as part of an export-led national plan. In 1966 the Party promised a new system of investment incentives to provide cash grants to expanding firms, especially in the manufacturing sector. In 1982, the Party committed itself to an array of employment subsidies to companies in order to help remedy the mass unemployment of the era. According to Labour, 'the advantage of such

---

[167] For example, in 2006, 921 new cases were registered with the Commission, a 36% increase on 2005.

[168] Ross (1995).

[169] Mouffe (1996).

subsidies is that they are quick-acting, they can be targeted precisely on those groups in the population in greatest need, and conditions can be attached to their use.'[170] It would therefore appear that the distribution of state aid was considered an indispensable tool of Labour economic policy. As Conor Quigley noted, the dividing-line between state aid and general economic policy is obscure.[171]

Secondly, and less obviously, state aid law tilts the constitutional playing field in favour of private enterprise. Paradoxically, this has been accomplished by means of Article 345 TFEU, the very article that supposedly guarantees respect for the systems of property ownership in the Member States. The Commission and ECJ have subtly manipulated Article 345, by somehow extracting from it the 'principle' that public and private sectors must be accorded the same treatment in the context of the competition rules.[172] Thus the Commission, when examining a particular operation under the rules on state aid, must neither prejudice nor favour public undertakings. Aid granted to public undertakings must therefore be subject to the same rules applying to all forms of aid granted by the Member States.[173] Yet the effect of non-discriminatory treatment is to deprive public ownership of its potential for distinctiveness and of its useful purpose.

As the ECJ itself acknowledged in *France, Italy and United Kingdom v Commission (Transparency Directive)*, there is an intrinsic difference between public and private sectors: whilst private undertakings decide their industrial and commercial strategies by reference to profitability, the public sector's decision-making may be determined by objectives of public interest.[174] But this difference in purpose makes the very nature of public ownership different from private ownership. Governments do not nationalise companies merely to effect a change in the formal identity of the owner. They do so in order to furnish investment that private actors would not provide, as well as sometimes to shelter employees and consumers from market forces. Forcing public ownership into the mould of the private sector prejudices the system of property ownership in the Member States—the very thing that Article 345 seeks to prohibit. Thus EU law discriminates against public ownership by treating public and private ownership alike when they are essentially different. In this way, the jurisprudence of the Commission and ECJ has illegitimately manipulated the idea of 'property ownership' and arguably impoverished it. The question of whether society's conception of 'property ownership' should preclude the right for the state to manage property in ways other than those that conform to free market orthodoxy is a contestable one. As Charles Lipson has demonstrated, the very meaning of 'property' is not a settled matter: rather, it is socially constructed and therefore subject to constant revision as social relations and expectations change.[175]

---

[170] Labour Party (1982) 27.
[171] Quigley (1988) 252–53.
[172] Commission of the European Communities (1984a) para 5.
[173] *Ibid*, para 1; Hancher, Ottervanger and Slot (2006) 195.
[174] Cases 188–90/80 [1982] ECR 2545.
[175] Lipson (1985) 3.

The exposure of the public sector to EU state aid law also has a more subtle ideological impact. Rather than conceptualising the public sector as part of the state (as would be the case, say, with the armed forces), state aid law *detaches* the public sector from the state, and re-attaches it to an ostensibly autonomous market. By creating distance between the state and its industrial activities, whilst subjecting the latter to the rules of the free market, this conceptualisation conforms to ideas of a minimalist state.

Article 107 TFEU (previously Article 87 EC) does not prohibit state aid outright but only insofar as it is 'incompatible with the internal market', in that it distorts (or threatens to distort) competition. Article 107 goes on to delineate certain types of aid that shall or may nonetheless be regarded as lawful. The state aids that are per se lawful are not of great relevance to our present analysis and need not detain us.[176] More important for our purposes are the areas in which state aid *may* be considered compatible with the internal market. These include 'aid to promote the economic development of areas where the standard of living is abnormally low or where there is serious underemployment' (Article 107(3)(a)); 'aid to promote the execution of an important project of common European interest or to remedy a serious disturbance in the economy of a Member State' (Article 107(3)(b)); and 'aid to facilitate the development of certain economic activities or of certain economic areas, where such aid does not adversely affect trading conditions to an extent contrary to the common interest' (Article 107(3)(c)). The power to decide whether state aids offered on these grounds are lawful lies exclusively with the Commission (Article 108). The Commission's power is reinforced by two factors. The first is that the EU judiciary allows the Commission a wide margin of appreciation in this field, so it will normally uphold Commission decisions.[177] The second relates to the way in which the system deploys national courts. It is not open to national courts to determine whether the state aid can be justified on the discretionary grounds, since to do so would infringe the Commission's monopoly on decision-making.[178] Conversely, however, national courts must play their part in ensuring respect for the Commission's position. They must enforce both the duty to notify the Commission of proposed aids and the prohibition on prior implementation of planned aids. They must also ensure that unlawful aids are repaid to the state.

Quite apart from its discretionary power over individual state aid decisions, the Commission enacts legislation on state aids in order to guide national policymaking. This has the merits of reducing caseload and obviating the need for formal

---

[176] Art 107(2) TFEU permits aid having a social character that is granted to individual consumers; aid to make good natural disasters and exceptional occurrences; and aid required for the reunification of Germany.

[177] See, eg, Case C-142/87 *Belgium v Commission (Tubemeuse)* [1990] ECR I-959, para 56.

[178] See Case C-39/94 *Syndicat français de l'Express International (SFEI) and Others v La Poste and Others* [1996] ECR I-3547. By contrast, national courts have the right to apply and interpret Art 101 TFEU (concerted practices) and Art 102 TFEU (abuse of a dominant position), subject to the preliminary reference procedure. Art 15(2) of Regulation 1/2003 requires Member States to forward to the Commission a copy of any written judgment issued by national courts deciding on the application of these two Articles.

Council legislation.[179] Yet Commission legislation reduces Member States' room for manoeuvre. When, as is frequently the case, the Commission legislates in the form of regulations (as opposed to, say, guidelines), the doctrine of the supremacy of EU law applies with full force, just as it would in the case of regulations made by the Council and European Parliament.

Defining State Aid: Article 107(1) TFEU

The Commission's jurisprudence on the definition of state aid provides a good illustration of its homogenisation of public and private sectors. In 1993 the Commission declared that it would be seeking a 'reinforced application of policy towards state aids', which would focus upon the applicability of state aid rules to the public sector, an aspect previously neglected. To this end, the Commission declared that whenever a state provided financing to a public undertaking in circumstances that would not be acceptable to an investor operating under normal market conditions, this would be deemed to constitute state aid.[180] This has become known as the 'market economy investor principle', and it militates in favour of a wide interpretation of state aids, bringing a larger proportion of cases within the scope of the Commission's discretionary power under Article 107(3).

The principle applies not only to capital injections but to all other forms of public funding, and it covers aid to profitable public undertakings as well as loss-making ones.[181] In 1984 the Commission announced that the acquisition of shareholdings by public authorities in private companies would also normally amount to state aid. Thus when a public authority injects capital by acquiring a holding in a company, and it is not merely providing equity capital under normal market conditions, the case must be assessed under the state aid rules. This position was endorsed by the ECJ in *Intermills v Commission*.[182] Conversely, straightforward partial or total acquisition of a holding in the capital of an existing company, without any injection of fresh capital, does not constitute state aid, nor does the contribution of fresh capital in circumstances that would be acceptable to a private investor operating under normal market economy conditions.[183]

Against this backdrop the Commission has legislated, in the face of national resistance, to compel Member States to be transparent in their funding of public undertakings.[184] The Commission maintains that it must be in a position to judge whether a transaction between a Member State and a public undertaking is a normal commercial transaction or whether there are elements of aid. Thus governments put themselves wholly beyond reproach only if they act like private

---

[179] Craig and de Búrca (2008) 1086.
[180] Commission of the European Communities (1993).
[181] *Ibid.*
[182] Case 323/82 *Intermills SA v Commission* [1984] ECR 3809.
[183] Commission of the European Communities (1984b).
[184] Joined cases 188 to 190/80 *France, Italy and United Kingdom v Commission (Transparency Directive)* [1982] ECR 2545.

investors. Yet, as Leigh Hancher, Tom Ottervanger and Piet Jan Slot have observed, states will inevitably be in a different position from private investors. They give the example of very large governmental investments, for instance on infrastructure, in which there is often no private investor that could have taken the place of the government.[185]

The trend towards contracting out of public service obligations has led the ECJ to expand the conception of state aid even further. In *Altmark* it held that there is state aid whenever there is over-compensation for the provision of a service relative to the costs that an efficient company would have incurred. More specifically, the ECJ held that there was no state aid if four conditions were met.[186] First, the public service obligation must be clearly defined. Second, the parameters for the compensation must be objective, transparent and established in advance. Third, the compensation should not exceed costs plus a reasonable profit. And finally, the compensation must be determined either through public procurement, or if no public tender has taken place, the firm should be compensated on the basis of the costs of a typical 'well-run' firm. Since the *Altmark* criteria apply as much to the public as to the private sector, the message of the judgment would appear to be, once again, that public sector provision is acceptable so long as it is managed as if it were private sector. Indeed, as Tony Prosser has observed, *Altmark* will in all likelihood lead Member States to increase their use of competitive tendering for public services, in view of the uncertainty over whether the Commission will deem payments commensurate with the costs of an efficient and well-run company.[187] Thus once again the consequence is to promote private sector provision. Overall, therefore, the choice of template to define state aids reflects the more general preference for private sector provision as the dominant economic paradigm.

Justifying State Aid: Article 107(3) TFEU

The Commission's power over the Article 107(3) derogations gives it a startlingly wide discretion. First, the Commission determines the legitimacy of Member States' objectives in granting aid. It has ruled that state aid, if it is to be declared compatible with the Treaty, must fulfil clearly defined objectives of the common interest.[188] Secondly, the Commission discerns the existence of and therefore essentially defines the essential element of 'market failure'. Thirdly, the Commission balances the negative effects of aid on competition with its positive effects in terms of common interest.[189]

---

[185] Hancher, Ottervanger and Slot (2006) 74.
[186] Case C-280/00 *Altmark Trans GmbH and Regierungspräsidium Magedeburg v Nahverkehrsgesellschaft Altmark GmbH* [2003] ECR I-7747.
[187] Prosser (2005)
[188] Commission of the European Communities (2005) 1.1.10.
[189] *Ibid,* 1.1.11.

The Commission's *State Aid Action Plan 2005–2009* spells out its policy when applying the discretionary derogations under Article 107(3): 'less and better targeted state aid'. It appears to view legitimate state aid as a means of meeting the needs of the business community, in terms of research and development, innovation and risk capital. In its *Report on Competition Policy 2006*, the Commission's stated aim was to channel an ever larger share of total state aid budgets into research, development and innovation, whilst approving rescue and restructuring aid only if strict conditions were satisfied.[190] According to the *State Aid Action Plan*, the object of supranational regulation is to create a level playing field between all undertakings active in the European single market.[191] Thus Member States cannot be permitted to give selective advantages to domestic firms at the cost of overall European competitiveness. At the same time, however, the Commission recognises that there can be market failures, and state aid can help to correct these failures. State aid can also help promote social and regional cohesion and sustainable development. The Commission therefore permits state aid that fulfils 'clearly defined objectives of common interest'.[192] However, the *Action Plan* does not explain how this 'common interest' is to be determined, nor does it reveal how the Commission performs its balancing exercise between market-failure-correcting gains in one Member State and adverse effects in other Member States.[193] The bottom line appears to be that governments are welcome to *service* the market, provided they do not *distort* it.

The Commission had adopted a 'refined economic approach' to its decision-making. Essentially this means that the Commission accepts that when markets do not achieve economic efficiency, intervention is appropriate to correct market failures. It is not enough, however, for a Member State to demonstrate the existence of market failure: it must also show that other, less distortive measures could not remedy that failure. The Member State must show that state aid is the appropriate policy tool and that such aid will be designed so that it effectively solves the market failure by creating an incentive effect and being proportionate. To this end, the Commission uses a range of numerical indicators, which lay down the maximum permissible 'aid intensity' (the value of the aid as a percentage of the total project cost) for each type of aid (eg, regional aid; small and medium enterprise aid; aid for research development and innovation, etc).[194] Thus the Commission's 'economic analysis' involves an examination of the relevant sector, weighing up a range of considerations:

> In general, the positive impact of an aid depends on: i) how accurately the accepted objective of common interest (whether social, regional, economic or cultural) has been identified; ii) whether state aid is an appropriate instrument for dealing with the prob-

[190] Commission of the European Communities (2006), para 20. Cf para 30.
[191] Commission of the European Communities (2005) 3.
[192] *Ibid*, 4.
[193] Hancher, Ottervanger and Slot (2006) 23
[194] Commission of the European Communities (2007b); Commission of the European Communities (2008).

lem as opposed to other policy instruments; and iii) whether the aid creates the needed incentives and is proportionate. On the other hand, the level of distortion created by an aid generally depends on i) the procedure for selected beneficiaries and the conditions attached to the aid; ii) the characteristics of the market and of the beneficiary; and iii) the amount and type of aid. For example, restructuring aid or investment aid to large companies should be carefully monitored to clearly address an objective of common interest, since the impact of such measures on competition and trade will normally be significant.[195]

On the basis of such an analysis, 'the Commission has now established a clear general framework, with a methodology enshrined in the so-called "balancing test".'[196] In 2008, the Commission encapsulated its approach into a general block exemption regulation.[197]

However, the technocratic vocabulary of the 'refined economic approach' ought not to obscure the fact that 'balancing' cannot be a value-free exercise. Rather, it requires the allocation of an a priori weight to the importance of an undistorted free market on the one hand and the interests of social welfare on the other. On this score, the Commission appears to start from the assumption that market failure is exceptional, and market success is the rule. Hence it perceives the Treaty as permitting state aid only 'in exceptional circumstances'.[198] In its *State Aid Action Plan*, the Commission explained that the Treaty prohibition on state aid is part of a competition policy based upon 'the idea that a market-based economy provides the best guarantee for raising living conditions in the EU to the benefit of citizens'.[199] Yet the optimum *degree* of the free market element required to ensure optimum living conditions is contestable, depending in part on what level of social equality is perceived as desirable. Whilst the Commission lays great store by 'the free interplay of market forces',[200] it is likewise contestable whether markets optimise welfare. For instance, the adoption of a market-based economy tends to widen the gap between the better-off and the poor, the acceptability of which will vary between those of differing political views. As Prosser has observed, 'a market failure approach is too narrow: it treats the primary value as that of competitive markets, to which other values are secondary and only come into play as a means of mopping up residual problems which the market cannot solve.'[201]

However, an even more fundamental objection to EU arrangements relates to democracy: the relative merits of free-market competition as against governmental intervention ought to be the stuff of routine political debate and periodic elections. In the field of state aids, as elsewhere, the EU system purports to elevate

---

[195] Commission of the European Communities (2005) para 20.
[196] Commission of the European Communities (2007a) para 100.
[197] Commission Regulation (EC) No 800/2008 of 6 August 2008, declaring certain categories of aid compatible with the common market in application of Arts 87 and 88 of the Treaty, OJ 9.8.2008, L 214/3.
[198] Commission of the European Communities (2007b) 2.
[199] Commission of the European Communities (2005) 1.1.6.
[200] Case 323/82 *SA Intermills v Commission* [1984] ECR 3809, para 39.
[201] Prosser (2005) 244.

such eminently contestable matters above politics by entrusting them to an unaccountable agency.

State Aid and the Credit Crunch

In 2009 the European Commission decided that in view of the financial crisis, it was important to unblock bank lending to companies and to encourage companies to continue investing. The Commission therefore resolved to relax its policy on state aid in several important respects.[202] It did so in the form of 'temporary adaptations of existing rules'. Accordingly, it relaxed its de minimis regulation, permitted subsidised loan guarantees in certain circumstances, allowed certain aid in the form of subsidised interested rates, facilitated the grant of aid for the production of environmentally friendly products and so on. A charitable interpretation of the Commission's leniency might regard the Commission as responding to the democratic pressures of the national governments and the needs of their citizens. However, the Commission's policy shift, which it repeatedly emphasised was only a temporary expedient at a time of crisis, is also wholly compatible with the dominant form of neoliberalism—the political project to do whatever is necessary to restore the power of an economic elite, even if to do so means going against classical neoliberal principles.[203] The bailouts of the credit crunch era were needed in order to maintain the economic elite in the wake of its calamitous 'herding' in favour of investment in the subprime mortgage market, even at the cost of compromising 'free market fundamentalism', which would insist on companies paying the price for their business mistakes. Toleration of lavish state aid was the price worth paying in order to avoid the greater evil of nationalisation and governmental control of the financial sector.

Neoliberalism and the Open Method of Co-ordination

Much of this chapter has been devoted to the substance of EU law, its tendency towards neoliberalism and the way in which this restricts democracy in a manner that seems incompatible with British constitutional traditions. A few brief remarks need to be made about the *process* by which these rules came about. The 'Classic Community Method' of lawmaking, involving legislation by the Council and European Parliament on proposals from the Commission and subject to the jurisdiction of the ECJ, is clearly alive and well: ultimately, most neoliberal measures have been embodied in legislation of this type. This familiar method in itself reduces accountability, since, as Harlow notes, 'first, an issue of internal, domes-

---

[202] Commission of the European Communites (2009).
[203] Harvey (2005) 19.

tic politics is moved into the less accountable area of foreign policy; secondly, accountability may be diminished because the rambling and inchoate structures of the EU lend themselves . . . to unaccountable government.'[204]

Yet whatever the shortcomings of the Classic Community Method, there has in any event been a shift in the last twenty years 'away from the monopoly of traditional politico-legal institutions' in favour of more flexible forms of governance.[205] We have already considered one aspect of this 'new governance'—the delegation of product standards to private organisations. Another element is the 'Open Method of Co-ordination' (OMC), which takes place between Member States. OMC involves experimental techniques of cooperation and convergence to kick-start the integration process. Hailed by the EU as a new approach to problem-solving, OMC embraces iteration, mutual cooperation, standard-setting, mutual learning and enforcement through peer pressure. Ultimately, much of the 'soft law' generated by OMC has eventually been concretised into 'hard-law' measures using the Classic Community Method. As David Trubek, Patrick Cottrell and Mark Nance have observed, 'soft law sets the stage for hard law, establishing non-binding standards that can eventually harden into rules.'[206]

No attempt will be made here to review the general merits or demerits of OMC. There is a vast literature on the subject. What needs to be noted, however, is the way in which the use of OMC reinforces the neoliberalism that has become increasingly embedded in EU law. First, it is generally accepted that OMC offers a way of extending the reach of EU law into 'the sacred domain of sensitive areas of policymaking', thereby evading conventional battle-lines over questions of competence;[207] it has been used, for example, to 'steer Member States towards ideas of convergence on economic policies, conventionally seen as unsuitable, unthinkable and untouchable by EC lawmaking processes'.[208] Yet this low-profile 'competence creep' can be used to avoid debates in the Member States as to whether further integration is desired. Moreover, it may be used by governments to bypass national representative assemblies and thereby insulate themselves from democratic pressures on matters traditionally the preserve of the Member States. It creates an 'embeddedness' of the EU within the British governing system in which conventional boundaries between 'the domestic' and 'the European' are losing their meaning.[209]

Secondly, the use of peer pressure as a means of enforcement stands on its head the normal democratic practice whereby governments are accountable to their electorates for their own choice of policy.[210] Instead, policy is determined collectively by the executives of the Member States, who then become accountable to the EU institutions and to each other for its implementation. Against the backdrop of

---

[204] Harlow (2002) 80.
[205] De Búrca and Scott (2006) 2.
[206] Trubek, Cottrell and Nance (2006) 89.
[207] Szyszczak (2006).
[208] *Ibid*, 90.
[209] Moran (2003) 164.
[210] Cf Sabel and Simon (2006) 400.

insulation from the voting public, peer pressure can be deployed to enforce neoliberal measures, such as the use of the 'State Aid Scoreboard' by which states that grant illegitimate aid to their domestic industries are named and shamed.

Thirdly, despite talk of involving citizens, OMC gained acceptance and became institutionalised because it was endorsed by the political elites of Europe, and the practical reality appears to be of an elite, opaque and unpublicised form of governance in which technocratic participants such as civil servants and experts loom large, whilst parliaments (European and national) are sidelined. Finally, it appears that the most powerful OMC is that dealing with economic policy and that its domination marginalises other OMCs dealing with such matters as social exclusion and pensions.[211] This would appear to reflect neoliberal priorities of the market prevailing over the social.

Conclusion

From the very foundation of the EEC—and despite the reassuring tones of Article 345 TFEU—the logic of the common market has appeared to rule out a general socialisation of the economies of its Member States. At the same time, however, the founding states (impatient for integration and not wanting to get bogged down in disagreement) left unresolved the precise balance between market forces and permissible state intervention. It was inevitable, however, that as European integration deepened, the 'fallacy of ideological neutrality' could no longer be maintained.[212] In the 1980s and 1990s, the growth of a neoliberal consensus among Europe's leaders and their willingness to embrace the constitutional demands of transnational corporations meant that the European project developed along neoliberal lines. By sidelining Article 345 and altering the meaning of 'property ownership', EU law demarcated a constitutional hierarchy of values that gave pride of place to private enterprise and the operation of market forces.[213]

These values have, in very significant fields, taken the place of democratic rule in the Member States.[214] They form a normative package that no national general election can unpick and is heavily entrenched within the European construct itself, both culturally (because the 'fundamental freedoms' have for so long been considered the very core of the European project) and in terms of the crude constitutional mechanics whereby the approval of all Member States is required for Treaty amendment. Sadly, therefore, EU economic policymaking does not replace national democratic deliberation with European democratic deliberation. Rather, it embodies a considerable predestination of economic politics by dint of consti-

---

[211] De Búrca (2003) 831.
[212] Weiler (1999a) 90.
[213] Ross (1995) 80.
[214] Armstrong and Bulmer (1998) 315.

tutional entrenchment. Nor is the EU likely to undergo the transformation that would make its own structures conform to democratic principles. The result has been a constitutionalism that seeks to separate economic policy from political accountability and makes governments more responsive to market forces and less responsive to democratic processes.[215]

In recent years, some commentators have contended that the EU is beginning to strike a more reasonable balance between the market and a more pro-public service ethos.[216] However, any such trend ought not to be exaggerated. Liberalisation remains the fundamental basis of the EU economic settlement, and liberalisation is inseparable from privatisation, particularly in the context of Britain, where a national programme of privatisation preceded the completion of the European single market. Moreover, there is a far more fundamental objection to the notion that the EU should be applauded for having embodied some sort of 'reasonable balance' between market liberalism and social welfare. Those who advance this argument make the assumption, whether consciously or unconsciously, that the striking of such a balance constitutes a satisfactory replacement for democracy. Yet reasonable people differ as to what that balance should be. The entrenchment as supreme law of *any* economic and social balance—be it faultlessly social democratic, uncompromisingly free market or unimpeachably half way between the two—is profoundly undemocratic. The very fact that important elements of substantive policy are entrenched at supra-legislative level is in itself democratically suspect. Democratic constitutions ought not to commit their political communities to specific economic and social policies: they should merely enshrine procedures whereby those policies can be chosen, allowing such policies to be generated by the democratic interplay between elected institutions. Since the ECJ has characterised the EC Treaty as 'constitutional', it would seem highly improper that this constitution should compel adherence to one particular economic policy whilst forbidding alternatives. The criticism would therefore be that in a democracy, the constitution ought not to entrench any economic programme, whatever its ideological content. Even the most fundamental elements of economic and social policy ought not to be set above the normal, everyday process of politics, elections and accountability.

The reality, however, is that democratic choice—over public versus private, economic versus social—has to a substantial extent been replaced by constitutional norms.[217] These norms have overridden the traditional British version of democracy in which 'parliamentary sovereignty functioned as a kind of empty vessel into which the (temporary) victors in the endless political fray could pour their ever-contingent versions of right and wrong'.[218] The result has been the construction of a teleological Britain within which neoliberal policy is significantly entrenched, irrespective of the outcomes of democratic politics.

---

[215] Gill (2001) 47.
[216] Prosser (2005). See also Ross (2007).
[217] Banquero Cruz (2005) 212.
[218] Gearty (2004) 23.

4

'The Fundamental Right of the Well-to-Do': Property as a Human Right

T HE WORLD TRADE ORGANIZATION (WTO) and the European Union (EU) protect the private ownership of industry and service provision in a way that might be described as *indirect*. The WTO Agreements and EU Treaties do not enshrine the right of private property as such. Instead, they guarantee rights of free trade in goods and services and undistorted competition in such a way as to afford protection to private enterprise. Since corporations from other states must be enabled to enter the market, this insures against a general socialisation of specific economic sectors. Private enterprise can, however, be protected in a *direct*, arguably more brazen, fashion, by declaring property ownership to be a fundamental human right, which states must guarantee. The United Kingdom adheres to the European Convention on Human Rights (ECHR), and one of the rights that it protects is the right to private property. The relevant provision is Article 1 of the First Protocol:

> Every natural or legal person is entitled to the peaceful enjoyment of his possessions. No one shall be deprived of his possessions except in the public interest and subject to the conditions provided for by law and by the general principles of international law.

> The preceding provisions shall not, however, in any way impair the right of a state to enforce such laws as it deems necessary to control the use of property in accordance with the general interest or to secure the payment of taxes or other contributions or penalties.

It should be observed that this provision (along with the other ECHR rights) benefits not only individuals but also private companies.[1] (By contrast, the property rights of the public sector are excluded from protection.[2]) It is questionable, however, whether in principle 'human' rights should apply to businesses at all. There is a danger that the economic interests of corporations will be mistaken for fundamental rights.[3] In particular, it seems contrived to argue that the values of individual autonomy and human dignity, which underlie human rights guarantees, should apply to the protection of the property rights of corporations.

---

[1] Art 34 ECHR.
[2] Van den Broek (1986) 89.
[3] Hiebert (2002) 80.

Human Rights at the Service of Neoliberalism

In chapter one, the constitutional protection of capitalism was described as an insurance policy, a guarantee of continuing neoliberal policies in the event of an ending of the neoliberal consensus among politicians. This insurance policy contains provisions that underpin the security of private-sector power. Yet there is a danger that some of these provisions could be perceived as weak in terms of legitimacy. Deploying free trade agreements and EU treaties to stifle the alternative policies of democratically elected governments might well be seen as anti-democratic. In the event of a political change of mood, political communities may be hostile to the idea that they have unwittingly pre-committed themselves on economic policy. By contrast, the language of fundamental human rights enjoys a high (albeit contested) degree of legitimacy. Such rights are widely perceived as forming a set of norms that, in an era of failed ideologies, are 'now probably as significant as the Bible in shaping modern, Western values'.[4]

The general public and even their politicians often assume—irrespective of the precise constitutional position in a specific state—that fundamental human rights reign supreme over ordinary law. Fundamental human rights have the capacity to overcome arguments based on the democratic will, since they famously counter the 'tyranny of the majority'. Yet at the same time, the primacy accorded to fundamental rights dovetails neatly with the requirements of the neoliberal constitution. Friedrich A Hayek insisted that the functioning of competition depended upon the existence of an appropriate legal system that recognised the principle of private property.[5] Indeed, Hayek saw private property as an essential condition for the prevention of coercion.[6] According to the Washington Consensus, the neoliberal state should favour strong private property rights,[7] and the strongest form of right—the only one that in principle cannot be overturned by the vagaries of normal majoritarian democracy—is the fundamental human right. The idea of fundamental human rights is thus ideally suited to service the needs of neoliberalism.

The suggestion that the European Convention on Human Rights has been deployed to advance neoliberal ideology may seem unpalatable. Conventional opinion assumes that human rights law ought to transcend disagreements between Right and Left. Indeed, insofar as human rights assume a partisan shape at all, a human rights ethos might be associated with anti-poverty approaches, since they share a focus on human dignity and on the things we need as a very minimum to flourish as human beings. To be sure, the ECHR appears to lack the explicit capitalistic aggressiveness of the WTO and the EU Treaties. Yet the fact remains that *it is human rights law that accommodates itself to neoliberal globalisation*, and not the

---

[4] Klug (2000) 18.
[5] Hayek (1986) 28.
[6] Hayek (1978) 140.
[7] Harvey (2005) 64.

other way around. Put bluntly, the established rights discourse conforms to the requirements of neoliberal globalisation and thereby serves to legitimate it.[8] For, as Krisztina Morvai put it, 'there is nothing UNlawful in the fact that, for many people, life is a degrading experience and the world is a pretty inhuman place to live'.[9] In fact, human rights law can be seen to play a legitimising role for the transnational constitution in three respects.

First, it acts as the human face of neoliberal globalisation. Neoliberalism is harsh; human rights law promises to soften that harshness. Yet it does so without confronting in any serious way the existing distribution of wealth. Secondly, human rights law provides window-dressing for the principle of supranational-ism, legitimising the expansion of international regulation into the realm previ-ously occupied by states. It thereby opens a vital bridgehead. If the European Court of Human Rights (ECtHR) can regulate compliance with the Convention rights, why should not the judicial institutions of the WTO and EU police the privatised free movement of services and goods? Thirdly, quite apart from the supranational element, human rights law lends legitimacy to the very notion of a higher-order law prevailing over the vagaries of political democracy. The state is depicted as violator of an incontestable and enduring higher law. The common and pervasive assumption is that constitutional law needs to take power away from the representative institutions of the state, despite the latter's democratic creden-tials. This focus, combined with the failure to adopt a 'horizontal' application of human rights to transnational corporations, serves to obscure the domination of corporate power. Furthermore it alienates the state, distancing its representatives from those to whom they are accountable. Thus, all in all, the ECHR fulfils an ide-ological function that reinforces rather than undermines the constitutionalised free market of the WTO and EU.[10]

It must also be added that one must never underestimate the fluidity of the notion of 'fundamental human rights'. For some scholars, the free trade rights in the WTO and EU law *constitute* fundamental human rights. Ernst-Ulrich Petersmann, for example, envisages a human right to free trade, which in his opinion is better pro-tected by international economic law than by national constitutions, which give governments too much power over economic policy.[11] Petersmann has thereby deployed the rhetorical and normative 'pull' of human rights to win legitimacy to a highly capitalist settlement, one that would see both national autonomy and parlia-mentary sovereignty as potent threats to rights.[12] His 'fundamental human right to capitalism' is embodied in Article 16 of the EU Charter of Fundamental Rights, which enshrines the human right to conduct a business. Petersmann's arguments

---

[8] Brown (2004) 451, 461–62.
[9] Morvai (1998) 247–48.
[10] This is confirmed by the landmark *Bosphorus* case in which the European Court of Human Rights declared the existence of a presumption that EC law complies with ECHR law: *Bosphorus Airways v Ireland* (Application no 45036/98) (2006) 42 EHRR 1.
[11] Petersmann (1991).
[12] Bellamy (2003).

provide a nice illustration of the fact that human rights—one of the most potent phrases in modern politics—does not mean one thing but many things.[13]

Property and Democracy: Four Possibilities

At the level of general principle, it is possible to envisage at least four approaches to the idea of property ownership as a fundamental right. Each has different implications for the democratic right of a political community to choose its own economic policy. The first possible approach does not regard property as a human right at all. This was the position favoured by the 1945–51 UK Labour government at the time of the ECHR negotiations. Labour was suspicious of enshrining a fundamental right to property that would mainly benefit the wealthy classes. The government essentially took the view that the distribution of property should remain democratically contestable. Clearly, ministers regarded the question of property ownership as being too intensely controversial and indeed too party-political to be elevated to the status of a constitutional right. The Attlee government's record of nationalisation bore testament to this argument of contestability.

This absence of fundamental protection of property rights might be thought to conform to the democratic traditions of the British constitution. Tom Allen has argued that in the Middle Ages and later, there were constitutional principles that protected property rights against sovereign power.[14] Most writers, he has contended, believed that a right to property formed part of the fundamental law of England, which bound both Parliament and the Crown, although the courts had only a limited power to enforce it against either body. It might be argued, however, that a 'fundamental law' that cannot be enforced might be better regarded not as a fundamental law as such but rather as a durable political consensus. In any event, Allen has observed that the idea of property rights as fundamental law has declined considerably in more recent times. On the basis of Allen's account, it might be argued that any such fundamental law in favour of property ownership should in fact be regarded as a relic of our pre-democratic past. With the establishment of the universal franchise, those with little or no property were entitled to vote, and their enfranchisement meant that ultimately Parliament's respect for private property became less reliable. This was especially the case when the Labour Party replaced the Liberals in the two-party system, since whatever its track record, Labour was formally committed to the 'common ownership of the means of production, distribution and exchange' until 1995.

The democratic argument against the absence of fundamental property rights would appear to rest primarily on the possibility of Britain becoming a dictatorship. Totalitarian regimes tend to use the seizure of possessions in order to destabilise

---

[13] Dembour (2006).
[14] Allen (2005) 8.

their opponents, with the ultimate result of destabilising democracy itself. Property rights should therefore be entrenched in order to preserve democracy. Yet there are compelling objections to this argument. One is that, in the unlikely circumstances that such a regime were to come to power in the UK, it could in fact easily renounce the ECHR as a whole, in view of the emergence of a public ambivalence towards human rights that the Convention framers never anticipated. A second objection stems from the risk that the protection of property ownership would not be interpreted merely as an anti-dictatorship device but would in fact make serious inroads into the economic policymaking of governments with impeccably democratic credentials. Human rights would then have become the very means of *subverting* democracy and would therefore be doing the dictator's job for him.

The second possible approach to the idea of property ownership as a fundamental right is that everyone should own property. Jeremy Waldron, in his book *The Right to Private Property*, usefully distinguished between very different conceptions of private property as a fundamental right. One he dubs a 'general-right-based argument' for private property, the argument that everyone should, as a matter of human rights, own property. He describes this conception of the property right as being based on an argument against inequality and in favour of a 'property-owning democracy'.[15] The 'general-right-based argument' is radical in its redistributive implications: everyone must own property, though not necessarily the same amount of property. It is nonetheless transformatively egalitarian. Accordingly, it would meet the objection that a right of property ownership ought not to be deployed so as to consolidate the existing, extremely inegalitarian distribution of wealth, to the detriment of those with little or no property. In 1999, for instance, the top 10 per cent of the population owned over half of personal wealth in the UK; and the top 1 per cent owned 23 per cent.[16] It is questionable whether that top 1 per cent should have a fundamental human right to preserve its ownership of its 23 per cent in the face of demands from the remaining 99 per cent of the British population for a more equitable sharing-out of property ownership. The 'general-right-based' conception of property ownership would evidently offer a greater degree of social equality. From the point of view of democracy, however, its entrenchment would appear to be profoundly undemocratic. The democratic will may be hostile to redistribution, and it should be open to a political community to opt for a society based on self-reliance. If property becomes an entitlement, this precludes any democratic decision to orientate society in such a direction.

The third possible approach to the idea of property ownership as a fundamental right is that human rights law should guarantee the existing distribution of property. Waldron referred to this conception as a 'special-right-based argument'.[17] This argument assumes that the question of the acquisition and allocation of property has been settled independently. In other words, the argument is that,

[15] Waldron (1988)
[16] Institute of Public Policy Research (2002).
[17] Waldron (1988).

given a pre-existing distribution of property, individual property-holders have a right against the government that their holdings be respected. The fundamental right therefore consists of an immunity against expropriation, protecting existing rights of property without in any way guaranteeing a universal entitlement to hold property.[18] Having analysed the arguments of Hegel, Locke, Nozick and others, Waldron was compelled to the conclusion that this 'special-right-based argument' cannot convincingly be defended from the point of view of political philosophy. As he put it, 'under serious scrutiny, there is no right-based argument to be found which provides an adequate justification for a society in which some people have lots of property and many have next to none'.[19] For Waldron, the slogan that property is a human right can be deployed only disingenuously to legitimise the massive inequality that we find in modern capitalist countries.

By contrast with the 'general-right-based' conception of property rights, the 'special-right-based' conception is, in distributional terms, conservative. But, in common with the 'general-right-based' approach, it is once again wholly undemocratic. By consolidating an economic system and distribution under which the right of property ownership is denied to a large proportion of the population, the 'special-right-based' conception would undermine the ability of a democratic political community to choose to establish a more egalitarian society.

A fourth possible approach represents a compromise between the general-right-based approach and the special-right-based approach to property. This compromise would not require a redistribution of property but would nonetheless permit it, thereby posing less of a restriction to the democratic choice of socioeconomic policy. It would also be premised on the idea that only a certain minimum amount of property is necessary for the flourishing of individual dignity, autonomy and responsibility. On this assumption, it might be legitimate to immunise against expropriation the modest property holdings of the broad mass of the people, insofar as they already own property, but without protecting *all* the property of the wealthy. Formulating such a right might be a little clumsy but would not be excessively difficult. It would be possible, for instance, to guarantee property against expropriation up to a certain index-linked value, corresponding perhaps to the price of an average dwelling in the relevant territory. Any property above such a value would not benefit from the protection of the human rights guarantee but only from the force of ordinary law.

In sum, it is striking that the concept of a fundamental human right of private property ownership can give rise to such very different conceptions, which if developed would lead to starkly different kinds of society. Above all, these different conceptions would have diverse consequences for democracy. There is a danger that as one ideology achieves dominance, the diversity of possible conception of the property right comes to be disregarded, and the concept of the property right is taken to mean the same thing as a particular conception thereof. This

---

[18] *Ibid*, 17.
[19] *Ibid*, 5.

conflation might be taken as evidence of the tendency of 'rights-talk' to obscure the real issue—the kind of society we are trying to create or preserve.

Disagreements over the Right of Property Ownership, 1950–51

In view of the controversial nature of the right to property and its various conceptions, it is hardly surprising that the subject proved highly contentious at the time of the ECHR negotiations. Some delegates and ministers shared the position of the UK Labour Party in not wanting a right of property ownership at all, since they were anxious to preserve national autonomy in the sphere of economic policy. But even among those who sought such a right, it was readily apparent that different negotiators were motivated by very different considerations. Many declared themselves to be driven primarily by the way in which totalitarian regimes had used the confiscation of property to undermine their opponents. They wanted a property right to prohibit seizures of that kind. By contrast, others wanted property ownership to be protected not only against dictatorships but also against what they considered to be the 'extreme' redistributive efforts of democratically-elected governments. These differences over the nature of the property right reflected a broader divergence regarding the nature of the ECHR as a whole. For some, the ECHR was intended to be merely an inoculation against totalitarianism, an anti-dictatorship device that would rarely if ever impinge on the activities of democratically elected governments. Others sought a fully-fledged, interventionist Bill of Rights that would play a regular part in the governance of all states.[20]

The controversial nature of the right of property ownership was evident from the start of the negotiations. In fact, it was one of three rights—along with the rights of parents in the education of their children and the right to vote in the election of the legislature—that were proposed by the Council of Europe's Consultative Assembly for inclusion in the ECHR only to be vetoed by the Council of Ministers. This veto led to considerable dissatisfaction. Some French and German Assembly members boycotted the signing of the ECHR altogether, in protest at the 'missing' rights. Furthermore, three of the ministers used the occasion to express regret that the Convention was still 'incomplete'.[21] As a compromise, the Council of Ministers agreed to refer the three rights to a committee of experts for further study, with a view to drawing up what became the First Protocol.

It is important to appreciate that the debates within the Consultative Assembly in 1950–51 regarding the right of property ownership were dominated by a

---

[20] Nicol (2005).
[21] Council of Europe (1985) vol VII, 46. The ministers were Mr Schuman (France), Mr MacBride (Ireland) and Mr Stikker (Netherlands).

Left–Right split. Whilst Assembly members with centre-right inclinations sought a Bill-of-Rights-style entrenchment of property rights to protect property against totalitarian expropriation and redistributive democratic socialism alike, left-leaning Assembly members were anxious not to set in stone the existing distribution of property ownership.[22] At first these members opposed point blank the very inclusion of a property right, arguing that the matter was party-political.[23] They doubtless envisaged that, irrespective of how cautiously such a right were framed, the Court might accord it an expansive interpretation, protecting the prosperous at the expense of the less fortunate by fashioning a fundamental 'right of the well-to-do'.[24] A right of property ownership might, for example, be exploited by private companies in order to thwart nationalisation designed to serve the public interest—for example, steel nationalisation in Britain[25] and ownership of the railways in Sweden.[26] To guarantee private property would be to defend a system whereby a 'tiny handful of people own the means by which millions of others live'.[27] Socialists also argued that if the right to own property were to be protected, then so too should the right to an adequate standard of living; otherwise the ECHR would be lopsided and reactionary.[28] Later in the course of the negotiations, they sought to water down the property right so as to distinguish Nazi-style expropriations from the array of socialist measures that, in their opinion, formed part of legitimate democratic politics. This in turn led to complaints that such a dilution of the property right would be 'the thin end of the Moscow wedge' and 'a kind of fellow traveller policy'.[29]

In view of the rather basic nature of the disagreement over the property right, it would clearly not be easy for the negotiators to draw a dividing line between the fundamental core right and the democratically contestable. As one Assembly member put it, 'who can say what is legal taxation and what is confiscation?'[30] Some claimed that the decisions of a democratically elected parliament limiting property rights could never be arbitrary,[31] whereas others urged that the ECHR should engage in the battle against the abuse of legislative power.[32] Thus the division between negotiators of different political persuasions was readily apparent. As one delegate put it with customary British understatement, 'perhaps unfortunately,

[22] Eg, *ibid*, vol II, 76 (Mr Nally, UK).

[23] Eg, *ibid*, vol II, 70 (Mr Sundt, Norway); 106 (Mr Lapie, France); 72 (Mr Philip, France); 60–62 (Mr Ungoed-Thomas, UK); 254 (Mr Schuman, France); and vol VII, 218 (Mr Unden, Sweden).

[24] *Ibid*, vol II, 98 (Mr Callas, Greece).

[25] *Ibid*, vol II, 194 (Mr Nally, UK); 252 (Mr Ungoed-Thomas UK); and vol VI, 94–96 and vol VII, 138 (Mr Mitchison, UK).

[26] *Ibid*, vol II, 86 (Mr Edberg, Sweden).

[27] *Ibid*, vol II, 80 (Mr. Nally, UK).

[28] *Ibid*, vol II, 60–62 (Mr. Ungoed-Thomas, UK); 62 (Mr de la Vallée-Poussin); 72 (Mr Philip, France); 80 (Mr Elmgren, Sweden).

[29] *Ibid*, vol II, 104 (Mr Crosbie, Ireland).

[30] *Ibid*, vol II, 84 (Mr Edberg, Sweden).

[31] *Ibid*, vol II, 122 (Mr Lapie, France); 128 (Mr Dominedo, Italy); 250 (Mr Ungoed-Thomas, UK).

[32] *Ibid*, vol II, 134 (Mr Benvenuti, Italy). See also vol II, 126–30 (exchanges between the President of the Assembly and various members) and vol VII, 206.

in the course of this session of the Assembly, party feeling has been somewhat acute'.[33]

In deference to the sharp disagreements that the property right had encountered, the final version of Article 1 was framed so as seemingly to impose only modest restrictions on governmental freedom. The bare words of the Article seem to preserve sweeping powers to expropriate 'in the public interest', provided that such expropriation complied with domestic and international law. There was deliberately no commitment to provide compensation. Furthermore, the Contracting States explicitly retained their right to enact laws to control the use of property, as well as to secure the payment of taxation and other penalties.

The First Protocol came into force and was signed by the UK on 20 March 1952, by which time the Conservatives had replaced Labour in office. Whilst the government entered a reservation in respect of Article 2, the right to education, its adhesion to the property right was unqualified. One reason for this would have been the change in governing party. Whilst the Conservative Party of the day largely tolerated the new public sector in Britain, it would not have shared any great enthusiasm for further extensions of public ownership. A second reason for the lack of British anxiety was that the text appeared in any event to preserve extensive national powers.

Predominant Purpose of the Property Right: The Protection of Existing Entitlements

Once the Contracting States of the ECHR settled on a form of words for the First Protocol, this did not in itself resolve the disagreement over what Article 1 actually meant. Rather, it transferred power from the negotiators to the European Court of Human Rights to determine the nature of the property right by way of interpretation. In this context, it is possible to characterise Article 1 of the First Protocol as a 'standard' rather than a 'rule'. Whereas rules require a clear decision on the part of negotiators, standards may serve to mask disagreement, enabling both sides in the negotiating process to think they have got their way. With rules, negotiators often 'make' the decision, whereas with standards, an adjudicator—here the ECtHR—interprets the standard, thereby 'making' the decision.[34] In its early years the Court adopted a 'self-limiting strategy', because it was anxious to build up the confidence of governments in the new Strasbourg system. But once the system had gained greater acceptance and the larger states were safely enmeshed within the system of individual petition, the Court was in a position to expand the substantive content of the Convention rights, including the property right.[35] It seems to

---

[33] *Ibid*, vol II, 56 (Mr Ungoed-Thomas, UK). See also vol II, 106 (Mr Lapie, France), who highlighted party differences.

[34] Trachtman (2006) 450–52.

[35] Madsen (2007).

be generally agreed that, despite the UK government's best efforts at the time of the negotiation, the Court has given the Article 1 right a wide reach.

On the most fundamental issue of all, however, the Court has remained profoundly conservative. Unsurprisingly, its jurisprudence has emphatically confirmed that the right contained in Article 1 of the First Protocol is essentially a guarantor of the existing distribution of property. It therefore operates as an instrument for ensuring the stability of entitlements, where the foundation for those entitlements is not itself questioned.[36] In Waldron's classification, it eschews a 'general-right-based' conception of property ownership in favour of a 'special-right-based' one. A vivid illustration is provided by *The Former King of Greece and Others v Greece*, in which the former King complained that Greek legislation, under which the Greek State became owner of his movable and immovable property without compensation, violated his rights under Article 1 of the First Protocol.[37] The Greek government denied that the former King's real property constituted his 'possessions', arguing that royal property had a semi-public quality. The Court felt unable to agree with the government that the members of the royal family did not have any property in Greece; rather, the disputed properties were owned by the royal family as private persons, and therefore Article 1 of the First Protocol was engaged. Judges Koumantos and Zupanāiā dissented, arguing that a large proportion of the property was only acquired by dint of the exercise of royal power, and the property therefore formed part of a sui generis regime, part public and part private, which excluded the application of the Convention right. The majority, however, disagreed and went on to hold that Greece's failure to pay compensation to the King was disproportionate and meant that Article 1 had been violated. Thus, in general Article 1 of the First Protocol protects the existing possessions of a corporation or an individual: it is not a right to be put in possession of things one does not already have.[38]

In general, therefore, the Court appears to take the existing pattern of property rights as a given. It is not usually prepared to look behind the formal status of property owners to examine the legitimacy of ownership.[39] Whilst there have been a few cases in which the judicial focus has shifted to other values, such as autonomy, dignity and fairness, such case law remains remarkably limited and strictly secondary.[40] Overwhelmingly, the primary focus of Article 1 jurisprudence has been to consolidate and legitimise the property-owning status quo.

---

[36] Allen (2005) 5.
[37] *The Former King of Greece and Others v Greece* (Application no 25701/94), judgment of 23 November 2000.
[38] Harris, O'Boyle, Bates and Buckley (2009) 660.
[39] The Court has not, however, been wholly consistent on this score. In *Jahn v Germany* (Application nos 46720/99, 72203/01 and 72552/01), judgment of 30 June 2005 the Court was prepared to question the historical legitimacy of the applicants' modest holdings deriving from the Communist era in a way that formed rather a striking contrast to the relatively uncritical treatment of the former Greek Royal Family's far more substantial acquisitions.
[40] Allen (2005) 293.

Transforming the Property Right

The Concept of 'Fair Balance'

The extent to which the property right strengthens the existing distribution of property ownership might be mitigated if Contracting States were allowed a large measure of discretion to limit or restrict that right. The bare text of Article 1 indicates that the Contracting States intended to give themselves more leeway in this respect than in the case of other ECHR rights. The Court, however, has done much to effect a 'judicial upgrade' of the property right, thereby narrowing the gap designed by the ECHR framers.

The leading case is *Sporrong and Lönnroth v Sweden*.[41] Land belonging to Mrs Lönnroth and to the estate of the late Mr Sporrong had been subject to long-term expropriation permits and prohibitions on construction under Swedish town-planning legislation. The expropriation permits gave discretion to the local authority to effect an expropriation with compensation, within a certain time limit. However, the Swedish government allowed these permits to be repeatedly renewed. As a result, in the case of Mr Sporrong's property, the expropriation permit and the prohibition on construction were in force for total periods of 23 and 25 years respectively. In the case of Mrs Lönnroth, the periods were 8 and 12 years. In the end, in fact, the local authority did not exercise its right to expropriate. Nonetheless, during these periods, Sporrong and Lönnroth suffered adverse effects, since they lost the possibility of selling their properties at normal market prices.

The Court held by ten votes to nine that Sweden had violated Article 1 of the First Protocol. The narrowness of the vote was remarkable in view of the profound effect of the judgment in expanding the power of the Court vis-à-vis the Contracting States. The majority held that only the first 'rule' of Article 1 ('Every natural or legal person is entitled to the peaceful enjoyment of his possessions') was relevant to the case. The second 'rule' ('No one shall be deprived of his possessions except in the public interest and subject to the conditions provided for by law and by the general principles of international law') was inapplicable, since the effects of the Swedish measures were not such as to constitute 'deprivation'. Controversially, the Court went on to hold that the third 'rule' of Article 1 ('The preceding provisions shall not, however, in any way impair the right of a state to enforce such laws as it deems necessary to control the use of property in accordance with the general interest or to secure the payment of taxes or other contributions or penalties.') was also inapplicable, since 'the expropriation permits were not intended to limit or control' the use of property. This element of the judgment was heavily criticised by the minority.

---

[41] *Sporrong and Lönnroth v Sweden* (Application nos 7151/75 and 7152/75), judgment of 23 September 1982.

The Court held that whilst Contracting States enjoyed a margin of appreciation in the field of town-planning policy, the Court had power of review and had to determine whether the 'requisite balance' had been maintained in a manner compatible with the right to peaceful enjoyment of one's possessions. Accordingly, the Court held that the combination of the lengthy expropriation permits and construction prohibitions created a situation that upset the 'fair balance', which should be struck between the protection of the right to property and the requirements of the general interest, and this had led to a violation of Article 1 of the First Protocol.

The minority held that the majority had reached its conclusion in a way that did not correspond to the underlying intention and real meaning of the Convention provision. In particular, they were unconvinced by the majority's finding that the third rule of Article 1 was inapplicable, since the expropriation permits, considered in combination with the prohibitions on construction, did indeed have the single objective of limiting property rights in order to facilitate town development. The minority accused the majority of having eliminated the third rule so that they could discard the test agreed by the Convention framers in favour of one of their own liking, namely 'whether a fair balance was struck between the demands of the general interest of the community and the requirements of the protection of the individual's fundamental rights'. The minority believed that the third rule *was* applicable. Furthermore, this rule was expressed in very emphatic terms, such as to leave the States a very wide margin of appreciation. Since modern town planning involves the most difficult considerations and evaluations, the Swedish authorities had not gone beyond their margin of appreciation, and there had been no violation.

It is difficult to disagree with the minority's view that in *Sporrong and Lönnroth* the Court effectively rewrote Article 1 of the First Protocol. It seems reasonably clear that the ECHR framers had not intended the property right to involve the same degree of restriction on state action as is the case with the other rights guaranteed by the Convention. Confronted with the strong disagreements over the property right, the Convention framers intended to give states more freedom of action in the sphere of property ownership than in other fields. The wording, drafting history and debates on Article 1 tend to confirm this.

In *Lithgow v United Kingdom*, the UK government tried to resist the universalisation of the 'fair balance' test by arguing that only if the second and third rules were inapplicable would it be appropriate to examine whether a fair balance had been struck. The Court rejected this argument, confirming that the search for a fair balance imbued Article 1 as a whole.[42] In *James v United Kingdom*, the Court reiterated that the fair balance test applied to all three rules of Article 1, since 'the three rules are not . . . distinct in the sense of being unconnected. The second and third rules are concerned with particular instances of interference with the right to

---

[42] *Lithgow and Others v United Kingdom* (Application nos 9006/80, 9262/81, 9263/81, 9265/81, 9266/81, 9313/81 and 9405/81), judgment of 8 July 1986. See also Mendelson (1986) 49.

peaceful enjoyment enunciated in the first rule.'[43] Since the 'fair balance' test now pervades Article 1, the Court takes increasingly little interest in which of the three rules is engaged and simply considers the question of 'fair balance'. Thus the test provides a framework for resolving issues, however the interference is characterised.[44]

It is perhaps significant that *Sporrong and Lönnroth* was decided only three years after the European Court of Justice (ECJ) decided *Cassis de Dijon*.[45] We can discern echoes of *Cassis* in *Sporrong and Lönnroth*. In both cases, the courts adopted balancing exercises, and this is in itself significant, since such balancing tests involve a shift in polycentric decision-making power from governments and legislatures to the judiciary. Furthermore, in both cases the weighting involved in the balancing test was such as to favour aspects of neoliberal policy—free trade in the case of *Cassis* and property rights in the case of *Sporrong and Lönnroth*. In *Cassis*, the ECJ's balancing test explicitly gave pride of place to the free movement of goods. By contrast, in *Sporrong and Lönnroth* the ECtHR could not go quite so far. Faced with a divided Court and an unpromising text, it was not in a position to give the right of property ownership a corresponding degree of priority over competing concerns; yet by downgrading the importance of the actual wording of Article 1, the majority at least managed to eradicate a balancing test in which the presumption would be in favour of the pursuit of the public interest by the state. At the same time, however, the test of 'fair balance' is so indeterminate and subjective as to permit the Court, under the cover of a neutral test, to privilege property rights if it so wished, which was seemingly what happened in *Sporrong and Lönnroth* itself.

'Fair Balance' Fused with Proportionality

The advent of the 'fair balance' test marked a decisive turning point in the evolution of Article 1 of the First Protocol. Four years later, in *James v United Kingdom*, the Court modified this test in such a way as to empower itself to afford still greater protection to private property interests.[46] The Court declared that the test of 'fair balance' articulated in *Sporrong and Lönnroth* was essentially the same as the test of proportionality that it applied in other areas of Convention jurisprudence. When tackling a complaint under Article 1 of the First Protocol, therefore, the legal analysis was henceforth to be couched in the language of proportionality.

The test of 'fair balance' *simpliciter* had implied, at least at the level of legal formalism, that Contracting States were free as a matter of policy to privilege other values above property ownership. 'Proportionality' carries with it a different

---

[43] *James v United Kingdom*, Series A No 98 (1986) 8 EHRR 123 [37].

[44] Harris, O'Boyle, Bates and Buckley (2009) 667.

[45] Case 120/78 *Rewe-Zentrale AG v Bundesmonopolverwaltung für Branntwein* ('*Cassis de Dijon*') [1979] ECR 649. For further discussion, see ch 3 above.

[46] *James* (above n 43) [50].

nuance. In the context of the restriction of a fundamental right or freedom, the Court's introduction of the test of proportionality entails giving the protected right predominant weight *vis-à-vis* competing public interests. The right prevails *unless* the interference with it is judged proportionate. Thus the use of proportionality lacks the suggestion of even-handedness between competing considerations conveyed by the 'fair balance' test.

At the same time, however, the Court held that in the circumstances of *James*, the national authorities had a wide discretion, which they had not exceeded. *James* involved legislation that enabled the holders of long residential leases to buy out their landlord compulsorily so as to relieve tenants of the hardship or injustice caused by the expiry of long leases. Confronted with a complaint from the landlords that the compensation terms were inadequate and therefore constituted a disproportionate interference with their property rights, the Court ruled that measures designed to achieve greater social justice or economic reform may call for less than reimbursement at full market value and that the Court's power of review was limited to ascertaining whether the choice of compensation terms fell outside the state's wide margin of appreciation.[47]

Thus the use of the term 'proportionality', whilst it may connote more intense judicial scrutiny, does not necessarily do so. It does, however, maximise the degree of *choice* available to the Court. To be sure, the Court must determine whether the interference with the property right corresponds to a legitimate social need sufficiently pressing to outweigh the public interest in the right of property ownership guaranteed by the Convention. However, the Court also has to decide how intensively it is going to apply this test.[48] In general, when fundamental rights and freedoms have been unduly restricted, courts are likely to engage in vigorous scrutiny, whereas when economic policy choices are involved, review may be less intensive.[49] A case that counterposes the fundamental right of property ownership with the pursuance of an economic policy would presumably offer the Court the maximum degree of choice over whether to opt for anxious or relaxed scrutiny. Thus the significance of the adoption of proportionality is not that it always compels a standard of intense review but rather that it gives the judiciary power to apply such a standard of review should the Court deem that the context makes intense review appropriate.

Since the Court is entitled to look at all the circumstances to determine the appropriate intensity of scrutiny, this leads to a high degree of indeterminacy of judicial outcomes. In *The Former King of Greece*, the Greek government contended that in assessing proportionality and fair balance, the Court should allow the Contracting State a broad margin of appreciation, since Article 1 of the First Protocol does not contain the requirement, incorporated in many of the Convention rights, that any restriction on rights should be 'necessary in a democratic society' in order to fulfil

---

[47] *Ibid* [54].
[48] Craig and de Búrca (2008) 544–51.
[49] Craig (2006) chs 17–18.

competing public interests. The government argued that decisions in the area of property distribution commonly involved the assessment of political, economic and social questions on which opinions within a democratic society might genuinely and reasonable differ widely. The Greek government was thus advancing an argument pitched at a high level of generality, that national authorities should *always* enjoy a wide margin of discretion in respect of the proportionality of their limitations on property rights. The Court declined to respond to this argument at this level of general principle. Instead, it held that the government had failed to give a convincing explanation for its failure to compensate the former King, and whilst the State could have considered in good faith that exceptional circumstances justified the absence of compensation, this assessment had not been objectively substantiated. The Court's approach appears to connote a judicial unwillingness to give states an a priori wider degree of leeway over the right of property ownership. Instead, the Court reserves itself the right to examine each and every complaint under Article 1 of the First Protocol and to decide *on the basis of that individual case* what rigour of scrutiny is appropriate.

The full extent of the Court's freedom to vary the proportionality test was revealed in *Hentrich v France*, a 1994 case that Yutaka Arai-Takahashi has characterised as marking a crucial change in judicial policy.[50] Faced with tax evasion on an increasingly large scale, France introduced a law that allowed for the preemption of real property on the grounds that the sale price was too low. The French revenue service expropriated Mrs Hentrich's land, with compensation, on these grounds. The Court held that France had violated Article 1 of the First Protocol because of the availability of less burdensome measures capable of accomplishing the same objective, such as the institution of legal proceedings to recover unpaid taxes and the imposition of tax fines. Such a deployment of a 'least restrictive means' test in the context of property rights constitutes a profound shift in policymaking power in favour of the judiciary.[51]

Proportionality and Compensation

The feasibility of nationalisation often depends on compensation. If the law dictates that compensation must be full and prompt, this may well deter the acquisition of profitable firms. At the same time, however, an over-emphasis on compensation can undermine the legitimacy of property ownership as a human right. If property can readily be replaced with cash handouts, this calls into question the claim that property has an intrinsic worth in terms of human dignity and autonomy. Furthermore, if compensation becomes too central to the scheme of things, this can also raise suspicion—particularly in cases in which corporations claim to be victims of violations of property rights—that what is really at stake is not human rights but rather commercial interests.

[50] Arai-Takahashi (2002).
[51] Stone Sweet (2004) 244.

Many constitutions that protect the right to property ownership require compensation on expropriation. So too do some free trade agreements. A supranational guarantee of compensation, since it acts as a deterrent to expropriation, is an incentive to foreign direct investment. It will be recalled that during the abortive attempt to create an International Trade Organization (ITO) in the 1940s, US businessmen had pressed for the inclusion of such a provision in the ITO agreement but were dissatisfied with the content of what was agreed, since they considered that the obligation to pay (undefined) 'just compensation' for nationalisations amounted to an affirmation of a national right to expropriate.[52] More recently, Article 1110 of the North American Free Trade Agreement (NAFTA) 1994 requires that expropriations should be compensated at the equivalent of fair market value immediately before the expropriation takes place, and that compensation should be paid without delay and be fully realisable.

By contrast, Article 1 of the First Protocol does not provide for compensation in express terms. Indeed, at the time of the negotiations there was an explicit difference of opinion over whether to enshrine a right to compensation when property was nationalised. The Belgian delegation had proposed that Article 1 should make expropriation 'subject to fair compensation which shall be fixed in advance'.[53] This suggestion was vehemently opposed by the UK, France and the Saar, who did not wish national compensation decisions to be reviewed by international organs.[54] By way of compromise, Germany and Belgium proposed that compensation should at least be available for non-nationals, contending that this commitment was in any event already imposed upon states by the general principles of international law.[55] The British negotiators accepted this proposal in preference to an express reference to a right of compensation for all. Thus the final text provided that 'no one shall be deprived of his possessions except . . . subject to the conditions provided for by . . . the general principles of international law.'

It was made emphatically clear at the negotiations that by agreeing to this form of words, the Contracting States were *not* committing themselves to compensate their own nationals in similar circumstances: the general principles entailed an obligation to pay compensation only to *non*-nationals in cases of expropriation. The British therefore believed that the chosen formulation would largely ward off judicial intervention in the domestic sphere. The Court, however, has overturned this apparent compromise by expounding the principle that expropriation without compensation might violate the requirement of proportionality. In *James v United Kingdom*, it held that the right to property ownership would be largely illusory unless the Court read into Article 1 a requirement for compensation.[56] Thus the taking of property without payment of an amount reasonably related to its

---

[52] Aaronson (1996) 84–85. See also ch 2 above.
[53] Council of Europe (1985) vol VII, 194
[54] *Ibid*, 326
[55] *Ibid*, 326.
[56] *James* (above n 43).

value would normally constitute a disproportionate interference that could not be considered justifiable.

In order to justify its assertion of jurisdiction over compensation decisions, the Court would need to override the seeming agreement of the Convention framers to commit themselves to compensating only non-nationals. In *James*, therefore, the Court appealed to the existence of a European consensus, arguing that 'under the legal systems of the Contracting States, the taking of property in the public interest without payment of compensation is treated as justifiable only in exceptional circumstances.' The Court then went on to proclaim that the amount of such compensation must be reasonably related to the property's value. Yet, significantly, the Court did not attempt to justify this latter assertion by recourse to a European consensus. Under the British constitution, parliamentary sovereignty means that there can be no 'higher law' enshrining a standard for the reasonableness of compensation for nationalisation. The provision of compensation corresponding to value may well be desirable, but in view of the need to allocate scarce resources, it may not be possible, and under Britain's internal constitution its absence presents no obstacle to economic reform.

It is worth reflecting on the Court's holding in *James* that the protection of property would be largely illusory and ineffective without compensation. Ultimately, the enforcement of *all* the Convention rights benefits from the Court's power to award 'just satisfaction', a compensatory sum, if rights are violated.[57] In one sense, therefore, compensation is available for the protection of all Convention rights. Furthermore, the Contracting States are obliged to make available compensation for Convention violations at domestic level by virtue of their duty to provide an effective national remedy under Article 13 ECHR.[58] Plainly, therefore, the Court's statement presupposes a conceptual difference between 'just satisfaction' and compensation for deprivation of property. No doubt the Court was indicating that compensation should be part of the routine arrangement for nationalisation. In other words, compensation should not be restricted to the pathological situation in which a victim brings legal action against a state, but rather the legislative act of nationalisation should normally be accompanied by compensation arrangements.

The Court in *James* tried to balance the 'judicial activism' of assuming jurisdiction over compensation with the 'judicial restraint' of assuring states that they would enjoy a wide margin of appreciation over compensation decisions. Clearly political expediency explains why the Court would wish to 'soften the blow' by expressly declaring that it would give the Contracting States a generous degree of leeway. Yet it always remains open to the Court to tighten its control over compensation. As Peter Van den Broek has observed, the Court narrows the margin of appreciation when there is a degree of acceptance of certain values among the Contracting States. Thus if a right to compensation were to become more widely accepted, the Court will in all likelihood narrow the margin of appreciation in

---

[57] Art 41 ECHR.
[58] *Z v United Kingdom* (2001) 35 EHRR 487.

respect of *when* and *how* the States are to give compensation.[59] Indeed, the Court could adopt a stricter standard of compensation without even overturning its formal position that the margin of appreciation is wide. The Court could, for example, specify in more precise terms what was meant in *James* by 'payment of an amount reasonably related to [the property's] value'. It would also be open for the Court to take a restrictive view of the 'exceptional' circumstances in which compensation need not correspond to value.

Lithgow v United Kingdom involved the 1974–79 Labour Government's nationalisation of Britain's aerospace and shipbuilding industries. In the case of shipbuilding, Labour had long believed that essential changes to the sector could not come about whilst the industry was in fragmented private ownership; in the case of aerospace, the Party perceived a need for greater public accountability of an industry unusually dependent on public funds and believed greater efficiency would result from a merger of the two main groups involved.[60] After nationalisation, seven companies argued that the United Kingdom had violated Article 1 of the First Protocol by grossly under-compensating them. The Court reiterated that in principle compensation was a material factor in determining whether a given deprivation of property was disproportionate but that, exceptionally, legitimate objectives of public interest, such as economic reform or social justice, might call for less than full compensation.[61] Furthermore, the nationalisation of an entire sector might require legislation that applies across the board to all undertakings concerned, and this may lead to a different standard of compensation in nationalisation cases compared to other takings of property. In sum, therefore, states had a particularly wide margin of appreciation, and on this basis, the UK had not breached Article 1.

Noting the heavy criticism of the *Lithgow* case,[62] Allen has contended that the Court's relaxed approach on compensation was exceptional and had two causes: first, the scale and complexity of valuing the property; and secondly, the support given to the legislation by both the Labour Government and its Conservative successor.[63] The second factor suggested by Allen is disquieting from a democratic point of view. Britain has long had a political system in which one of the two main parties represents the social and economic status quo, and the other represents some degree of social change—or at least is perceived as so doing. If bipartisan support for a nationalisation programme is a prerequisite to not having to pay full compensation, the likely effect would be to discriminate against nationalisation programmes that form part of a blueprint for a more egalitarian society. This in turn would undermine the relative ideological neutrality of the constitution.

Since the 1990s, the Court has adopted a more robust approach to compensation.[64] In *Holy Monasteries v Greece*, the Greek Parliament failed to provide

---

[59] Van den Broeck (1986).
[60] Mendelson (1986) 34
[61] *Lithgow* (above n 42) [121].
[62] Eg, Mendelson (1986); Salgado (1987).
[63] Allen (2005) 184.
[64] Arai-Takahashi (2002) 162.

compensation for the expropriation of land from the monasteries of the Greek Church.[65] The European Commission on Human Rights considered that the absence of compensation was not 'manifestly without reasonable foundation', since there were exceptional circumstances such as the ways in which the property was acquired and used and the monasteries' dependence on the Greek Church and the Church's dependence on the State. The Court, however, disagreed. It noted that in 1952 the Greek legislature had taken measures to expropriate a large portion of agricultural property from the monasteries and had provided for compensation of one-third of the real value of the expropriated land, whereas there was no similar provision in the new law. It therefore followed that the legislation imposed a considerable burden on the monasteries that were deprived of their property; there was no 'fair balance'; and Greece had violated Article 1 of the First Protocol. The Court has also recently started to emphasise that states do not have an unlimited margin of appreciation in pitching the level of compensation. The Court's more strident approach to the adequacy of compensation has been highlighted in cases such as *Broniowski v Poland* and *Pincová and Pinc v Czech Republic*.[66]

We have seen that in the context of the WTO, the Agreement on Trade-Related Investment Measures (TRIMS) contains rather modest provisions, which fall short of a right of foreign firms to compensation on expropriation.[67] However, the Court's creation of a human right to compensation dovetails with the transnational business demand for compensation on expropriation, allowing human rights law to make good the deficiency of international trade law. Indeed, Article 1 of the First Protocol affords transnational enterprises particularly strong protection, due to the requirement that expropriations conform to the 'general principles of international law'. It is to this provision that we now turn.

The Elasticity of 'General Principles of International Law'

It will be recalled that at the time of the ECHR negotiations, the UK went along with a form of words that made expropriation subject to the 'general principles of international law'. The Convention framers seemingly accepted that the inclusion of this formula 'would guarantee compensation to foreigners even if it were not paid to nationals'.[68] The British delegation therefore probably believed that this formulation would prevent the Court reviewing the vast majority of domestic compensation decisions. But the dynamic nature of international relations and international law means that in the long term these expectations are likely to be

---

[65] *Holy Monasteries v Greece*, judgment of 9 December 1994, A 301-A, para 75.
[66] *Broniowski v Poland* (2004) 43 EHRR 1; *Pincová and Pinc v Czech Republic* (2002) 3 EHRC 1078.
[67] See ch 2 above.
[68] Council of Europe (1985) vol IV, 10.

disappointed. Admittedly we are in the realm of speculation here, but nonetheless we can be reasonably confident of two developments.

First, the proportion of individuals and corporations covered by the protection of international law principles is likely to increase. Since the 1950s, partly as a result of the General Agreement on Tariffs and Trade (GATT) and the EEC, there has been an intensification of world trade and an upsurge in foreign direct investment. Consequently, with the passage of time, an increasing proportion of corporate property owners in each state are non-nationals and can therefore stand to benefit from the inclusion of the reference to general principles of international law. As the Court explained in *Lithgow*, the inclusion of these principles in Article 1 enables non-nationals to resort directly to the machinery of the Convention to enforce their rights, whereas otherwise they would have to seek recourse to diplomatic channels or to other available means of dispute-settlement.[69]

Quite apart from this globalisation of ownership, there is also the possibility that the Court (which is not bound by its previous decisions) may simply overturn its holding in *Lithgow* that the general principles of international law do not apply to a state's own nationals. It could do so with some justification, by arguing that changes in the nature of international law should override considerations of the original intent of the ECHR framers. Anthony Salgardo argued that in this context the Court should be suspicious of the political compromises and accommodations involved in the ECHR negotiations and should in preference discern and deploy overarching goals.[70] In this respect, the Court could cite the growing trend for international and supranational law to benefit states' own nationals. We have seen instances of this trend in WTO law and EU law, where increasingly the requirement of a trans-frontier element is either extremely easily satisfied or entirely unnecessary. Above all, the ECHR itself applies to a state's own nationals, whose exclusion from the benefits of the general principles of international law therefore appears anomalous and archaic.

Secondly, the general principles of international law are liable to change over time, and this process may lead to a further upgrading of the property right. These principles are part and parcel of constitutional debate and as such are not static but dynamic.[71] They evolve in response to ideological changes. In the mid-nineteenth century, for example, international property rights preventing expropriation of foreign-owned companies were well established. They were codified as international law, imposing strict minimum codes of conduct on all states. The legitimacy of these rules was not seriously questioned until the First World War.[72] As for the aftermath of the Second World War, this was a time of evolution: the world was embarking on a new era of supranationalism based on free trade. At the time of the ECHR negotiations, the UK government did not perhaps fully appreciate the extent to which international law was being transformed. Nonetheless, it falls

---

[69] *Lithgow* (above n 42) [115].
[70] Salgado (1986–87) 890.
[71] Tsagourias (2007) 79.
[72] Lipson (1985) 4, 24, 141.

to the courts to extract 'general principles' from the contemporary legal material available to them, so inevitably changes in the international regime governing the treatment of foreign investment will alter the content of such principles. Moreover, since the general principles are open-textured, their development allows ample scope for judicial legislation.[73]

In 1986, Judge Pettini, in his Dissenting Opinion in *Lithgow*, felt able to distil from the general principles of international law that, at least in relation to industrialised countries, compensation for non-nationals had to be full, adequate, equitable, prompt and appropriate, so as to arrive at an objective assessment of the actual loss suffered.[74] Today, legal globalisation has advanced yet further, and there is an increasing likelihood that principles of EU law or WTO law, as part of the global legal system, will 'spill over' to influence judicial perceptions of the general principles of international law. Under the Treaty on the Functioning of the European Union or the General Agreement on Trade in Services (GATS), for example, it may be impossible for states to nationalise sectors, even with compensation, if the effect is to prevent a service operator from another Member State or WTO Member from lawfully providing services. If expropriation is unlawful under the WTO or EU systems because it would conflict with corporate rights under, for example, the free movement of services or goods, it is not entirely fanciful to suggest that there may come a time when the Court may judge these norms to have 'ripened' into general principles of the international legal system, so that nationalisation could itself be contrary to these principles when it hinders transnational trade, regardless of the adequacy of compensation. In fact, such a position would merely mark a return to the situation that prevailed in the mid-nineteenth century, when interference with foreigners' property was permissible only in exceptional circumstances.[75] But even if the Court did not acknowledge the general principles of international law as extending this far, it is likely that those principles would at least be held to mandate full and prompt compensation, and this would go some way towards deterring nationalisation of successful concerns.

Compliance: The Evolution of Effective Enforcement

We have seen that the Court has pushed Article 1 of the First Protocol far beyond its textual limits and the original intent of its framers. However, this substantive development would not have much impact were it not accompanied by the development of enforcement machinery. At the time when the First Protocol was negotiated, it was unacceptable to the UK government that an international tribunal should be empowered to review British economic and social legislation.

---

[73] Tsagourias (2007) 96.
[74] *Lithgow* (above n 42) Dissenting Opinion.
[75] Lipson (1985) 8.

This explains not only the British efforts to weaken the property right but also the British approach to the enforcement machinery of the Strasbourg system as a whole. Owing to the resistance of the UK and other delegations, the founding Contracting States were sharply divided over whether to establish a Court at all. As a result, the negotiators reached a compromise whereby acceptance of the jurisdiction of the Court and acceptance of the right of individual petition were both to be optional. In consequence, most states accepted the right of individual petition for limited durations only, and it was always open to them not to renew. Thus the Court was established on shaky foundations—so much so that by the mid-1960s even some of its own judges openly doubted its chances of survival.[76]

Against this backdrop, it is hardly surprising that the Court remained for a long time constitutionally conservative, determined to remain an international rather than a supranational tribunal. In conformity with traditional conceptions of international law, therefore, the Court largely left questions regarding the internal enforcement of the Convention rights within the Contracting States to the States themselves. Thus judges who argued for an ECHR supremacy doctrine within the national legal systems, in the style of *Costa v ENEL*, remained isolated.[77] Most significantly, and in contrast to the ECJ, the Court did not single out the national courts as agents on which it could rely to pursue European human rights standards. Instead—and again in line with conventional ideas of international law—it merely concerned itself with whether states conformed to the Convention, an approach that might be characterised as 'institution neutrality'. This formed a stark contrast to the strategy pursued by the ECJ, which has been based on the relentless 'directed use of judicial power', enlisting national judiciaries to police the compliance with EU law of national governments and Parliaments.[78]

It was only in the 1990s that the Court started letting go of its institution neutrality and feeling its way towards a new focus on the domestic courts as enforcers of Convention rights in the Contracting States.[79] The Court had a new sense of self-confidence. In part, this was due to a growing familiarity with and acceptance among national polities of ECHR institutions and case law. In part, it was due to the Eleventh Protocol of the ECHR, which came into force in 1998 and transformed the Strasbourg machinery, making the right of individual petition mandatory for all Contracting States. But these developments were in any event inseparable from the growth of legal globalisation. This was the same period in which the WTO dispute settlement procedure was brought into force, and the ECJ further enhanced respect for EC law by fashioning its remedy of state liability and developing its doctrines of effectiveness and equivalence. At a time of neoliberal hegemony, national politicians were receptive to shifts in legal authority from

---

[76] Rolin (1965).

[77] *The Observer and The Guardian v United Kingdom*, Series A No. 216, (1991) 14 EHRR 153, 207 (Dissenting Opinion of Judges de Meyer and Pettiti).

[78] Tridimas (1998) 14. See also the discussion above in ch 3.

[79] Nicol (2001b).

national, electorally-accountable institutions to supranational non-accountable ones.

In the case of the ECHR, this shift was brought about largely by recourse to the previously neglected Article 13, which provides:

> Everyone whose rights and freedoms as set forth in this Convention are violated shall have an effective remedy before a national authority notwithstanding that the violation has been committed by persons acting in an official capacity.

In *Smith and Grady v United Kingdom*, the Court made it clear that there would be a violation of Article 13 if national courts assessed the lawfulness of interferences with the Convention rights by employing traditional national administrative law tests such as irrationality.[80] Instead, domestic courts had to apply the tests formulated by the Court itself of whether the interference with the applicants' rights answered a pressing social need and was proportionate to the legitimate aims pursued. In short, national courts must enforce Convention rights in the same way as the Strasbourg Court; otherwise, they will attract the opprobrium of being held responsible for a human rights violation by their state.

In *Z v United Kingdom*, the Court emphasised that Article 13 assumed a crucial function in ensuring that the national systems themselves provided redress for Convention breaches.[81] This meant that national legal systems had to deal with the substance of any complaint of breach of Convention rights and that damages had to be available for non-pecuniary loss. The ECJ had already shown in its *Francovich* case law the potent deterrent force of making a state shell out money for its breaches of Community law,[82] and so seemingly, the Strasbourg Court had now followed suit by creating its own damages remedy. In the same spirit, the Court suggested in *Matthews v United Kingdom* that every Contracting State which is also a Member State of the European Union is responsible for every EU act that breaches the Convention rights of those within their jurisdiction.[83] In view of the ever wider fields in which EU law now operates, this was a significant assertion of ECHR supremacy, with the Strasbourg Court seemingly pressing national courts to give primacy to its conception of fundamental rights over any competing interpretations emanating from the ECJ. The Court tempered this judgment in *Bosphorous v Ireland* by creating a presumption that a state does not depart from ECHR requirements when it merely implements EU obligations. This presumption would be rebutted only if in the circumstances of the case, protection of the Convention rights is manifestly deficient.[84]

In sum, therefore, it would appear that ECHR law has conformed to the common pattern of enhanced effectiveness during the 1990s and beyond, which we have also seen in the case of the WTO and the EU. It is against this backdrop that

---

[80] *Smith and Grady v United Kingdom*, Judgment of 18 February 1999, (1999) 29 EHRR 493.

[81] *Z v United Kingdom* (Application no 29392/95), judgment of 10 May 2001.

[82] Cases C-6/90 and C-9/90 *Francovich and Bonifaci v Italy* [1991] ECR I-5357, [1993] 2 CMLR 66.

[83] *Matthews v United Kingdom*, Judgment of 21 January 1999, (1999) 28 EHRR 361.

[84] *Bosphorous* (application no 45036/98), (2005) 42 EHRR 1, paras 155–56.

the substantive transformation of Article 1 of the First Protocol needs to be viewed.

Conclusion

The Strasbourg judiciary has hitherto, in the main, accorded Contracting States a wide margin of appreciation in the field of property rights. The Court was wary of getting bogged down with the property claims of the rich.[85] We can therefore acquit the Court of having thus far used Article 1 of the First Protocol in order to stifle major radical or redistributive economic programmes. On the other hand, the *untapped potential* of Article 1, as judicially interpreted, to consolidate the economic status quo is very substantial. The wide margin of appreciation in property cases rests on exceedingly fragile foundations. By constitutionalising the right to peaceful enjoyment of one's possessions, the ECHR consolidated existing patterns of property ownership. Whilst this protection of private property is relatively weak, nonetheless the very creation of such a cause of action serves to legitimise the extremely unequal distribution of property, giving the established pattern of property ownership a moral legitimacy it might not otherwise possess.[86] We must not underestimate the impact of constitutionalising *a certain conception* of private property in making it better placed to become the cultural norm.

Moreover, in the neoliberal era of the last thirty years, the Court has thrown off the shackles of the text of Article 1 of the First Protocol and has essentially rewritten it. Thus the Court has constructed its own right to private property based on ideas of fair balance, proportionality and compensation, which bears little resemblance to the modest protection of property rights originally intended. At the same time, the Convention's enforcement machinery has become progressively stronger, making it increasingly difficult for Contracting States to deviate from Strasbourg policy. Whilst hitherto the Court has generally chosen to adopt a low intensity of review in property cases, it nonetheless remains entirely at liberty to harden its stance in favour of the protection of property ownership for the benefit of corporations. It has already fashioned the jurisprudential weapons required to do so. Perhaps the most potent weapon of all, however, is the assumption that 'fundamental human rights' prevail over majoritarian politics, and this permits a highly contestable conception of property rights to prevail over democracy.

---

[85] Mendelson (1986) 75.
[86] Allen (2005) 299.

5

Neoliberalism as the Constitution

A STUDY OF THE three transnational regimes featured in this book reveals that transnational law now reaches deeply into national economic policy, shaping its contours and determining its limits. Furthermore, the systems of enforcement within these regimes have been strengthened so as to form, in substance, a higher constitutional law. We have seen that this constitutional protection of capitalism has been created not by organic, inevitable forces but by human beings. The message of this chapter is that by the same token, it could be dismantled by human beings.[1]

Just as there was nothing inevitable about neoliberal constitutionalism, so too there was nothing inevitable about the trend towards neoliberal globalisation generally. It has not been some spontaneous economic and technological happening. Rather, it constituted a profoundly *political* choice.[2] We have seen how, in the second half of the twentieth century, national leaders established a myriad of international organisations with ambitious aims.[3] Transnational regimes such as the General Agreement on Tariffs and Trade (GATT) and the European Economic Community (EEC) created the permissive environment that shaped the character of transnational economic activities.[4] In particular, these regimes facilitated the rise of the transnational corporations, and these giant firms have then been able to assume the role not merely of political actors but of protagonists in constitutional transformation.

In the last thirty years, the trend towards transnational economic governance has dramatically intensified. In particular, since the 1980s, as David Harvey has observed, 'there has everywhere been an emphatic turn towards neoliberalism in political-economic practices and thinking . . . Neoliberalism has, in short, become hegemonic as a mode of discourse'.[5] Such has become the strength of this neoliberal consensus that neoliberalism's political victory has been upgraded to a *constitutional* triumph at transnational level. Neoliberal constitutionalism was intended to bring about a yet greater degree of neoliberal globalisation. It was also designed to place neoliberalism on a more secure footing. Thus constitutional change has facilitated economic restructuring, which in turn has prompted further constitutional change.

---

[1] Anderson (2005) 151.
[2] Gowan (1999).
[3] Alvarez (2005) 7
[4] Ruggie (1983).
[5] Harvey (2005) 2–3.

From the point of view of neoliberals, there were distinct advantages in placing a transnational constitution above national constitutions. The latter offered limited scope for neoliberal change, since issues of democratic legitimacy made it difficult to entrench substantive policies. The British constitution, with its traditional resistance to entrenchment, provides a good example of the difficulties that would have been encountered. Transnationalism also had the advantage of a low profile: constitutional change could be passed off as the 'mere' amendment of international agreements. The 'high politics' of constitution-building could masquerade as the 'low politics' of highly technical trade policy. The international quality of transnational constitutionalism meant that it was uniquely able to tackle trade barriers of numerous countries in one fell swoop. In so doing it could start to erode the public ownership of economic sectors, which stood as a bulwark to privatisation in favour of foreign and domestic undertakings. Thus neoliberals could secure fundamental corporate property rights through the pursuit of free movement and competition law.

Transnational constitutionalism possesses another advantage over domestic constitutions from the point of view of neoliberals. If a national constitution opts for a rights-based approach, it would normally be expected to place some form of 'human rights' at the pinnacle of its domestic legal hierarchy. Yet in fact, neoliberals have been able to exploit the fragmented nature of the transnational constitution in order to place free movement and competition rights at the apex of the system of norms. Indeed, human rights and business rights have started to blur into one another. What, after all, *is* a human right? Traditionally, a human right is thought of as a right that is a basic entitlement of individuals, owed to them in their capacity as human beings. Yet if a decision is made to fundamentalise a business right by force of transnational law, that decision in itself necessarily presupposes that such a right is considered an essential element of human existence. In other words, it is the very fact of constitutionalisation that raises such a right to the status of a human right. On this reading, the free movement and competition rights discussed in this book actually constitute the fundamental human rights of transnational constitutionalism. Some of the more forthright scholars of the law of the World Trade Organization (WTO), such as Ernst-Ulrich Petersmann, have expressly articulated this.[6] For politicians and judges, by contrast, it has usually been politic to manufacture a rhetorical distinction between business rights and human rights, even though transnational law has essentially transformed business rights into our supreme human rights.

Insofar as national leaders have played the decisive role in shifting lawmaking power from their states to the transnational regimes, states have in a sense been the central players in their own downsizing.[7] Contrary to the trite adage that those with power like to hang on to it, neoliberal leaders have in fact been enthusiastic to abandon their absolute policymaking discretion. After all, in so doing they were

---

[6] Petersmann (1991).
[7] De Sousa Santos (2002) 94.

merely relinquishing 'the right to pursue economic policies one regards as abhor-rent'.[8] On the other hand, such a surrender of policymaking autonomy has had the highly desirable consequence of locking in neoliberal reforms against the vagaries of democracy. In effecting these constitutional changes, national leaders were receptive to the promptings of the business sector in favour of a constitution that would guarantee greater security, stability and commercial liberty for corpora-tions. The institutional constraints of the state had become fetters on the develop-ment of capitalism,[9] since transnational capitalism needed a global environment unhampered by nation states and democracy.[10] Neoliberal leaders have also been aided by a new layer of transnational judiciary, eager to pursue the aims of the transnational regimes of which they form part.

Our study appears to confirm William Robinson's assessment that the state is neither retaining its primacy nor disappearing but is rather being transformed and absorbed into a larger structure.[11] In essence, the state is not being destroyed but is being rendered teleological. Instead of governmental objectives being deter-mined by general elections, the constitution entrenches durable aims in respect of many important fields of policy, which cannot be changed through the normal political process. These aims are not, however, based on Hayekian orthodoxy. We need to return to the two conceptions of neoliberalism put forward by David Harvey, which were discussed above in chapter one. Only a minority of neoliberals keep to the holy grail of neoliberal principle: the majority set their sights on the maintenance and strengthening of an economic elite, deploying neoliberal doctrine as an intellectual cover and abandoning it when class interests call for alternative policies, such as governmental bailouts for failing corporations.[12] There is an acceptance, therefore, that instruments of restraint have to be com-bined with the built-in flexibility required in order to prevent economic paraly-sis.[13] Thus states can lawfully manipulate the economy so as to maintain the status quo in times of crisis, but there must be constitutional limits as to the extent to which they can transform the economy in pursuit of egalitarian conceptions of social justice. On this reading, the primary political aim of globalisation is there-fore to promote a new constitutionalism that consolidates the power gains of capital on a world scale.[14]

---

[8] Mount (1993) 242.
[9] Robinson (2004) 102.
[10] *Ibid*, 113.
[11] Robinson (2004) 87–88.
[12] Harvey (2005) 19.
[13] World Bank (1997) 101.
[14] Gill (2000) 6.

The Binding of Parliament

Business stability, business security and the reviewability of regulation thereby appear to have become the fundamental ground rules of the constitution, even though they are not acknowledged as such. By putting in place 'forward-looking commitment mechanisms', transnational regimes have attempted 'to create a set of long-term economic and political reforms that gain constitutional status, thereby underpinning the extension of the disciplinary power of capital'.[15] The objective is to insulate the making of economic policy from democratic control, thereby guaranteeing the durability of 'sound', disciplined economic policy.[16] To do so has required, in the words of the World Bank, a 'locking-in of good policies'. The Bank explained: 'a number of possible lock-in mechanisms are available, all with the same basic logic: to provide checks that restrain any impulse to depart from announced commitments.'[17]

Viewed from a British constitutional perspective, this 'locking-in' phenomenon is not really compatible with the demands of democracy. The transnational regimes tie states to commitments made in earlier years, irrespective of the views of the present generation. All of this sits uneasily with the British doctrine of parliamentary sovereignty, which is based on the impermissibility of the UK Parliament being bound by its predecessors. Although parliamentary sovereignty is different from national autonomy—the one concerning the relationship between our national judiciary and our Parliament, the other relating to the United Kingdom's freedom of policymaking vis-à-vis the rest of the world—these concepts can nonetheless no longer be kept in hermetically sealed containers: globalisation forces us to acknowledge the melding and blurring of the de facto and the de jure and the futility of maintaining a rigid separation between the two.[18] Above all, parliamentary sovereignty and national autonomy share the same underlying democratic rationale: they both help to prevent the present generation being ruled from the grave by previous generations.

The impermissibility of self-binding is an essential part of democracy.[19] In the British context, it helps in turn to safeguard the three democratic attributes of our constitution: contestability, ideological neutrality and accountability. All policies remain contestable since they will not be protected merely by virtue of the fact that the political community adopted them at some point in history; the constitution remains relatively ideologically neutral, since the values of the past cannot prevail

---

[15] *Ibid*, 9.

[16] *Ibid*, 12.

[17] World Bank (1997) 50.

[18] Parliament may retain the purely *theoretical* ability to pass any statute it likes, but *in reality* its legislative competence must increasingly be exercised in conformity with the expanding legal requirements of the transnational regimes. But *good* theory works in practice: that is what differentiates it from bad theory.

[19] See generally Schwartzberg (2007).

over the values of the present; and those wielding power remain accountable for all the policies they implement, since they cannot deploy the binding nature of earlier decisions in order to shirk political responsibility. However, whilst the rule that Parliament cannot be bound by its predecessors arguably remains formally intact, the democratic principle underlying the rule—that the political community of the present should not be constrained by the decisions of the past—has in practice been undermined by other means, namely the evolution of transnational regimes and the corresponding loss of national autonomy.

In writing of the transnational constitution it is easy to become nostalgic for a golden age of British democracy that never was; nonetheless in view of the analysis in this book, the argument that British governments and Parliaments formerly had a superior degree of policy choice is not particularly extravagant. In particular our analysis has highlighted two themes that have pervaded the evolution of the transnational regimes. The first theme is widened scope. We have witnessed an abandonment of the idea that international law should focus exclusively on a country's external frontiers. Instead, transnational regimes have made ever greater inroads into domestic policy. Particularly over the last thirty years, most national leaders have developed a taste for international governance and have expanded its scope by treaty amendment and other means. In all three regimes juridical bodies further facilitated this substantive expansion, by adopting a teleological and evolutive approach to interpretation, eschewing simple literalism along with concern for original intent and state sovereignty. These juridicial bodies have all assumed the role of 'balancing' corporate interests against competing social concerns, a function previously discharged by accountable politicians. In *Shrimp–Turtle* the WTO Appellate Body asserted its right to balance free trade against competing considerations.[20] In *Cassis de Dijon* the European Court of Justice (ECJ) held that it would assess the legitimate purpose and proportionality of policies that would hinder free movement.[21] In *Sporrong* the European Court of Human Rights asserted a right to balance the right to private property against other social concerns.[22] 'Balance' does not equate to 'neutrality'. Indeed, agnosticism in such matters simply is not possible: in each case the juridicial body privileged the free movement or private property right concerned, either explicitly or implicitly.

The second theme that has arisen throughout the development of the transnational regimes is enhanced bindingness. We have seen how high levels of embeddedness, in which the means of enforcement have been taken out of the hands of national governments, have made it difficult for those governments to discard their judicialised commitments.[23] To be sure, the enforcement machinery

---

[20] *United States–Import Prohibition on Certain Shrimp and Shrimp Products,* WTO case nos 58 (and 61) WT/DS58/AB/R, paras 152–53. See also discussion above in chs 1 and 2.

[21] Case 120/78 *Rewe-Zentrale AG v Bundesmonopolverwaltung für Branntwein ('Cassis de Dijon')* [1979] ECR 649. See also the extensive discussion of this case above in ch 3.

[22] *Sporrong and Lönnroth v Sweden* (1982) 5 EHRR 35. See also the discussion of this case above in ch 4.

[23] Kahler (2001) 297.

evolved somewhat differently in each of the transnational regimes. In the case of GATT, the panel system emerged from unpromising beginnings and was strengthened by the reforms of the WTO Agreements. In the case of the EEC, the landmark doctrines of direct effect and supremacy were laid down by the ECJ early in the Community's history, were tolerated by the Member States and were subsequently extended and enhanced by the ECJ. As for the European Convention on Human Rights (ECHR), the story is one of gradual evolution prompted by the universality of the individual right of petition. Despite these differing paths of development, however, the common trend is self-evidently one of ever-stronger enforceability.

Overall, one can perceive the globalisation process as operating at two levels. First, a new administrative law has emerged within the state itself, embodying and embedding transnational dynamics at the heart of the state. Secondly, procedures have been fashioned that operate at the transnational level.[24] Our analysis of vital provisions of WTO law, EU law and ECHR law have furnished ample evidence of these two processes in action. In the case of the WTO, the Agreements lay down various domestic procedures that WTO members are obliged to establish, but these are coupled with the WTO dispute settlement procedure, which is transnational. EU law relies primarily on national judicial enforcement through doctrines such as direct effect and supremacy, working alongside the system of preliminary references. But this deployment of national judicial resources has gone hand in hand with enforcement proceedings by the Commission. As for the ECHR, the European Court of Human Rights has in recent years repeatedly emphasised the role of the national authorities in according individuals their Convention rights, but this is combined with the transnational remedy of complaint to the Court itself. Domestic incorporation can prevent numerous applications coming before the European Court of Human Rights by resolving them instead at the domestic level, so it is arguable that the logic of the Strasbourg system virtually necessitates incorporation, even though incorporation is not a formal requirement.[25] All in all, this complex picture confirms that, rather than seeing a sharp differentiation between the 'supranational' EU and the 'international' ECHR and WTO, we need to perceive transnational regimes as constituting a *spectrum*. To this end, Joel Trachtman has suggested that the very term 'international law' needs to be revisited, as increasingly it comes to mean transnational law—an integrated body of domestic and international law that regulates both private persons and states, competition in both the market for private goods and the market for public goods. This reconception, according to Trachtman, should allow us to see the world as a single system.[26]

It is not only the rise of international judicial systems that has been remarkable—so too the way in which litigation has been opened up to private companies, either covertly (in the case of the WTO) or overtly (in the case of the EU and

---

[24] Cerny (1999b) 17.
[25] *Ireland v United Kingdom*, Application No 5310/71, judgment of 18 January 1978 [236]–[243].
[26] Trachtman (2006) 17–18.

ECHR). This change has transformed international litigation from being merely 'one of the many arrows in the quiver of Foreign Affairs Ministries to resolve legal disputes' to 'a tool accessible to all international actors'.[27] Thus private companies can deploy litigation both to enforce the supreme law *and* to change it through jurisprudence. They have thus been raised to the status of important constitutional actors. This constitutional elevation fits well with Saskia Sassen's argument that there is currently an aggregation of economic rights that constitutes a form of economic citizenship; but this citizenship does not belong to citizens but to firms and markets.[28]

As transnational law has secured its widened scope and enhanced effectiveness, a blurring has taken place between the international and the constitutional. The transnational agreements have increasingly assumed the characteristics of a constitution, and with it they have started, at least to a certain extent, to garner some of the normative prestige of a constitution and to benefit from the psychological advantage of a constitution in conditioning political behaviour. Yet this has been at the cost of sacrificing the ideological neutrality traditionally associated with international law. A quarter of a century ago, Prosper Weil identified the risk that under the cloak of international law, certain states were striving to implant an ideological system of law that would negate the inherent ideological pluralism of international society.[29] Transnational law's undermining of political democracy has eroded the international law tradition of accommodating a diversity of states in terms of political and religious belief.[30] In short, transnational law is partisan law: it forms, indeed, a partisan supra-constitution over and above the democracy of states. This ought surely to make us question the normative superiority that international law has often (perhaps mistakenly) enjoyed.

The startling paradox of the last thirty years, however, has been the way in which constitutional globalisation has gone hand in hand with the rhetoric of an international law right to democracy. As Thomas Franck has observed, democracy is increasingly seen as the *sine qua non* for validating governance and is perhaps evolving into an international legal obligation. Arising from the building blocks of the rights to self determination, free expression and peace, the idea of an international democratic entitlement enjoys a growing degree of legitimacy.[31] Such a 'right to democracy' was deployed, to some extent, to justify the invasion of Iraq, especially once weapons of mass destruction failed to materialise.

Yet democracy requires policy choice. If transnational law's commitment to private enterprise compels governments to implement significantly homogenous economic policies, this undermines the supposed international commitment to democracy. Democracy should allow a permanent choice between ideologies, whereas the transnational provisions presently in force represent the entrench-

---

[27] Romano (1998–99) 749.
[28] Sassen (1996) 41.
[29] Weil (1983) 441.
[30] *Ibid*, 420.
[31] Franck (1992).

ment of a single global ideology. The transnational provisions thereby serve to undermine the right to differ, which is the emblem of sovereignty. They also pervert the traditional purpose of international law, which is ostensibly to establish orderly relations among sovereign and equal states and to serve the common aims of members of the international community. If aims are entrenched, there is less emphasis on ongoing state consent and more emphasis on 'universal' general rules.

In 1970 the United Nations General Assembly adopted a Resolution purporting to define the sovereign immunity of states. This emphasised that 'each state has the right freely to choose and develop its political, social, economic and cultural systems'.[32] The resolution's preamble recommended strict observance of the principle that states are to suffer no interference or coercion with regard to their political independence. By way of contrast, transnational economic law, by binding states in areas that fall emphatically within traditional domestic jurisdiction, compromises the independent development of those states' economic and political destinies. At the heart of the problem lies the disconnection between the perspectives of the business community, which seeks long-term business certainty, and those of the world of politics, where value is ascribed to political innovation and to the preservation of the means to innovate. This distinction has, however, diminished as the constitution has increasingly come to enshrine the concerns of the business community, and the evolution of the constitution has become 'business pursued by other means'.

Dismantling the Teleological State

In the 1940s Friedrich A von Hayek made a demand that, in the post-war era of socialism and social democracy, was outrageous: he insisted that democracy should in fact be limited, so as to constitutionalise the principal elements of neoliberalism. The limited democracy craved by Hayek has essentially come into existence, by virtue of the transnational regimes. But the problem is that democracy bereft of choice over fundamental aspects of economic governance is so limited as scarcely to constitute democracy at all. We have essentially replaced the democratic state with the teleological state. The time has come, therefore, for a second proposal, perhaps as outrageous in the present neoliberal climate as was Hayek's a generation ago. *The proposal is that we should acknowledge that the abandonment of full democracy has been a mistake and should press for the introduction of a new world system that guarantees the far greater autonomy of states.* This may seem like a radical proposal, but (as Hayek himself recognised) merely because proposals are radical

---

[32] Resolution No 2625 (XXV) Declaration on Principles of International Law concerning Friendly Relations and Co-operation among States in accordance with the Charter of the United Nations (A/8082), 24 October 1970.

is no reason to discount them; they should be assessed on their normative merits. The proposal is not merely that states should have more power vis-à-vis international organisations but more fundamentally that states should be liberated from their present teleology. In place of transnational law pre-committing states in perpetuity to a specific ideology, such choices should be constantly made and remade through states' democratic mechanisms.

The 'new constitutionalism' of the transnational regimes may seem to have succeeded, yet it contains irresoluble contradictions, which perhaps contain the seeds of its own destruction.[33] National politics still carries with it the promise of comprehensiveness: parties still go to the polls promising to solve the country's problems, not to do whatever they can within their ever more limited competence in order to improve things. Moreover, the state remains implicated in global economic developments, and questions of political legitimacy are endemic.[34] If we are content with a post-democratic society, then it is of course open to us to maintain the existing transnational constitution. But if so, there ought to be a more honest and open recognition that our transnational arrangements are in substance constitutional and that they bind us to a world of limited democracy. Conversely, if we wish to re-establish democracy, then this will require nothing short of the elimination of those transnational obligations that disable our political community from making ongoing ideological choices. The idea that the transnational regimes have exceeded the proper bounds of democratic governance has wide purchase. As Joseph Stiglitz, former Chief Economist at the World Bank, wrote in *Globalization and its Discontents,*

> Countries need to consider the [economic] alternatives, and through democratic processes, make these choices for themselves. It should be—and it should have been— the task of the international economic institutions to provide the countries with the wherewithal to make these informed choices on their own, with an understanding of the consequences and the risks of each. The essence of freedom is the right to make a choice—and to accept the responsibility that comes with it.[35]

As David Schneiderman has argued, it is possible to imagine a different global order—one in which state capacity with regard to most subject matters is deliberately left open rather than being constrained by constitution-like arrangements. In place of our transnational system for uniform economic governance, it would be possible to have a world system that facilitates and even encourages diversity, innovation and experimentation in all respects, including in respect of the relationship between politics and markets.[36] The role of states could thereby be revived as the democratic laboratories of humankind in which new experiments, including those concerning public and private provision of services and goods, can be contrasted and compared. In place of a world order that puts capitalism first

---

[33] Gill (2000) 19.
[34] Cooper (1998) 3.
[35] Stiglitz (2002) 88.
[36] Schneiderman (2008) 11.

and democracy second, it should be possible to create one that puts democracy first, capitalism second.

Not all critics of neoliberal globalisation would agree that the revival of the state offers the best remedy for globalisation's erosion of democracy. There is a fashionable disdain for the state. The alternative view is that the way to democratise globalisation is to have more globalisation. This view tends to be presented in one of two forms. Some commentators urge the creation of global social institutions to counteract and balance the existing institutions. Others insist that there should somehow be a 'globalisation from below' by focusing on the potential of transnational 'new social movements'.

The work of Noreena Hertz exemplifies the first tendency.[37] Hertz urges that politics be reframed at a global level, by establishing a World Social Organization (WSO) to counter the domination of the WTO. She proposes a new adjudication mechanism that would cover both organisations and would thereby seek to reconcile trade and other interests when the WTO and WSO inevitably clash. 'Balancing' has already been a pervasive theme of this book. As Carol Harlow has observed, to encourage a 'balancing' role for transnational agencies simply leads to more judicialisation and less democracy.[38] Harlow has pointed out that there has already been a substantial relocation of power from parliamentary institutions towards a non-elected judiciary, and this is a feature of transnational governance, linked to the dominance there of commercial interests.[39] When attempts are made to ward off accusations of bias towards economic and property interests in the judicial process by binding the judiciary, for example, through the standards of human rights, the inevitable consequence is a further accretion of judicial power. Harlow has noted that at national, transnational and international levels, these shifts are now occurring. She rightly warns that the erosion of democracy should not be allowed to continue without consideration of whether a heightened degree of legal accountability to individuals is likely to end in superseding the forms of collective political and democratic accountability that modern society has learned to value most highly.[40] In cases such as *Shrimp–Turtle, Cassis de Dijon* and *Sporrong,* the juridicial bodies of the transnational regimes have already been drawn into the task of adjudicating between trade and property rights and competing considerations.[41] To create anything in the nature of a World Social Organization would merely serve to endow the execution of such balancing exercises by non-accountable institutions with greater legitimacy.

Hertz's proposal therefore constitutes, in fact, an astonishingly undemocratic proposal to sanctify the transfer to the judiciary of adjudiciation between the

---

[37] Hertz (2001).

[38] Harlow (2002) 144.

[39] *Ibid,* 166.

[40] *Ibid,* 167.

[41] *Shrimp-Turtle* (above n 20); Case 120/78 *Rewe-Zentrale AG v Bundesmonopolverwaltung für Branntwein* [1979] ECR 649; *Sporrong and Lönnroth v Sweden,* Application no 7151/75, 7152/75, judgment of 23 September 1982.

economic and the social. Essentially, indeed, Hertz seeks to substitute a global 'fair balance' for the constraints of democracy. Such a rejection of democracy fits well with the theory advanced by Philip Cerny that democracy did not become a major mode of governance because of an abstract idea; rather, it sprung from the state. Cerny is pessimistic, therefore, at the prospects of transplanting democracy into the kind of world that is crystallising through globalisation, particularly in view of the domination of private interests therein.[42]

The second group of opponents of the revival of the state focuses attention on political strategy rather than institutional outcomes. They urge the replacement of state-based politics by an approach based on constructing global civil society 'from below'. The idea is that we should bypass state-based constraints as to what counts as politics by focusing instead on emerging transnational 'new social movements'. Involvement in state-based institutions such as political parties and parliaments is therefore to be rejected in favour of participation in transnational struggles. Iris Marion Young, for instance, argues that the worldwide demonstrations in opposition to the war in Iraq may herald the emergence of a global public sphere, and this is to be preferred to a return to Westphalian ideas of sovereignty.[43] Michael Hardt and Antonio Negri advocate 'a world beyond sovereignty, beyond authority', where both sovereignty and authority have (somehow) been destroyed.[44] They press for institutions of democracy that 'coincide with the communicative and collaborative networks that constantly produce and reproduce social life' (whatever that means).[45]

But these nebulous ideas ignore the fact that, as Leo Panicht has put it, 'insofar as there is any effective democracy at all in relation to the power of capitalists and bureaucrats it is still embedded in political structures that are national or sub-national in scope'.[46] Today's globalisation, Panicht has observed, is after all authored by states and is primarily about reorganising states.[47] In a particularly compelling critique of the 'global civil society' enthusiasts, David Chandler argues against their rejection of formal political institutions. He observes that they deploy the term 'global' primarily negatively, in the sense that their top priority is to refuse to operate within the political logic of the state. Furthermore, Chandler notes that their favoured transnational activity has a limited and transient impact and leaves control in the hands of the powerful. Chandler concludes that the rejection of state-based politics reflects a deeper problem: an unwillingness to engage in political contestation per se. The ultimate result is further to shrink the political sphere, reducing it to a small circle of unaccountable elites and leaving political conflicts isolated from any formal process of democratic accountability.[48]

---

[42] Cerny (1999b).
[43] Young (2007) 141.
[44] Hardt and Negri (2005) 237–38.
[45] *Ibid*, 353–55.
[46] Panitch (1997) 109.
[47] Ibid, 85.
[48] Chandler (2007).

The only prospect, therefore, for a more democratic world lies in confronting the necessity of dismantling the teleological state in favour of the democratic state. This requires the creation of an international order very different from the present transnational regimes. The world system would have to place a far higher value on democratic policymaking within the states themselves. The most potent objection to such a reorientation of world society towards the autonomy of states is that such a solution does not address the reality of an interdependent world. The essence of such an argument is that only near-global or very large regional structures, such as the three regimes that feature in this book, can hope to deal with the world's problems effectively. Yet there is a risk that such an accusation mischaracterises what is being proposed. The call is for the trend towards transnational governance to be reversed, not for collective action to be eliminated altogether. A world society based on far greater state autonomy does not mean a world society based on *total* state autonomy, which would be as unlikely as it is undesirable. In a transnational democracy there would still be room for collective action when such action is absolutely indispensable (such as on aspects of peace-making, health, environmental protection and anti-crime measures) and where such aims enjoy the ongoing support of the states concerned. But this would be a far cry from the 'globalised overkill' of the present era. Above all, however, international agreements would have to be designed to permit ideological diversity among states. Indeed, they would need to be designed not merely to tolerate but ultimately to facilitate the realisation of the full range of alternative economic strategies.[49]

Delineating the boundary line between issues that should be decided nationally and those that require a collective response cannot in fact be a matter of objective analysis. The very delineation of that boundary line is ideologically charged. Consider the provisions discussed in this book. Those who approve of the WTO/EU/ECHR economic policy will in all likelihood judge that provisions embodying free trade, competition and corporate private property rights relate to vital matters of interdependence; by contrast those less enamoured of transnational economic policy may well be more inclined to regard these policy areas as matters on which sovereign states should be allowed to make their own, independent decisions. In this regard, we have significantly underestimated the extent to which globalised interconnectedness represents a choice. It has not materialised as some inevitable consequence of a shrinking world and new technology. Instead it represents a deliberate *ideological* decision on the part of national leaders, at the bidding of transnational corporations and with the willing help of transnational and national judiciaries. It is therefore not possible objectively to calculate the appropriate level of constitutional globalisation on the basis of the 'new interconnecedness' of today's world.

The argument that an interdependent world necessitates extensive globalised decision-making is profoundly based on the assumption that there is agreement as to the set of good, correct and sound policies to be adopted in respect of those

---

[49] Panitch (1997) 112.

matters on which interdependence is alleged to exist. But, as this book has shown, the policies presently entrenched in transnational law are not self-evidently good, correct or sound: they are deeply controversial and deeply partisan, based as they are on the view that what is good for the transnational corporation is in the general good. If, however, the very direction of collective action is far from self-evident, then the interdependence argument is significantly undermined. Our present constitutionalism binds political communities in perpetuity in areas in which it is most vitally important that they retain ongoing choice. It is against the backdrop of this extreme teleology that we are led to the conclusion that the trend towards limited democracy has been a mistake and that the time has come for this mistake to be corrected.

BIBLIOGRAPHY

AARONSON, S (1996), *Trade and the American Dream* (University of Kentucky Press, Lexington).

ACHESON, D (1949), 'Economic Policy and the ITO Charter' xx Dept State Bull 626.

ACKERMAN, B (1991), *We the People: Foundations* (Harvard University Press, Cambridge, MA).

ADAMS BROWN, W (1950), *The United States and the Restoration of World Trade* (The Brookings Institution, Washington, DC).

ALDER, J (2007), *Constitutional and Administrative Law*, 6th edn (Palgrave Macmillan, Basingstoke).

ALTER, K (2001), *Establishing the Supremacy of European Law* (Oxford University Press, Oxford).

ALLAN, T (2000), 'The Politics of the British Constitution: A Response to Professor Ewing's Paper' *Public Law* 374.

—— (2001), *Constitutional Justice* (Oxford University Press, Oxford).

ALLEN, T (2005), *Property and the Human Rights Act 1998* (Hart Publishing, Oxford).

ALVAREZ, J (2005), *International Organizations as Law-Makers* (Oxford University Press, Oxford).

AMAN, A (2001), 'The Limits of Globalization and the Future of Administrative Law: From Government to Governance' 8 *Indiana Journal of Global Legal Studies* 379.

ANDENAS, M, GORMLEY, L, HADJIEMMANUIL, C, and HARDEN, I, (eds) (1997), *European Economic and Monetary Union: The Institutional Framework* (Kluwer Law International, London).

ANDERSEN, S and BURNS, T (1996), 'The European Union and the Erosion of Parliamentary Democracy: A Study of Post-parliamentary Governance', in S Andersen and K Eliassen (eds), *The European Union: How Democratic Is It?* (Sage, London).

ANDERSON, G (2005), *Constitutional Rights after Globalization* (Hart Publishing, Oxford).

ANTINORI, M (1994–95), 'Does *Lochner* live in Luxembourg? An Analysis of the Property Rights Jurisprudence of the European Court of Justice' 18 *Fordham International Law Journal* 1778.

APPELBAUM, R, and ROBINSON, W (eds) (2005), *Critical Globalization Studies* (Routledge, New York and London).

ARAI-TAKAHASHI, Y (2002), *The Margin of Appreciation Doctrine and the Principle of Proportionality in the Jurisprudence of the ECHR* (Intersentia, Antwerp).

ARMSTRONG, D, FARRELL, T and LAMBERT, H (2007), *International Law and International Relations* (Cambridge University Press, Cambridge).

ARMSTRONG, K, and BULMER, S (1998), *The Governance of the Single European Market* (Manchester University Press, Manchester).

ARROWSMITH, S (2004), 'An Assessment of the New Legislative Package on Public Procurement' 41 *Common Market Law Review* 1277.

Bibliography

ARTHURS, H (2008), 'Constitutionalism: An Idea whose Time has Come . . . and Gone?' 75 *Amicus Curiae* 3.

AZOULAI, L (2008), 'The Court of Justice and the Social Market Economy: The Emergence of an Ideal and the Conditions for its Realization' 45 *Common Market Law Review* 1335.

BAKER, D, GAMBLE, A, and LUDLAM, S (1993), 'Whips or Scorpions? The Maastricht Vote and the Conservative Party' 46 *Parliamentary Affairs* 151.

BALL, C (1996), 'The Making of a Transnational Capitalist Society: The Court of Justice, Social Policy, and Individual Rights under the European Community's Legal Order' 37 *Harvard International Law Journal* 307.

BAQUERO CRUZ, J (2005), 'Beyond Competition: Services of General Interest and European Community Law' in G De Búrca (ed), *EU Law and the Welfare State: In Search of Solidarity* (Oxford University Press, Oxford).

BARAV, A (1994), 'Omnipotent Courts' in D Curtin and T Heukels (eds), *Institutional Dynamics of European Integration: Essays in Honour of Henry G Schermers* (Martinus Nijhoff, Dordrecht).

BARNARD, C (1999), 'EC "Social" Policy' in P Craig and G de Búrca (eds), *The Evolution of EU Law* (Oxford University Press, Oxford).

BARTLE, I (2005), *Globalization and EU Policy-Making: The Neoliberal Transformation of Telecommunications and Electricity* (Manchester University Press, Manchester).

BAXI, U (2002), *The Future of Human Rights* (Oxford University Press, Oxford).

BEATSON, J and TRIDIMAS, T (1998), *New Directions in European Public Law* (Hart Publishing, Oxford).

BEDJAOUI, M (1994), 'On the Efficacy of International Organisations: Some Variations on an Inexhaustible Theme' in N Blokker and S Muller (eds), *Towards More Effective Supervision by International Organizations: Essays in Honour of Henry G Schemers* (Martinus Nijhoff, Dordrecht).

BEILER, A and MORTON, A (2001), *Social Forces in the Making of the New Europe* (Palgrave, Basingstoke).

BELLAMY, R (2003), 'Sovereignty, Post-Sovereignty and Pre-Sovereignty: Three Models of the State, Democracy and Rights within the European Union' in N Walker (ed), *Sovereignty in Transition* (Hart Publishing, Oxford).

BELLAMY, R (2007), *Political Constitutionalism* (Cambridge University Press, Cambridge).

BELLO, W (2005), 'The Crisis of the Globalist Project and the New Economics of George W Bush' in R Appelbaum and W Robinson (eds), *Critical Globalization Studies* (Routledge, New York and London).

BENHABIB, S (ed) (1996), *Democracy and Difference: Contesting the Boundaries of the Political* (Princeton University Press, Princeton).

BENN, T (1982), *Arguments for Democracy* (Penguin, Harmondsworth Middlesex).

BERLIN, I (2007), *Liberty* (Oxford University Press, Oxford).

BEVERIDGE, W (1944), *Full Employment in a Free Society* (Allen and Unwin, London).

BHAGWATI, J (1987), 'Services' in J Finger and A Olechowski (eds), *The Uruguay Round: A Handbook on the Multilateral Trade Negotiations* (The World Bank, Washington, DC).

BICKEL, A (1986), *The Least Dangerous Branch* (Yale University Press, New Haven and London).

BICKERTON, C, CUNLIFFE, P and GOURENVITCH A (eds) (2007), *Politics without Sovereignty* (UCL Press, London).

BINGHAM, Lord (2006), 'The Rule of Law Today', Sixth Sir David Williams Lecture, Centre for Public Law, University of Cambridge, 16 November 2006.

BLAIR, A (2002), *Saving the Pound? Britain's Road to Monetary Union* (Prentice Hall, London).

BLANK, A, and MARCEAU, G (1997), 'A History of Multilateral Negotiations on Procurement: From ITO to WTO' in B Hoekman and P Mavroidis (eds), *Law and Policy in Public Purchasing: The WTO Agreement on Government Procurement* (University of Michigan Press, Ann Arbor).

BLOKKER, N, and MULLER, S (eds) (1994), *Towards More Effective Supervision by International Organizations: Essays in Honour of Henry G Schemers* (Martinus Nijhoff, Dordrecht).

BOGDANOR, V (2004), 'Our New Constitution' 120 *Law Quarterly Review* 242

BOURGEOIS, J (2000), 'The European Court of Justice and the WTO: Problems and Challenges' in J Weiler (ed), *The EU, the WTO and the NATFA: Towards a Common Law of International Trade* (Oxford University Press, Oxford).

BRADLEY, A, and EWING, K (2003), *Constitutional and Administrative Law*, 13th edn (Pearson, Longman, Harlow).

BRADLEY, B, and LEUTWILER, F (1985), *Trade Policies for a Better Future: Proposals for Action* (World Trade Organization, Geneva).

BROWN, W, (1950), 'Why Private Business Should Support the ITO' xxii Dept State Bull 132.

—— (2004), ' "The Most We can Hope for . . ." Human Rights and the Politics of Fatalism' 103 *South Atlantic Quarterly* 451.

BROWNLIE, I (2003), *Principles of Public International Law*, 6th edn (Oxford University Press, Oxford).

BRUMMER, A (2008), *The Crunch* (Random House Business Books, London).

BUTT, R (1967), *The Power of Parliament* (Constable, London).

CAIRNCROSS, A (1985), *Years of Recovery: British Economic Policy, 1945–51* (Methuen, London).

CAMPBELL, T (1999), 'Human Rights: A Culture of Controversy' 26 *Journal of Law and Society* 6.

CAMPBELL, T, EWING, K and TOMKINS, A (eds) (2001), *Sceptical Essays on Human Rights* (Oxford University Press, Oxford)

CASS, D (2005), *The Constitutionalization of the World Trade Organisation* (Oxford University Press, Oxford).

CERNY, P (1999a), 'Globalization, Governance and Complexity' in A Prakash and J Hart (eds), *Globalization and Governance* (London, Routledge).

—— (1999b), 'Globalization and the Erosion of Democracy' 36 *European Journal of Political Research* 1.

CERNY, P, MENZ, G and SOEDERBERG, S (2005), 'Different Roads to Globalization: Neoliberalism, the Competition State and Politics in a More Open World' in S Soederberg, G Menz and P Cerny (eds), *Internalizing Globalization, The Rise of Neoliberalism and the Decline of National Varieties of Capitalism* (Palgrave Macmillan, London).

CHANDLER, D (2007), 'Deconstructing Sovereignty: Constructing Global Society' in C Bickerton, P Cunliffe and A Gourenvitch (eds), *Politics without Sovereignty* (UCL Press, London).

CHALMERS, D, HAJIEMMANUIL, C, MONTI, G and TOMKINS, A (2006), *European Union Law* (Cambridge University Press, Cambridge).

COMMISSION OF THE EUROPEAN COMMUNITIES (1980), *Communication from the Commission Concerning the Consequences of the Judgment given by the Court of Justice on 20 February 1979 in Case 120/78 ('Cassis de Dijon')* [OJ 1980, No C256/2].

Bibliography

COMMISSION OF THE EUROPEAN COMMUNITIES (1984a), Commission position paper, *Application of Articles 92 and 93 of the EEC Treaty to public authorities' holdings* (Bulletin EC 91984).

—— (1984b), Application of Articles 92 and 93 of the EEC Treaty to public authorities' holdings, the Commission's position (Bulletin EC 9–1984).

—— (1985), *Completing the Internal Market*, COM(85)310 14 June 1985.

—— (1993), Commission Communication to the Member States, *Application of Articles 92 and 93 of the EEC Treaty and of Article 5 of Commission Directive 80/723/EEC to public undertakings in the manufacturing sector* (93/C307/03).

—— (1994), *23rd Competition Report*.

—— (1995). *Communication on the Broader Use of Standardisation in Community Policy* COM (1995) 412 Final.

—— (2005), *State Aid Action Plan: Less and Better Targeted State Aid, A Roadmap for State Aid Reform (2005–2009)*.

—— (2006), *Report on Competition Policy 2006 including Commission Staff Working Document*.

—— (2007a), *Commission Staff Working Document, Annex to the Report from the Commission Report on Competition Policy 2006* (COM 2007 (358) final).

—— (2007b), *Vademecum Community Rules on State Aid*.

—— (2008), *Vademecum Community Law on State Aid*.

—— (2009), *Communication from the Commission: Temporary Community framework for State aid measures to support access to finance in the current financial and economic crisis*, Official Journal of the European Union, 22.1.2009, C 16/1.

CONSERVATIVE PARTY (1983), *The Resolute Approach* (Conservative Party, London).

COOPER, D (1998), *Governing Out of Order* (Rivers Oram Press, London).

COUNCIL OF EUROPE (1985), *Collected Edition of the Travaux Préparatoires of the European Convention on Human Rights* (Martinus Nijhoff, The Hague).

COWHEY, P (1993), 'Elect Locally, Order Globally: Domestic Politics and Multilateral Cooperation' in J Ruggie (ed), *Multilateralism Matters* (Columbia University, New York).

COWLEY, P (2002), *Revolts and Rebellions* (Politico's, London).

—— (2005), *The Rebels* (Politico's, London).

CRAIG, P (1990), *Public Law in the United Kingdom and the United States of America* (Oxford University Press, Oxford).

—— (1991), 'Sovereignty of the United Kingdom Parliament after *Factortame*' 11 *Yearbook of European Law* 221.

—— (1997a), 'Formal and Substantive Conceptions of the Rule of Law: An Analytical Framework' *Public Law* 467.

—— (1997b), 'Report on the United Kingdom' in A-M Slaughter, A Stone Sweet and J Weiler (eds), *The European Court and the National Courts: Doctrine and Jurisprudence* (Hart Publishing, Oxford).

—— (1999), 'The Nature of the Community: Integration, Democracy and Legitimacy' in P Craig and G de Búrca (eds), *The Evolution of EU Law* (Oxford University Press, Oxford).

—— (2006), *EU Administrative Law* (Oxford University Press, Oxford).

CRAIG, P and DE BÚRCA, G (2008), *EU Law: Text, Cases and Materials*, 4th edn (Oxford University Press, Oxford).

—— (eds) (1999), *The Evolution of EU Law* (Oxford University Press, Oxford).

CREMONA, M (1999), 'External Relations and External Competence: The Emergence of an Integrated Policy' in P Craig and G De Búrca (eds), *The Evolution of EU Law* (Oxford University Press, Oxford).

—— (2000), 'EC External Commercial Policy after Amsterdam: Authority and Interpretation within Interconnected Legal Orders' in J Weiler (ed), *The EU, the WTO and the NATFA: Towards a Common Law of International Trade* (Oxford University Press, Oxford).

CROOME, J (1995), *Reshaping the World Trade System: A History of the Uruguay Round* (World Trade Organization, Geneva).

CROUCH, C (2005), *Capitalist Diversity and Change: Recombinant Governance and Institutional Entrepreneurs* (Oxford University Press, Oxford).

CULPEPPER, P (2006), 'Capitalism, Coordination and Economic Change: The French Political Economy since 1985' in P Culpepper, A Hall and B Palier (eds), *Changing France: The Politics that Markets Make* (Palgrave Macmillan, Basingstoke).

CULPEPPER, P, HALL, A and PALIER, B (eds) (2006), *Changing France: The Politics that Markets Make* (Palgrave Macmillan, Basingstoke).

CURZON, G (1965), *Multilateral Commercial Diplomacy* (Michael Joseph, London).

DAHRENDORF, R (1999), 'The Third Way and Liberty: An Authoritarian Streak in Europe's New Center' *Foreign Affairs* 16.

DAINTITH, T (1997), 'Between Domestic Democracy and an Alien Rule of Law? Some Thoughts on the "Independence" of the Bank of England' in M Andenas, L Gormley, C Hadjiemmanuil and I Harden (eds), *European Economic and Monetary Union: The Institutional Framework* (Kluwer Law International, London).

DAM, K, (1970), *The GATT: Law and the International Economic Organization* (University of Chicago Press, Chicago).

—— (2005) 'Cordell Hull, the Reciprocal Trade Act and the WTO' in E-U Petersmann (ed), *Reforming the World Trading System: Legitimacy, Efficiency and Democratic Governance* (Oxford University Press, Oxford).

DASHWOOD, A (2001), 'The Constitution of the European Union after Nice: Law-making Procedures' 26 *European Law Review* 215.

DAVIES, A (2008), 'One Step Forward, Two Steps Back? The *Viking* and *Laval* Cases in the ECJ' 37 *Industrial Law Journal* 126.

DAVIES, D (1995), *The World Trade Organization and GATT '94* (Carlton, Pinner).

DE BÚRCA, G (1999), 'The Institutional Development of the EU: A Constitutional Analysis' in P Craig and G De Búrca (eds), *The Evolution of EU Law* (Oxford University Press, Oxford).

—— (2003), 'The Constitutional Challenge of New Governance in the European Union' 28 *European Law Review* 814.

—— (ed) (2005), *EU Law and the Welfare State: In Search of Solidarity* (Oxford University Press, Oxford).

DE BÚRCA, G and GERSTENBERG, O (2006), 'The Denationalization of Constitutional Law' 47 *Harvard International Law Journal* 243.

DE BÚRCA, G and SCOTT, J (2006), *Law and New Governance in the EU and the US* (Hart Publishing, Oxford).

—— (eds) (2001), *The EU and the WTO: Legal and Constitutional Issues* (Hart Publishing, Oxford).

DE HANN, J and GORMLEY, L (1997), 'Independence and Accountability of the European Central Bank' in M Andenas, L Gormley, C Hadjiemmanuil and I Harden (eds), *European*

Economic and Monetary Union: The Institutional Framework (Kluwer Law International, London).

DE SOUSA SANTOS, B (2002), *Toward a New Legal Common Sense*, 2nd edn (Butterworths, London).

DE WITTE, B (1999), 'Direct Effect, Supremacy and the Nature of the Legal Order' in P Craig and G De Búrca (eds), *The Evolution of EU Law* (Oxford University Press, Oxford).

—— (2006), 'Non-Market Values in Internal Market Legislation' in N Nic Shuibhne (ed), *Regulating The Internal Market* ((Edward Elgar, Cheltenham).

DE ZWAAN, J (1986), 'The Single European Act: Conclusion of a Unique Document' 23 *Common Market Law Review* 747.

DEMBOUR, M-B (2006), *Who Believes in Human Rights? Reflections on the European Convention* (Cambridge University Press, Cambridge).

DESTLER, I (2005), *American Trade Politics*, 4th edn (Institute for International Economics, Washington, DC).

DICEY, A (1962), *Introduction to the Law of the Constitution* (Macmillan, London).

DIDIER, P (1997), 'The Uruguay Round Government Procurement Agreement: Implementation in the European Union' in B Hoekman and P Mavroidis (eds), *Law and Policy in Public Purchasing: The WTO Agreement on Government Procurement* (University of Michigan Press, Ann Arbor).

DIEBOLD, W (1952), *The End of the ITO* (Princeton University Press, Princeton).

DORLING, D, THOMAS, B, FAHMY, E, GORDON, D and LUPTON, R (2007), *Poverty, Wealth and Place in Britain, 1968 to 2005* (Polity Press, London).

DOUZINAS, C (2000), *The End of Human Rights* (Hart Publishing, Oxford).

DRESNER, D (2004), 'The Global Governance of the Internet: Bringing the State Back In' 119 *Political Science Review* 477.

DRYZEK, J (2000), *Deliberative Democracy and Beyond: Liberals, Critics, Contestations* (Oxford University Press, Oxford).

DUNKLEY, G (2000), *The Free Trade Adventure: The WTO, the Uruguay Round and Globalism—A Critique* (Zed Books, New York).

DUNN, J (1999), 'Situating Political Accountability' in A Prezeworski, S Stokes and B Manin (eds), *Democracy, Accountability and Representation* (Cambridge University Press, Cambridge).

DWORKIN, R (1977), *Taking Rights Seriously* (Duckworth, London).

—— (1986), *Law's Empire* (Fontana, London).

EDWARD, D and HOSKINS, M (1995), 'Article 90: Deregulation and EC Law: Reflections Arising from the XVI FIDE Conference' 32 *Common Market Law Review* 157.

ELSTER, J (ed) (1998), *Deliberative Democracy* (Cambridge University Press, Cambridge).

EMBERLAND, M (2006), *The Human Rights of Companies* (Oxford University Press, Oxford).

EVANS, M (2005), 'Neoliberalism and Policy Transfer in the British Competition State: The Case of Welfare Reform' in S Soenderberg, G Menz and P Cerny (eds), *Internalizing Globalization: The Rise of Neoliberalism and the Decline of National Varieties of Capitalism* (Palgrave Macmillan, Basingstoke).

EVERLING, U (1996), 'Will Europe Slip on Bananas? The *Bananas* Judgment of the Court of Justice and National Courts' 33 *Common Market Law Review* 401.

EWING, K, (2000), 'The Politics of the British Constitution' *Public Law* 405

—— (2001), 'The Unbalanced Constitution' in T Campbell, K Ewing and A Tomkins (eds), *Sceptical Essays on Human Rights* (Oxford University Press, Oxford)

—— (2004), 'The Futility of the Human Rights Act' *Public Law* 829.

EWING, K and THAN, J-C (2008), 'The Continuing Futility of the Human Rights Act' *Public Law* 668.

FALK, R (2005), 'Reimagining the Governance of Globalization' in R Appelbaum and W Robinson (eds), *Critical Globalization Studies* (Routledge, New York and London).

FASSBENDER, B (2007), 'The Meaning of International Constitutional Law' in N Tsagourias (ed), *Transnational Constitutionalism* (Cambridge University Press, Cambridge).

FEKETEKUTY, G (2000), 'Assessing and Improving the Architecture of GATS' in P Sauvé and R Stern (eds), *GATS 2000: New Directions in Services Trade Liberalization* (The Brookings Institution, Washington, DC).

FELDMAN, D (2004), 'The Internationalization of Public Law and its Impact on the United Kingdom' in J Jowell and D Oliver (eds), *The Changing Constitution*, 5th edn (Oxford University Press, Oxford).

—— (2005), 'None, One or Several? Perspectives on the UK's Constitution(s)' 64 *Cambridge Law Journal* 329.

FINGER, J, and OLECHOWSKI, A (1987), *The Uruguay Round: A Handbook on the Multilateral Trade Negotiations* (The World Bank, Washington, DC).

FITZPATRICK, P and BERGERON, J (eds) (1998), *Europe's Other: Between Modernity and Post-Modernity* (Ashgate, Dartmouth).

FLETCHER, I, MISTELIS, L and CREMONA, M (2001), *Foundations and Perspectives of International Trade Law* (Sweet & Maxwell, London).

FLINDERS, M (2002), 'Shifting the Balance? Parliament, the Executive and the British Constitution' 50 *Political Studies* 23.

FRANCK, T (1992), 'The Emerging Right to Democratic Governance' 86 *American Journal of International Law* 46.

FREEDLAND, M (1998), 'Law, Public Services and Citizenship: New Domains, New Regimes?' in M Freedland and S Sciarra (eds), *Public Services and Citizenship in European Law* (Clarendon Press, Oxford).

FREEDLAND, M and SCIARRA, S (eds) (1998), *Public Services and Citizenship in European Law* (Clarendon Press, Oxford).

FREEMAN, J (2000), 'The Private Role in Public Governance' 75 *New York University Law Review* 5434.

FUKUYAMA, F (1992), *The End of History and the Last Man* (Penguin Books, London).

GARDNER, A (1995), 'The Velvet Revolution: Article 90 and the Triumph of the Free Market in Europe's Regulated Sectors' 16 *European Competition Law Review* 78.

GARDNER, R (1956), *Sterling-Dollar Diplomacy* (Clarendon Press, Oxford).

GEARTY, C (2004), *Principles of Human Rights Adjudication* (Oxford University Press, Oxford).

GEE, G (2008), 'The Political Constitutionalism of JAG Griffith' 28 *Legal Studies* 20.

GEORGE-BROWN, Lord (1971), *In My Way* (Victor Gollancz, London).

GERADIN, D (2000a) 'The Opening of State Monopolies to Competition: Main Issues of the Liberalization Process' in D Geradin (ed), *The Liberalization of State Monopolies in the European Union and Beyond* (Kluwer Law International, The Hague).

—— (ed) (2000b), *The Liberalization of State Monopolies in the European Union and Beyond* (Kluwer Law International, The Hague).

GERADIN, D (ed) (2004), *The Liberalization of Postal Services in the European Union* (Kluwer Law International, The Hague).

GERADIN, D and HUMPE, C (2004), 'The Liberalization of Postal Services in the European Union: An Analysis of Directive 97/67' in D Geradin (ed), *The Liberalization of Postal Services in the European Union* (Kluwer Law International, The Hague).

GILL, S (2000), 'The Constitution of Global Capitalism', http://www.theglobalsite.ac.uk.

—— (2001), 'Constitutionalizing Capital: EMU and Disciplinary Neo-liberalism' in A Beiler and A Morton (eds), *Social Forces in the Making of the New Europe* (Palgrave, Basingstoke).

GLYN, A (2006), *Capitalism Unleashed: Finance, Globalization and Welfare* (Oxford University Press, Oxford).

GOLDSTEIN, J (1993), 'Creating the GATT Rules: Politics, Institutions and American Policy' in J Ruggie (ed), *Multilateralism Matters* (Columbia University, New York).

GOLDSTEIN, J, KAHLER, M, KEOHANE, R and SLAUGHTER A-M (eds) (2001), *Legalization and World Politics* (MIT Press, Cambridge, MA).

GOLDSTEIN, J and MARTIN, L (2001) 'Legalization, Trade Liberalization and Domestic Politics: A Cautionary Note' in J Goldstein, M Kahler, R Keohane and A-M Slaughter (eds), *Legalization and World Politics* (MIT Press, Cambridge, MA).

GOLDSWORTHY, J (1999), *The Sovereignty of Parliament: History and Philosophy* (Clarendon, Oxford).

GORMLEY, L (2006), 'The Internal Market: History and Evolution' in N Nic Shuibhne (ed), *Regulating The Internal Market* ((Edward Elgar, Cheltenham)

GOWAN, P (1999), *The Global Gamble: Washington's Faustian Bid for World Domination* (Verso, London).

GRAHAM, C and PROSSER, T (1991), *Privatizing Public Enterprises: Constitutions, the State and Regulation in Comparative Perspective* (Oxford University Press, Oxford).

GRANT, C (1994), *Delors: Inside the House that Jacques Built* (Nicholas Brearly Publishing, London).

GRIECO, J and IKENBERRY, G (2003), *State Power and World Markets* (Norton, New York).

GRIFFITH, J (1979), 'The Political Constitution' 42 *Modern Law Review* 1.

—— (1997), *The Politics of the Judiciary* (Fontana Press, London).

GUISINGER, G (1987), 'Investment Related to Trade' in J Finger and A Olechowski (eds), *The Uruguay Round: A Handbook on the Multilateral Trade Negotiations* (World Bank, Washington, DC).

HAAS, E (2004), *The Uniting of Europe* (University of Notre Dame Press, Notre Dame, Indiana).

HABERMAS, J (2001), *The Postnational Constellation* (Polity, Cambridge).

HACKETT, C (ed) (1995), *Monnet and the Americans* (Jean Monnet Council, Washington, DC).

HALL, P and SOSKICE, D (eds) (2001), *Varieties of Capitalism: The Institutional Foundations of Comparative Advantage* (Oxford University Press, Oxford).

HANCHER, L, (1999) 'Community, State and Market' in P Craig and G De Búrca (eds), *The Evolution of EU Law* (Oxford University Press, Oxford).

HANCHER, L, OTTERVANGER, T and SLOT, P (2006), *EC State Aids*, 3rd edn (Sweet and Maxwell, London).

HARDEN, I, VON HAGEN, J and BROOKES, R (1997), 'The European Constitutional Framework for Member States' Public Finances' in M Andenas, L Gormley, C Hadjiemmanuil and I Harden (eds), *European Economic and Monetary Union: The Institutional Framework* (Kluwer Law International, London).

HARDT, M and NEGRI, A (2000), *Empire* (Harvard University Press, Cambridge, MA).
—— (2005), *Multitude* (Penguin, London).
HARLOW, C (1999), 'European Administrative Law and the Global Challenge' in P Craig and G De Burca (eds), *The Evolution of EU Law* (Oxford University Press, Oxford).
—— (2002), *Accountability in the European Union* (Oxford University Press, Oxford).
HARRIS, D, O'BOYLE, M, BATES, E and BUCKLEY, C (2009), *Law of the European Convention on Human Rights*, 2nd edn (Oxford University Press, Oxford).
HARVEY, D (2005), *A Brief History of Neoliberalism* (Oxford University Press, Oxford).
HAYEK, F (1978), *The Constitution of Liberty* (University of Chicago Press, Chicago).
—— (1982), *Law, Legislation and Liberty* (Routlege and Kegan Paul, London)
—— (1986), *The Road to Serfdom* (Ark Paperbacks, London).
HELD, D, MCGREW, A, GOLDBLATT, D and PERRATON, J (1999), *Global Transformations: Politics, Economics and Culture* (Polity Press, Cambridge).
HENDERSON, D (1999), *The MAI Affair: A Story and its Lessons* (Royal Institute of International Affairs, London).
HENIG, S (1997), *The Uniting of Europe* (Routledge, London)
HENKIN, L (1979), *How Nations Behave: Law and Foreign Policy* (Columbia National Press, New York).
HERTZ, N (2001), *The Silent Takeover: Global Capitalism and the Death of Democracy* (Arrow, London).
HIEBERT, J (2002), *Charter Conflicts: What is Parliament's Role?* (McGill-Queen's University Press, Montreal and Kingston).
—— (2008), 'The UK's Human Rights Act: Ideas Meet Practice', conference paper, Canadian Political Science Association, 4–6 June 2008, Vancouver.
HIRSCHL, R (2004), *Towards Juristocracy* (Harvard University Press, Cambridge, MA).
HOEKMAN, B and KOSTECKI, M (2001), *The Political Economy of the World Trading System*, 2nd edn (Oxford University Press, Oxford).
HOEKMAN, B and MAVROIDIS, P (1997), *Law and Policy in Public Purchasing: The WTO Agreement on Government Procurement* (University of Michigan Press, Ann Arbor).
HOLLAND, S (1975a), *The Socialist Challenge* (Quartet, London).
—— (1975b), *Strategy for Socialism* (Spokesman Books, Nottingham).
HOLMES, P (2001), 'The WTO and the EU: Some Constitutional Comparisons' in G De Búrca and J Scott (eds), *The EU and the WTO: Legal and Constitutional Issues* (Hart Publishing, Oxford).
HONIG, B (1993), *Political Theory and the Displacement of Politics* (Cornell University Press, Ithaca).
HOWSE, R (2000), 'Adjudicative Legitimacy and Treaty Interpretation in International Trade Law: The Early Years of WTO Jurisprudence' in J Weiler (ed), *The EU, the WTO and the NATFA: Towards a Common Law of International Trade* (Oxford University Press, Oxford).
HUDEC, R (1990), *The GATT Legal System and World Trade Diplomacy* (Butterworth Legal, Salem, NH).
—— (1993), *Enforcing International Trade Law: the Evolution of the Modern GATT Legal System* (Butterworth Legal, Salem, NH).
—— (2000), *The Adequacy of WTO Dispute Settlement Remedies for Developing Country Complaints* (The World Bank, Washington D.C.).
HULL, C (1937), *Economic Barriers to Peace* (Woodrow Wilson Foundation, New York).

INSTITUTE FOR PUBLIC POLICY RESEARCH (2002), *Wealth Distribution: The Evidence* (IPPR, London).

IRWIN, D (1996), *Against the Tide: An Intellectual History of Free Trade* (Princeton University Press, Princeton).

JACKSON, J (1994), 'The Legal Meaning of a GATT Dispute Settlement Report: Some Reflections' in N Blokker and S Muller (eds), *Towards More Effective Supervision by International Organizations: Essays in Honour of Henry G Schemers* (Martinus Nijhoff, Dordrecht).

—— (1998), *The World Trade Organization: Constitution and Jurisprudence* (Pinter, London).

—— (2000), *The Jurisprudence of the GATT and the WTO: Insights on Treaty Law and Economic Relations* (Cambridge University Press, Cambridge).

—— (2006a), *Sovereignty, the WTO and Changing Fundamentals of International Law* (Cambridge University Press, Cambridge).

—— (2006b), 'The World Trade Organization after 10 Years: The Role of the WTO in a Globalized World' 59 *Current Legal Problems* 427

JENKINS, S (2007), *Thatcher and Sons* (Penguin, London).

JENNINGS, I (1947), *The Law and the Constitution*, 3rd edn (University of London Press, London).

JOERGES, C (2004), 'What is Left of the European Economic Constitution? A Melancholic Eulogy', European University Institute LAW Working Paper 13/07, Florence.

JOERGES, C and RÖDL (2004), ' "Social Market Economy" as Europe's Social Model?', European University Institute LAW Working Paper 2004/8, Florence.

JOERGES, C, SAND, I-J and TEUBNER, G (eds) (2004), *Transnational Governance and Constitutionalism* (Hart Publishing, Oxford).

JONES, G (2005), *Multinationals and Global Capitalism* (Oxford University Press, Oxford).

JOWELL, J, and OLIVER, D (2004), *The Changing Constitution*, 5th edn (Oxford University Press, Oxford).

KAHLER, M (2001), 'Conclusion: The Causes and Consequences of Legalization' in J Goldstein, M Kahler, R Keohane and A-M Slaughter (eds), *Legalization and World Politics* (MIT Press, Cambridge, MA).

KELEMAN, R and SIBBERT, E (2004), 'The Globalisation of American Law' 58 *International Organization* 103.

KELLY, W (1987), 'Functioning of the GATT system' in J Finger and A Olechowski (eds), *The Uruguay Round: A Handbook on the Multilateral Trade Negotiations* (World Bank, Washington, DC).

KENNEDY, D (1986–87), 'The Move to Institutions' 8 *Cardozo Law Review* 842.

KEOHANE, R, MACEDO, S and MORAVCSIK, A (2007), 'Democracy-Enhancing Multilateralism', IILJ Global Administrative Law Series Working Paper 2007/4, http://www.iilj.org.

KEOHANE, R, MORAVCSIK, A and SLAUGHTER, A-M (2001), 'Legalized Dispute Resolution: Interstate and Transnational' in J Goldstein, M Kahler, R Keohane and A-M Slaughter (eds), *Legalized and World Politics* (MIT Press, Cambridge, MA).

KLUG, F (2000), *Values for a Godless Age* (Penguin, London).

KOH, H (1998), 'Bringing International Law Home' 35 *Houston Law Review* 623.

KOSKENNIEMI, M (2005), *From Apology to Utopia: The Structure of International Legal Argument* (Cambridge University Press, Cambridge).

—— (2007), 'The Fate of Public International Law: Between Technique and Politics' 70 *Modern Law Review* 1.

KOVAR, R (1988), 'Nationalisations: privatisations et droit communautaire' in J Schwarze (ed), *Discretionary Powers of the Member States in the Field of Economic Policies and their Limits under the EEC Treaty* (Nomos Verlagsgesellschaft, Baden-Baden).

KRASNER, S (ed) (1983), *International Regimes* (Cornell University Press, Ithaca).

KREIJEN, G (ed) (2002), *State Sovereignty and International Governance* (Oxford University Press, Oxford).

KU, C (2001), 'Global Governance and the Changing Face of International Law' Academic Council on the United Nations System Report & Papers 26.

LABOUR PARTY (1942), *The Old World and the New Society* (Labour Party, London).

—— (1945), *Let Us Face the Future* (Labour Party, London).

—— (1950), *Let Us Win through Together* (Labour Party, London).

—— (1966), *Time for Decision* (Labour Party, London).

—— (1972), *Labour's Programme for Britain* (Labour Party, London).

—— (1974), *Britain Will Win with Labour* (Labour Party, London).

—— (1979), *The Labour Way is the Better Way* (Labour Party, London).

—— (1982), *Labour's Programme 1982* (Labour Party, London).

—— (1983), *The New Hope for Britain* (Labour Party, London).

LALONE, N (2004), 'Variable Geometry in the Community's Foreign Economic Relations: The CCP and Effectiveness in International Trade Negotiations', London School of Economics conference on European Foreign Policy, 2–3 July 2004.

LAMONT, N (1999), *In Office* (Little, Brown and Company, London).

LANE, R (2006), 'The Internal Market and the Individual' in N Nic Shuibhne (ed), *Regulating The Internal Market* (Edward Elgar, Cheltenham).

LAWS, J (1995), 'Law and Democracy' *Public Law* 72.

—— (1996), 'The Constitution: Morals and Rights' *Public Law* 622.

LE SUEUR, A (2004), 'Developing Mechanisms for Judicial Accountability in the UK' 24 *Legal Studies* 73.

LESTER, A (2005), 'The Utility of the Human Rights Act: A Reply to Keith Ewing' *Public Law* 249.

LEYS, C (2001), *Market-Driven Politics: Neoliberal Democracy and Public Interest* (Verso, London).

LINDAHL, H (2007), 'Book Review: Constitutional Rights after Globalization; Sovereignty and its Discontents: On the Primacy of Conflict and the Structure of the Political' 16 *Social and Legal Studies* 149.

LINDBERG, L (1963), *The Political Dynamics of European Economic Integration* (Stanford University Press, Stanford).

LIPSON, C (1985), *Standing Guard: Protecting Foreign Capital in the Nineteenth and Twentieth Centuries* (University of California Press, Berkeley).

LORD, C (1998), *Democracy in the European Union* (Sheffield Academic Press, Sheffield).

LOUGHLIN, M (2003), *The Idea of Public Law* (Oxford University Press, Oxford).

LOVELAND, I (2006), *Constitutional Law, Administrative Law and Human Rights*, 4th edn (Butterworths, London).

LOWE, V and WARBRICK, C (eds) (1994), *The United Nations and the Principles of International Law* (Routledge, London and New York).

LUARD, E (1977), *International Agencies: The Emerging Framework of Interdependence* (Oceana, New York).

LUKASHUK, I, (1989), 'The Principle *Pacta Sunt Survanda* and the Nature of Obligation under International Law' 83 *American Journal of International Law* 513.

MADISON, J, HAMILTON, A and JAY, J (1987), *The Federalist Papers* (Penguin Classics, London).

MADSEN, M (2007), 'From Cold War Instrument to Supreme European Court: The European Court of Human Rights at the Crossroads of International and National Law and Politics' 32 *Law & Social Inquiry* 137.

MAJONE, G (1993), 'The European Community between Social Policy and Social Regulation' 31 *Journal of Common Market Studies* 153.

MAJOR, J (1999), *The Autobiography* (HarperCollins, London).

MALMBERG, J and SIGEMAN, T (2008), 'Industrial Actions and EU Economic Freedoms: The Autonomous Collective Bargaining Model Curtailed by the European Court of Justice' 45 *Common Market Law Review* 1115.

MANDEL, M (1998), 'A Brief History of the New Constitutionalism, or "How We Changed Everything so that Everything Would Remain the Same" ' *Israel Law Review* 250.

MARTELL, L (2008), 'Britain and Globalization' 5 *Globalizations* 449.

MARTINICO, G and POLLICINO, O (2008), 'Between Constitutional Tolerance and Judicial Activism: The "Specificity" of European Judicial Law' 10 *European Journal of Law Reform* 97.

McRAE, D (1996), 'The Contribution of International Trade Law to the Development of International Law' 260 *Academy of International Law Recueil des Cours* 114.

McRAE, D (2000), 'The WTO in International Law: Tradition Continued or New Frontier?' *Journal of International Law* 30.

McCRUDDEN, C (2007), *Buying Social Justice* (Oxford University Press, Oxford).

McGEE, A and WEATHERILL, S (1990), 'The Evolution of the Single Market: Harmonisation or Liberalisation?' 53 *Modern Law Review* 578.

McGOLDRICK, D (1997), *International Relations Law of the European Union* (Longmans, London).

MENDELSON, M (1986), 'The United Kingdom Nationalisation Cases and the European Convention on Human Rights' 57 *British Yearbook of International Law* 33.

MEUNIER, S (2005), *Trading Voices: The European Union in International Commercial Negotiations* (Princeton University Press, Princeton).

MILLER, A (1997), 'Ideological Motivations of Privatization in Great Britain versus Developing Countries' 50 *Journal of International Affairs* 391.

MITTELMAN, J (ed) (1997), *Globalization: Critical Reflections* (Rienner, Boulder, CO).

—— (1997), 'The Dynamics of Globalization' in J Mittelman (ed), *Globalization: Critical Reflections* (Rienner, Boulder, CO).

MONBIOT, G (2000), *Captive State: The Corporate Takeover of Britain* (Macmillan, London).

MORAN, M (2003), *The British Regulatory State* (Oxford University Press, Oxford).

MORAN, T (1998), *Foreign Direct Investment and Development: The New Policy Agenda for Developing Countries and Economies in Transition* (Institute for International Economics, Washington, DC).

MORVAI, K (1998), 'The Construction of the Other in European Human Rights Enterprise: A Narrative about Democracy, Human Rights and My Neighbour Uncle Blaze' in P Fitzpatrick and J Bergeron (eds), *Europe's Other: Between Modernity and Post-Modernity* (Ashgate, Dartmouth).

MOUFFE, C (1996), 'Democracy, Power and the "Political" ' in S Behabib (ed), *Democracy and Difference: Contesting the Boundaries of the Political* (Princeton University Press, Princeton).

MOUNT, F (1993), *The British Constitution Now* (Mandarin, London).

MUCHLINSKI, P (2001), 'Human Rights and Multinationals: Is there a Problem?' 77 *International Affairs* 31

NARLIKAR, A (2005), *The World Trade Organization* (Oxford University Press, Oxford).

NATIONAL FOREIGN TRADE COUNCIL (1950), *Position of the National Foreign Trade Council on the ITO Charter* (National Foreign Trade Council, New York).

NAU, H (1987), 'Bargaining in the Uruguay Round' in J Finger and A Olechowski (eds), *The Uruguay Round: A Handbook on the Multilateral Trade Negotiations* (World Bank, Washington, DC).

NIC SHUIBHNE, N (ed) (2006), *Regulating The Internal Market* ((Edward Elgar, Cheltenham).

NICOL, D (1996), 'The Industrial Tribunals: Disapplying with Relish?' *Public Law* 579.

—— (2001a), *EC Membership and the Judicialization of British Politics* (Oxford University Press, Oxford).

—— (2001b), 'Lessons from Luxembourg: Federalisation and the European Court of Human Rights' 26 *European Law Review (Human Rights Survey)* 3.

—— (2004), 'The Human Rights Act and the Politicians' 24 *Legal Studies* 451.

—— (2005), 'Original Intent and the European Convention on Human Rights' *Public Law* 152.

—— (2009), 'Democracy, Supremacy and the "Intergovernmental" Pillars of the European Union' *Public Law* 218.

NORTON, P (1975), *Dissention in the House of Commons 1945–1974* (Macmillan, London).

NORTON, P (1985), *Parliament in the 1980s* (Basil Blackwell, Oxford).

OBORNE, P (2007), *The Triumph of the Political Class* (Simon & Schuster, London).

O'CINNEADE, C (2004), 'Democracy, Rights and the Constitution: New Directions in the Human Rights Era' 57 *Current Legal Problems* 175.

OSTERHAMMEL, J and PETERSSON, N (2005), *Globalization: A Short History* (Princeton University Press, Princeton).

ORREGO VINCŪNA, F (2004), *International Dispute Settlement in an Evolving Global Society: Constitutionalization, Accessibility, Privatization* (Cambridge University Press, Cambridge).

PANITCH, L (1997), 'Rethinking the Role of the State' in J Mittelman (ed), *Globalization: Critical Reflections* (Rienner, Boulder, CO).

PELKMANS, J (1987), 'The New Approach to Technical Harmonization and Standardization' 25 *Journal of Common Market Studies* 249.

PETERSMANN, E-U (1991), *Constitutional Functions and Constitutional Problems of International Economic Law* (University Press, Fribourg).

—— (1994), 'Settlement of International Environmental Disputes in GATT and the EC: Comparative Legal Aspects' in N Blokker and S Muller (eds), *Towards More Effective Supervision by International Organizations: Essays in Honour of Henry G Schemers* (Martinus Nijhoff, Dordrecht).

—— (2001), 'European and International Constitutional Law: Time for Promoting "Cosmopolitan Democracy" in the WTO' in G de Búrca and J Scott (eds), *The EU and the WTO* (Hart Publishing, Oxford)

—— (ed) (2005), *Reforming the World Trading System: Legitimacy, Efficiency and Democratic Governance* (Oxford University Press, Oxford).

PETTIT, P (1997), *Republicanism: A Theory of Freedom and Government* (Oxford University Press, Oxford).

POLLOCK, A and PRICE, D (2003), 'The Public Health Implications of World Trade Negotiations on the General Agreement on Trade in Services and Public Services' 362 *The Lancet* 1072.

POOLE, T (2007), 'Book Review of *Constitutional Rights after Globalization* by Gavin W Anderson' *Public Law* 606.

PROSSER, T (2005), *The Limits of Competition Law: Markets and Public Services* (Oxford University Press, Oxford).

PRZEWORSKI, A, STOKES, S and MANIN, B (eds) (1999), *Democracy, Accountability and Representation* (Cambridge University Press, Cambridge).

QUIGLEY, C (1988), 'The Notion of a State Aid in the EEC' 13 *European Law Review* 242.

RACINE, R (1954), *Vers une Europe nouvelle par le plan Schuman* (Editions de la Baconnière, Neuchâtel).

ROBINSON, W (2004), *A Theory of Global Capitalism: Production, Class and State in a Transnational World* (Johns Hopkins University Press, Baltimore).

RODRIK, D (1997), *Has Globalization Gone Too Far?* (Institute for International Economics, Washington, DC).

ROLIN, H (1965), 'Has the European Court of Human Rights a Future?' (1965) *Howard Law Journal* 442.

ROMANO, C (1998–1999), 'The Proliferation of International Judicial Bodies: The Pieces of the Puzzle' 31 *New York University Journal of International Law and Politics* 709.

ROSENFELD, M (2008), 'Rethinking Constitutional Ordering in an Era of Legal and Ideological Pluralism' 6 *International Journal of Constitutional Law* 415.

ROSS, M (1995), 'State Aids: Maturing into a Constitutional Problem' 15 *Yearbook of European Law* 79.

—— (2007), 'Promoting Solidarity: From Public Services to a European Model of Competition?' 44 *Common Market Law Review* 1057.

RUBENFELD, J (2004), 'Unilateralism and Constitutionalism' *New York Law Review* 1971.

RUGGIE, J (1983), 'International Regimes, Transactions and Change: Embedded Liberalism in the Postwar Economic Order' in S Krasner (ed), *International Regimes* (Cornell University Press, Ithaca).

—— (ed) (1993), *Multilateralism Matters* (Columbia University Press, New York).

SABEL, C and SIMON, W (2006), 'Epilogue: Accountability without Sovereignty' in G de Búrca and J Scott (eds), *Law and New Governance in the EU and the US* (Hart Publishing, Oxford).

SAH, M and DAINTITH, T (1993), 'Privatisation and the Economic Neutrality of the Constitution' *Public Law* 465.

SALGADO, A (1986–7), 'Protection of Nationals' Rights to Property under the European Convention on Human Rights: *Lithgow v United Kingdom*' 27 *Virginia Journal of International Law* 865.

SAMPSON, G (ed) (2001), *The Role of the World Trade Organization in Global Governance* (United Nations University Press, New York).

SAND I-J (2004), 'Polycontextuality as an Alternative to Constitutionalism' in C Joerges, I-J Sand and G Teubner (eds), *Transnational Governance and Constitutionalism* (Hart Publishing, Oxford).

SANDHOLTZ, W and ZYSMAN, J (1989), '1992: Recasting the European Bargain' 42 *World Politics* 95.

SAROOSHI, D (2005), *International Organizations and Their Exercise of Sovereign Powers* (Oxford University Press, Oxford).

SASSEN, S (1996), *Losing Control?* (Columbia University Press, New York).

SAUTER, W, (1998), 'Universal Service Obligations and the Emergence of Citizens' Rights in European Telecommunications Liberalization' in M Freedland and S Sciarra (eds), *Public Services and Citizenship in European Law* (Clarendon Press, Oxford).

SAUVÉ, P (1996), 'Assessing the GATS: Half-Full or Half-Empty?' 29 *Journal of World Trade* 125.

SAUVÉ, P and STERN, R (eds) (2000), *GATS 2000: New Directions in Services Trade Liberalization* (Brookings Institution, Washington, DC).

SCHEPEL, H (2005), *The Constitution of Private Governance* (Hart Publishing, Oxford).

SCHERMERS, H (2002), 'Different Aspects of Sovereignty' in G Kreijen (ed), *State Sovereignty and International Governance* (Oxford University Press, Oxford).

SCHMIDT, V (2006), *Democracy in Europe: The EU and National Polities* (Oxford University Press, Oxford).

SCHNEIDERMAN, D (2008), *Constitutionalizing Economic Globalization* (Cambridge University Press, Cambridge).

SCHWARTZBERG, M (2007), *Democracy and Legal Change* (Cambridge University Press, Cambridge).

SCHWARZE, J (1988), *Discretionary Powers of the Member States in the Field of Economic Policies and their Limits under the EEC Treaty* (Nomos Verlagsgesellshaft, Baden-Baden).

SCOTT, C (2000), 'Accountability in the Regulatory State' 27 *Journal of Law and Society* 38.

SHAFFER, G (2003), *Defending Interests: Public–Private Partnerships in WTO Litigation* (Brookings Institution Press, Washington, DC).

SHAPIRO, M (2002), 'The Success of Judicial Review and Democracy' in M Shapiro and A Stone Sweet (eds), *On Law, Politics and Judicialization* (Oxford University Press, Oxford).

SHAPIRO, M and STONE SWEET, A (eds) (2002), *On Law, Politics and Judicialization* (Oxford University Press, Oxford).

SIMPSON, A (2001), *Human Rights and the End of Empire* (Oxford University Press, Oxford).

SLAUGHTER, A-M (2000), 'A Liberal Theory of International Law' *ASIL Proceedings of the 94th Annual Meeting* 240.

SLAUGHTER, A-M, STONE SWEET, A and WEILER, J (eds) (1997), *The European Court and the National Courts: Doctrine and Jurisprudence* (Hart Publishing, Oxford).

SMITH, A (2006), 'The Government of the European Union and a Changing France' in P Culpepper, A Hall and B Palier (eds), *Changing France: The Politics that Markets Make* (Palgrave Macmillan, Basingstoke).

SNYDER, F (1999), 'EMU Revisited: Are We Making a Constitution? What Constitution are We Making?' in P Craig and G De Búrca (eds), *The Evolution of EU Law* (Oxford University Press, Oxford).

SNYDER, F (2003), 'The Gatekeepers: The European Courts and WTO Law' 40 *Common Market Law Review* 313.

SOEDERBERG, S, MENZ, G and CERNY, P (eds) (2005), *Internalizing Globalization: The Rise of Neoliberalism and the Decline of National Varieties of Capitalism* (Palgrave Macmillan, Basingstoke).

SOMEK, A (2008), *Individualism: An Essay on the Authority of the European Union* (Oxford University Press, Oxford).

STEIN, E (1981), 'Lawyers, Judges and the Making of a Transnational Constitution' 75 *American Journal of International Law* 1.

STEIN, E and NICHOLSON, T (1960), *American Enterprise in the European Common Market: A Legal Profile* (University of Michigan Press, Ann Arbor).

STEYN, Lord (1997), 'The Weakest and Least Dangerous Branch of Government' *Public Law* 89.

STIGLITZ, J (2002), *Globalization and its Discontents* (Penguin, London).

STONE SWEET, A (2000), *Governing with Judges* (Oxford University Press, Oxford).

—— (2004), *The Judicial Construction of Europe* (Oxford University Press, Oxford).

SWANN, D (2000), *The Economics of Europe, From Common Market to European Union*, 9th edn (Penguin, London).

SZYSZCZAK, E (2006), 'Competition and the Liberalised Market' in N Nic Shuibhne (ed), *Regulating The Internal Market* (Edward Elgar, Cheltenham).

—— (2007), *The Regulation of the State in Competitive Markets in the EU* (Hart Publishing, Oxford).

TEUBNER, G (2004), 'Social Constitutionalism: Alternatives to State-Centred Constitutional Theory?' in C Joerges, I-J Sand and G Teubner (eds), *Transnational Governance and Constitutionalism* (Hart Publishing, Oxford).

THATCHER, M (1995), *The Downing Street Years* (HarperCollins, London)

TOMKINS, A (2005), *Our Republican Constitution* (Hart Publishing, Oxford).

TRACHTMANN, J (2006), *The International Economic Law Revolution and the Right to Regulate* (Cameron May, London).

TREBILCOCK, M and HOWSE, R (2005), *The Regulation of International Trade*, 3rd edn (Routledge, London).

TREPTE, P (2004), *Regulating Procurement: Understanding the Ends and Means of Public Procurement Regulation* (Oxford University Press, Oxford).

TRIDIMAS, T (1998), 'Damages for Breach of Community Law' in J Beatson and T Tridimas (eds), *New Directions in European Public Law* (Hart Publishing, Oxford).

TRUBEK, D, COTTRELL, P and NANCE, M (2006), 'Soft Law, Hard Law and European Integration' in G de Búrca and J Scott (eds), *Law and New Governance in the EU and the US* (Hart Publishing, Oxford).

TSAGOURIAS, N (2007), 'The Constitutional Role of General Principles of Law in International and European Jurisprudence' in N Tsagourias (ed), *Transnational Constitutionalism* (Cambridge University Press, Cambridge).

—— (ed) (2007), *Transnational Constitutionalism* (Cambridge University Press, Cambridge).

UNITED NATIONS DEVELOPMENT PROGRAMME (1998), *Human Development Report 1998* (Oxford University Press, Oxford).

VAN DEN BOSSCHE, P (2005), *The Law and Policy of the World Trade Organization: Text, Cases and Materials* (Cambridge University Press, Cambridge).

VAN DEN BROEK, P (1986), 'The Protection of Property Rights under the European Convention on Human Rights' *Legal Issues of European Integration* 52.

VAN MIERT, K (2000), 'Liberalization of the Economy of the European Union: The Game is Not (Yet) Over' in D Geradin (ed), *The Liberalization of State Monopolies in the European Union and Beyond* (Kluwer Law International, The Hague).

VIBERT, F (2007), *The Rise of the Unelected: Democracy and the New Separation of Powers* (Cambridge University Press, Cambridge).

WALDRON, J (1988), *The Right to Private Property* (Clarendon Press, Oxford).

—— (1993), 'A Right-Based Critique of Constitutional Rights' 13 *Oxford Journal of Legal Studies* 18.

—— (1999), *Law and Disagreement* (Oxford University Press, Oxford).

WALKER, N (ed) (2003), *Sovereignty in Transition: Essays in European Law* (Hart Publishing, Oxford).

WARBRICK, C (1994), 'The Principle of Sovereign Equality' in V Lowe and C Warbrick (eds), *The United Nations and the Principles of International Law* (Routledge, London).

WARD, I (1996), *A Critical Introduction to European Law* (Butterworths, London).

WARE, A (1979), *The Logic of Party Democracy* (Macmillan, London).

WATERS, M (2001), *Globalization*, 2nd edn (Routledge, London).

WEIL, P (1983), 'Towards Relative Normativity in International Law?' 77 *American Journal of International Law* 413.

WEILER, J (1991), 'The Transformation of Europe' 100 *Yale Law Journal* 2403.

—— (1999a), *The Constitution of Europe* (Cambridge University Press, Cambridge).

—— (1999b), 'The Constitution of the Common Market Place: The Free Movement of Goods' in P Craig and G De Búrca (eds), *The Evolution of EU Law* (Oxford, Oxford University Press).

—— (ed) (2000), *The EU, the WTO and the NATFA: Towards a Common Law of International Trade* (Oxford University Press, Oxford).

WILCOX, C (1949), *A Charter for World Trade* (Arno Press, New York).

WINARD, P (1995), 'Eisenhower, Dulles, Monnet and the Uniting of Europe' in C Hackett (ed), *Monnet and the Americans* (Jean Monnet Council, Washington, DC).

WINHAM, G (1998), 'The World Trade Organization: Institution-Building in the Multilateral Trade System' 21 *World Economy* 349.

WOOLSTONECRAFT, M (1792), *A Vindication of the Rights of Women* (Johnson, London).

WORLD BANK (1996), *World Development Report 1996: From Plan to Market* (Oxford University Press, Oxford).

—— (1997), *World Development Report 1997: The State in a Changing World* (Oxford University Press, Oxford).

WRISTON, W (2002), *The Twilight of Sovereignty: How the Information Revolution is Transforming Our World* (Charles Scribner's Sons, New York).

WULFF, O (1988), 'National Economic Policy: An Obstacle to the European Community?' in J Schwarze (ed), *Discretionary Powers of the Member States in the Field of Economic Policies and their Limits under the EEC Treaty* (Nomos Verlagsgesellschaft, Baden-Baden).

YENKONG, N (2006), 'World Trade Organization Dispute Settlement Retaliatory Regime at the Tenth Anniversary of the Organization: Reshaping the "Last Resort" against Compliance' 40 *Journal of World Trade* 365.

YOUNG, A (2008), *Parliamentary Sovereignty and the Human Rights Act* (Hart Publishing, Oxford).

YOUNG, IM (2007), *Global Challenges* (Polity, London).

INDEX

Index

Index